This book is dedicated to my beloved husband

Harold Arthur Bennett

Red Spy

Anhua Gao

Remembering Publishing LLC

Copyright © 2023 by Remembering Publishing, LLC. USA

Red Spy

Anhua Gao

ISBN: 978-1-68560-062-4 (Print)
978-1-68560-063-1 (eBook)

LCCN: 2023 905390

March 2023, First Edition, First Printing

Remembering Publishing, LLC
RememPub@gmail.com

All rights reserved.
No part of this book may be reproduced in any form or by any electronic or mechanical means including information storage and retrieval systems, without permission in writing from the publisher. The only exception is by a reviewer, who may quote short excerpts in review.

PREFACE

Gao Qing, 1950 in Hong Kong.

In China, the family name comes first, so my birth name was, Gao Anhua. Please note that although Gao Qing and I share the same family name of Gao, we are not related.

The Red Spy is based on the true story of a Chinese/Soviet Special Agent named Gao Qing, code-name, Bashan. As far as I am aware, the Chinese Communists have never released his name nor have they admitted his existence. Reading from his notes, Yu Tianming, who was imprisoned with Gao Qing, wrote and published a book in Chinese which was soon banned by the Communist regime. I compiled Yu's Chinese version into English and it becomes this book.

I had to be careful when researching the story. In China, every Communist leader of any rank has absolute power over his/her section. Any suspicious leader could have had me arrested and imprisoned without charge. I could only gently draw out old-people memories, but what I did hear was sufficient for me to have no doubts that this was, in essence, a true story. In 2005 I found a reference to Gao Qing on a Chinese/American Mandarin language website that confirmed some of what Yu Tianming had told me. Sadly I didn't make a note of the site name and have never found it again.

The story begins in north-west China in 1966 with a bewildered Yu Tianming, the storyteller, being taken to prison where his aging and unkempt cellmate turns out to be Gao Qing, who Yu Tianming has been investigating for anti-Communist activities. It quickly becomes clear that Yu has been arrested and placed in that particular cell to extract information from Gao Qing. When he gets it, Yu will be released.

However, the two men form a friendship that culminates in Gao trusting Yu with his story, but only after Yu gives his word not to tell the prison authorities but to take it with him if/when Yu is released.

Gao's story begins in 1939 when he and 19 other Chinese are sent to Spy School in Moscow. There, under the supervision of Stalin, through the direct control of the section known in the West as the Communist International – shortened to The Comintern, Gao learns the skills needed to be a successful Special Agent. He was the best and one of only four of his group to make it through to graduation. He is given the codename, Bashan (Palm Hill). The failures, apparently, were executed.

His orders were simple. Everything he did, or learned, was secret and must not be divulged to anyone except his Soviet Controller or his contact in Moscow. They reported directly to Stalin. However, he chose to remain true to China and the Chinese Communist Party, which meant that he had to betray all others, including the Soviets. For his protection, only a select few Chinese Communists knew of his existence.

Gao, posing as a rich multilingual businessman, is sent to Chongqing, the provisional Capital City of the Chinese Kuomintang (Nationalist) Government during the Anti-Japanese War. His first task is to set up an important radio link between Moscow and the many Soviet spies based far and wide throughout Asia and the Orient. That done, he is given increasingly more dangerous assignments that bring him into close contact with Mao Zedong, Zhou En-lai, Chiang Kai-shek, top Kuomintang and American Generals. Some Japanese, and the British, Chinese and American intelligence agencies.

Gao has an active love life. In spy school he meets and falls in love with Natasha. When she is killed on a Russian battlefield, he turns to the beautiful Zhao Ying – a member of his team, for solace. She too is later killed - tortured to death. He eventually marries Little Dove, a girl whose life he saved whilst on his way from spy school to Chongqing, several years previously.

Gao was involved in a number of complicated and dangerous espionage activities, which sometimes resulted in him narrowly escaping death.

Yu Tianming kept his word, but he had to wait almost forty years before it was safe for him to reveal what he knew about Gao Qing. *The Red Spy* is that story.

The USSR intended to use The Comintern both for extensive propaganda and spying. Stalin rapidly became disenchanted with its efforts at espionage and shifted the responsibility for that to the NKVD. The greatest (known) triumph of Soviet espionage in China was through the work of the brilliant Richard Sorge, the founder of the first major Soviet espionage net in China. Perhaps Gao Qing was never a part of this network – it would have been typical of Stalin to keep everybody divided and working in ignorance of each other.

TABLE OF CONTENTS

PRELOGUE

Yu Tianming.

Northwest China, autumn 1966.

Siren screaming, the large army truck crammed full of soldiers carrying rifles with fixed bayonets sped out of the gate, closely followed by a Soviet-made jeep. Behind the jeep came another truck filled with more soldiers.

From my place in the jeep, I could see the steel bayonets reflecting the dim lights of the street-lamps. My back was crushed against the hard wooden rear seat, but I was not about to change position. Only my eyes moved. On either side of me sat an army officer poking a pistol-barrel into my ribs, cold eyes staring at me as if to repeat what had already been said, "Stay still, or I will shoot you! "

In the shafts of brightness from the vehicle headlights, the carpet of paper slogans and leaflets left behind by the many thousands of demonstrating Red Guards who daily marched these streets, rose up like ghostly apparitions, flapping and swirling as though angry at being disturbed.

The wheels of the vehicles rolled through the rubbish, heading to…I didn't know where. And I didn't know why. What I did know was that fate was forcing me to depart the battlefield of big-character posters, loudspeakers, street demonstrations, violence and disorder. One of the officers had said I was being taken to attend "Study Courses of Mao Zedong Thought", whatever that meant.

I was very much afraid, but despite not knowing what the future held, my strongest feeling was relief. During the past months my belief in the sacred ideals of Communism had been shocked out of me, to be replaced by a never-to-be-spoken fear and loathing of everything relating to Chairman Mao and his cursed Cultural Revolution. The siren stopped its incessant clamour. Strangely, the sudden silence felt more dangerous than the noise.

We left the city behind and veered left onto a dirt road that took us up a mountain into a thick white mist, causing the driver to switch on the screen wipers. Through the fan-shaped area of visibility, the red rear lights of the truck in front of us made me think of the eyes of a monster waiting to swallow me up. And in a way there really was a monster. I had heard the stories of torture and mistreatment of prisoners resulting in secret night-time body disposals. Who would tell my story? Or, for that matter, who would care?

My mother, living in a far away village, would cry when she heard the news of my downfall and death. I pictured her working in the fields, worrying about the son from whom she never got a letter, and promised myself that I would write to her every week if I ever got another chance. There was my girl friend. She would care when she realised I was no longer around, but for how long? I cast my eyes down. Only two people to miss me.

As suddenly as it had come, the mist was gone. I looked at the sky. There was the Great Bear and the Pole Star, so we were moving north. The latest revolutionary song was "Looking at the Pole Star, thinking of Chairman Mao". We had sung it with deep class feelings, exactly as we had been taught, but this time the stars couldn't tell me my direction in life. Heading straight to death, perhaps?

Many kilometres later, the vehicles stopped in front of an old temple. In the breaking dawn, I could clearly see the gull-wing shapes of the roof and the intricately latticed frontage. The once beautiful building was in a bad state of repair.

I thought, "Nobody in China cares about beauty anymore. "

Guilt hit me as I remembered that I too had stopped caring. Only politics was allowed to fill our lives, nothing else. Pistol barrels nudged me out of the jeep into a circle of soldiers pointing bayonet-topped rifles at me. The pistols prodded me to the brightly-lit back yard of the temple. I was sure that I was about to be shot.

"Stop!" yelled someone. I was facing a green metal door. "This is your cell. You are number 74. You no longer have a name. You are nothing…rubbish…dog-shit! Your cell-mate will tell you the rules. Break them and you die. Get in!"

Relief flowed through me. I wasn't about to be shot. A soldier handed me a smelly old blanket whilst another opened the door. Pistols prodded from behind. I moved forward and the door slammed shut. I stood in almost total darkness. For the first time since my arrest, fear left me, to be replaced by anger. My angry heart wanted to burst out of my chest. How could this be? I was a trusted follower of Communism and this was absurd. Had they read my thoughts? Or sensed my despair? I muttered a curse.

By a wall, a match flared and a skinny arm reached out to light a candle. Then a bony ghost-like man with long matted snow-white hair and beard rose up and moved towards me. His sharp eyes were sunk into his thin white face. Above the eyes a thick pair of white eyebrows joined forces in his frown.

I stared, dumbstruck. The fear was back in charge. My legs turned to wobbly bean curd and I was about to mess my pants.

When just half a meter away from me, he stopped and placed the candle in a nearby hole in the wall. He seemed to be old. Under a mildew-splotched army overcoat resting on his shoulders he wore a tattered V-neck sweater over a grubby once-white shirt. Thin rope held up his black peasant trousers and he was barefoot. Never had I seen anyone filthier. He stared at me.

What he saw was a bespectacled very frightened man aged twenty-seven holding a blanket and dressed like everyone else in Cultural Revolutionary China in army style uniform jacket and trousers.

"What do you want?" I barked, trying to appear tough and ready to defend myself.

No reply, just those sharp eyes staring. I felt as if they were trying to see into my soul. For what seemed a long time but was probably no more than ten seconds, he stared, checking me out. Turning away, he retrieved the candle and shuffled back to his bed, an old blanket spread over a mound of hay.

Feeling braver now that he had retreated, I tried again but this time in a much quieter, more respectful tone. "Old man, what should I do?"

He raised his hand and pointed to another mound of hay. In a firm, authoritative, but quiet voice, he said, "Go to your bed. You will know soon enough."

That was how I met the man I was never, ever, going to forget.

*

With no option but to obey, I went to where the finger pointed, dropped the blanket on the hay and sat on it. Then I saw the rats. With a frightened cry I jumped to my feet, not knowing where to go to escape. My head met a thick clinging spider web, making me duck back down, frantically brushing it away. At the same time I farted. Suddenly the old man was by my side, soothing me with his hand on my arm.

"Take it easy young comrade, nothing here will hurt you," he said quietly. "I know because I have been here for a long time." He gently sat me down, then knelt beside me. His voice came again. "Don't be afraid of the rats, they will not harm you. If you treat them with respect, they will become your friends."

Of course I didn't believe him, but his voice settled me.

"Please forgive my appearance," he chuckled, pulling at his beard. "There are no barbers here." He sniffed then joked, "I think you need to use the bucket."

He pointed. My eyes followed his finger and saw a wooden bucket standing in the corner. I rose and went to it. The smell told me what it was used for, so I dropped my trousers, squatted and let my bowels do their job. Straw took the place of paper.

Feeling better, I returned to my bit of hay to find the blanket laid out waiting for me. "This time I do it, tomorrow I will show you how," said the old man. His unexpected kindness left me speechless. I had just been separated from a mad world where there was only violence, to find gentleness in… "Where am I?" I asked, almost childlike.

The old man replied as he shuffled away, "You will have to wait. When they are ready, you will be told everything they want you to know."

I sat down and took off my shoes, all the while shifting my gaze, looking at the rats, the thick spider webs, the damaged walls letting in cold mountain air, the stinking bucket and the high wooden beams holding up the corrugated iron roof. Tentatively I lay down, still not knowing where I was, or why.

In minutes my whole skin area turned into a trembling, agitated itch. I sat up, scratching fiercely at my neck, my arms, my back. "Bloody Hell," I thought, "What's happening to me? "

Once again the old man was by my side, whispering, "I see that the fleas have found you." With an almost soundless titter he continued, "Don't worry, you will soon get accustomed to them. And the ants, and the midges, and the flies, and the creepy-crawlies, and the dirt, and the filth, and the lack of water for washing, and no haircuts or shaving. Soon, Comrade, you will be as mouldy as me!"

Still tittering, he returned to his bed.

*

I awoke to gentle shaking. "Little Comrade, come and eat," said the already familiar soft voice. I sat up, stretched and yawned.

"What time is it?" I asked, not yet fully tuned in to my surroundings.

"Feeding time," said the old man, handing me a small bowl of boiled rice.

From somewhere the tantalising smells of cooking hit my nostrils, making me feel hungry. I looked questioningly at the rice, at him and back to the rice.

With a grin, he said, "Ignore the smells. They eat the best food and plenty of it. We get poor quality rice and sometimes, if we're lucky, leftover soup. We drink water rationed to one cup a day. They drink as much tea as they want."

He checked the door before making the "hush" sound with his upright forefinger to his lips, then whispered, "Welcome to the West Hill Dictatorship Team."

That woke me up.

"What?" I whispered back as though shouting, "Oh no…oh, shit, no. It can't be!"

He hushed me again and pointed. Through the damaged outer wall, soldiers on guard were clearly visible.

I was locked up in the worst possible place. The biggest enemies of Communism were sent here, including those who had opposed our "Guide", our "Red Sun", our "Saviour", Chairman Mao.

"I have fallen from Communist heaven into reactionary hell!" I mouthed in my loudest whisper. "Somehow I have offended the Iron Wall of the Republic (a nickname Mao had given to the People's Liberation Army), and now I am at their mercy!"

Chinese conversation was littered with such political phraseology during the Mao years. My fear returned as terrible visions of my immediate future life, and death, flashed through my imagination. I hurried to use the bucket then spent the rest of that day and most of the night wallowing in self-pity and dismay, and an even longer time dealing with my terror. Prison routine continued as normal. Food was delivered, put beside me by the old man and eaten by the rats. Water also came and was sipped. Shouted orders signalled some kind of prisoner movement. The bucket was emptied, refilled and emptied again. The guard changed at regular intervals, and I scratched.

I sat upright; full of anger. It was dark outside. For perhaps an hour, tears streamed down my face, then I was over it. Yes I was frightened of what the future had in store for me. Yes I hated being where I was. But no, I was not about to cave in. My last thought before I fell asleep was, "You won't break me, you bastards! "

The next morning the old man again brought me food. I took it and ate every grain of the mouldy rice and drank all of the water. He was surprised and pleased. He asked me how I was feeling and, because of his kindness and concern, I told him about my battle with fear and my remembered last thought. He nodded and smiled his understanding.

"That was a good response," he said. "Don't let them beat you down. I hope you don't mind me asking, what's your name?"

"I don't mind," I replied. "My name is Yu Tianming."

That put a look of surprise on his face, whilst my surprise was about to be revealed.

He responded with, "Yu Tianming? The same Yu Tianming who checks case histories for Military Intelligence?"

When I nodded, he laughed softly before looking at me with a mischievous smile and saying, "I've heard of you. My name is Gao Qing."

He waited expectantly for me to react. When my face showed that I had, his extreme amusement caused his face to crease into hundreds of lines. He dared not laugh loudly so he banged the floor with his hands and rocked backwards and forwards in silent belly-shaking merriment.

*

Two years previously, I, as a new graduate from the Army Engineering Institute, had been selected by the Military Intelligence section of the Party and sent to their office in the city of Lanzhou, northwest China. My first assignment seemed, on the face of it, simple. In reality it was nothing of the kind. I had to check out a "vicious reactionary" without ever being allowed to meet him.

Comrade Kang Sheng, Head of Chinese Communist Intelligence, informed me that Gao Qing was an extremely dangerous man. For many years he had been deeply hidden within the Chinese Communist Party, awaiting orders from an unknown foreign power to do damage to the Chinese revolution.

Kang Sheng had looked up at me from behind his desk, saying, "This case is special. If you reveal even the smallest hint of what you know about Gao Qing to anyone, severe punishment will surely follow."

After his arrest, Gao Qing had been transported fourteen hundred kilometres away from Beijing to Northwest China and imprisoned in the oddly named "West Hill Dictatorship Team" where all the important counter-revolutionaries were jailed.

The Special Case Office clerk didn't question Kang Sheng's hand-written authority giving me unlimited access to Gao Qing's personal file. This was my first case and the first time I had ever seen a personal file. I hadn't even seen my own. I carried the package away to my desk and, for a long while, just sat and looked at it. Delving into the life of another human being was not something I wished to do. Then, as though opening an old book, I carefully turned to the first item and began to read. And like a good book, as page followed page, the more engrossed I became until, suddenly, it ended, leaving me deeply troubled and not at all sure that I could carry out my orders.

From the file and especially after reading the transcripts of Gao Qing's interrogations and all of his compulsory self-criticisms that every Communist must write in his or her own handwriting, I did not get any suggestion of a bad element. Instead, Gao Qing impressed me with his thoughts on loyalty to the Party and his comrades. He was also totally committed to the principles of socialism as laid down by Karl Marx. I thought him to be a deep, intense man, with a finely tuned sense of humour. Reports by his superiors proved that he had been a very fine officer. Bravery mixed with compassion and a strong sense of right and wrong.

For many days I deliberated until, not knowing what else to do, I decided to seek help and advice. Standing to attention before my Political Commissar, I made my report.

"There is nothing in the file to help me." I barked, military style - my voice hoarse with nervousness. "Gao Qing's military history stopped twenty-six years ago, leaving me with insufficient information to arrive at a correct conclusion or to make any sort of recommendation."

The Political Commissar frowned as he said, "Is it so difficult?"

"Yes. From the age of twelve, Gao Qing proved himself to be a first class soldier with a promising military career. He was quickly promoted to senior rank, then, nothing. It is as though he died in 1939 and came alive again in 1952. How can I prove that this man is the real Gao Qing? How can I prove that he is a spy? How can I arrive at a conclusion if I am not allowed to interrogate the prisoner? I have nothing to go on. Where to start? How can I investigate a big black empty hole?"

As I spoke, I knew I was disobeying Kang Sheng's orders, but thought a "Political Commissar" must be a man of discretion and silence.

The reply I received was, "If you cannot make any recommendations, you can at least keep an eye on the prisoner. Perhaps, during interrogation, he will let slip information that will help you."

I had to accept his advice. From that day, until my arrest, I received regular reports from the West Hill Dictatorship Team about Gao Qing's general behavior, together with the transcripts of his many hours of interrogation. Oh yes, I knew the name of Gao Qing!

*

Two weeks went by. Gao Qing and I got along very well. He seemed not to resent the fact that I had spent two years trying to prove his guilt. His easy manner helped me settle into prison life as we quietly exchanged opinions, mostly about the cinema, music and art. We avoided politics other than for him to tell me how he knew my name and that I had the job of trying to prove him guilty of something… Anything.

"Simple" he chuckled. "During a session, it is usual for the interrogating officers to have my file open on the desk and I have good eyesight. I can read upside-down writing as fast as right-way up writing. It's a useful tool when you're in prison."

One morning an army officer appeared in the doorway and shouted, "Number 74!" I stood up and followed him outside. Escorted by soldiers, we crossed the courtyard and entered a room.

The officer sat down behind a desk and lit a cigarette. I stood in front of the desk. Having been a heavy smoker before my incarceration, I sucked his smoke deep into my lungs. The officer had an open file in front of him, reminding me of how Gao Qing knew of my existence. Exasperatingly I couldn't read a single character. The officer spoke first.

"Do you understand that by being sent here, your case is considered serious?"

"Yes" was my answer.

"Do you also know that we treat you better than the other prisoners?"

"No, I didn't know that."

"Well, we do. Your case is being looked at as a possible miscarriage of justice. To help prove your innocence, you must dig out the secret life of Gao Qing and give us the information we need to prove him guilty. For example, you must find out about his relationship with the evil Black Gang members such as Marshal He Long."

It was then that I understood exactly why I had been arrested. I was actually guilty of nothing except of falling into their trap. My "crime" was asking the Political Commissar for advice. My prearranged "punishment" was imprisonment with Gao Qing. My release depended upon me getting the evidence needed to prove the guilt of Gao Qing, and through him, help create a case against Marshal He Long.

The Marshal was a legendary hero and his arrest was one of the many reasons why I was no longer a committed Communist. He had been one of the leaders involved in the August the First Uprising of 1927. It had begun in the city of Nanchang in protest against the continued and systematic slaughter of Communists by the Nationalist Government led by Chiang Kai-shek.

The Marshal was much loved and respected by the whole Chinese people. That was probably the only reason why Mao had branded him a "Warlord" and a "Capitalist Roader" (someone who favours following the capitalist economic system.) For some years I had suspected that, himself apart, Mao hated everyone held in high esteem by the people. Now very old, Marshal He Long and his wife were in prison awaiting trial. Obviously they had found no real evidence to present before the court.

Rebellion began to build in me. Not only for the unfair way I was being treated but also at the preposterous suggestion that the Marshal was a criminal. Inside my head an angry voice told me, "No! I cannot do what they ask. Why should I help send good men like the Marshal and Gao Qing to their deaths? "

In as firm and an even voice as I could muster, I replied, "Comrade Zhou En-lai led the Nanchang Uprising. Comrade Marshall He Long was his deputy. The Marshal was a hero. How can he ever be considered a member of any Black Gang? You, as a senior army officer, must surely know this."

Expecting me to be grateful for the chance to gain my freedom, the officer was taken aback by my response. After a long pause, he gave me an obvious stock answer.

"No matter how much of a hero he has been in the past, today he is a Revisionist and a Capitalist Roader. Today he is a harmful influence on our proletarian revolution."

"I'm sorry" I said. "I don't understand the meaning of revisionist, or exactly what a capitalist roader is."

I did know. I was just using up the time allocated to my interrogation.

"Stupid fool! A capitalist roader is someone who wants to replace Communism with Capitalism - to go down the capitalist road."

"Yes, I understand. What about revisionist?"

I knew. Revisionism is a form of Communism that prefers to use persuasive argument, not violent revolution. Did he?

I asked, as innocently as I could, "Does it mean that Chairman Mao has outlawed men of peace? Is non-violence now a crime?"

He stared blankly at me. It was quite obvious that he had no idea what, exactly, was the meaning of revisionism. He had probably heard the word during political instruction and had simply incorporated it into his Communistic jargon.

After a long pause he came back to me with, "Do you want to die here?"

I shrugged my shoulders. "From birth our only certainty is death. Both of us will die someday. In the future there will be no difference between two dead men."

The officer leapt to his feet. "You are crazy to talk this way! Your future is in your own hands. I will give you a chance to think about your perilous position and the punishment that is waiting for you."

With these words he took me back to my cell.

*

As week followed week, a true friendship and trust built up between Gao Qing and me. He showed me his daily fitness routine, which helped keep him in good health despite the poor diet and continuous confinement. It was important, he said, to keep fit. "We prisoners are considered to be less than nothing - lower than garbage. There are no doctors, dentists or nurses here. If you have a toothache, all you can do is suffer. If you cut yourself, there is no bandage. If your cut gets infected, they won't care. If you fall ill, they will let you die."

In silence we worked at it together, all the while mindful of the guards. Our captors would have banned such activity if they knew.

Then came the day we trusted each other enough to discuss politics. In low whispers we confided our views on Communism versus Capitalism, the pros and cons of Mao Zedong and Chiang Kai-shek, and in particular, Mao's Cultural Revolution.

By this time I knew that my cell-mate was aged about fifty. It was his white hair and beard that made him look older. I was the younger man so he called me "Little Comrade" and I addressed him as "Old Gao".

One evening, I said, "I don't think the Communist Party is always correct, nor do I believe that the Nationalists were always wrong."

"Hush!" he whispered. "I'm glad to know that you can still use your reasoning powers, but please be careful. Communist propaganda has brainwashed our people into accepting the distorted thinking of a madman. He has promoted the dregs of society - the bullies, the killers and the thugs, into positions of absolute authority. This has resulted in wholesale rape, murder, torture and false imprisonment. Nobody is safe. In a country where even the most loyal of Mao's supporters fear for their lives, you are in danger of being shot where you stand."

"Why?" I asked.

"You are too honest and outspoken. You must learn to hide your thoughts, control your emotions, keep your views to yourself and never show anything on your face. If you don't, you will die."

I looked at his dirty wasted face, knowing he was right.

"Old Gao" I asked him. "Can you teach me?"

"Of course!" was his reply.

He began by teaching me the art of meditation. It was a wonderful way to combat the boredom. We sat on our hay, cross legged, eyes closed, as still as clay statues. Sometimes he would recite poems that had been passed down from the Tang and Song Dynasties. When I began reciting some remembered schoolboy poems; he smiled at me like a father to his son.

*

Compared to what was going on outside, living in the cell was bearable. For one thing it was peaceful. From overhearing the guards, we knew that the Cultural Revolution was continuing apace, causing huge difficulties for the ordinary people. Everywhere there was total chaos. The streets were becoming ever more dangerous. Basic commodities were running out and there was widespread hunger. We had our daily ration of rice and water. No cooking or cleaning for us. The cell was large, perhaps six metres square. It had once been the milling shed where soya beans and grains had been ground down to powder. In the centre of the cell, a huge grinder was still in place. Strangely, we were forbidden to touch it. The floor was hard mud with hay spread over it. Three thick wooden posts held up the roof and at some time in the past the wooden walls had been reinforced with thick bamboo slats. Years of neglect had resulted in the outside walls rotting away, allowing us to see out. When it rained, leaks in the roof caused pools of water to form, forcing us to keep to one end of the cell. We used our tin cups to collect, and drink, as much water as we could. When it was windy, debris and dust fell from the rotting roof. In summer it was an oven. In winter it was a freezer. Always, it was uncomfortable.

On the positive side, it was also our refuge from the madness taking place in Chairman Mao's Cultural Revolutionary China.

There was nothing unstable about our lives. One day followed another in monotonous similarity. Apart from sporadic bouts of interrogation when, with the approval of Old Gao, I said I would co-operate but didn't, we were left alone. Only food deliveries and bucket changes allowed a little of the outside world into ours.

Nevertheless, both of us had our off days.

One miserable rainy day it was my turn. Thoughts of how my arrest had ruined my promising future and fond memories of home, good food, deep satisfying draws on a cigarette and the warm responsive body of my girlfriend, enveloped me in a black cloud.

"I'm bored." I said to nobody in particular. "What a waste of a life."

Old Gao came over and whispered softly, "Little Comrade, don't be too sad. There is something worthwhile for you to do whilst you are here."

"What would that be?"

"I don't think I will ever get out of here alive. From my file you already know the official Chinese version, but it only tells a small part of my story. Much more detail is to be found in Moscow. My Russian file, with all my written reports, is locked away in the KGB vaults. If I am executed, my Chinese and Russian files are unlikely to be seen again and my story will die with me. I don't want that to happen and with your help it won't. If I tell you my story, you are young enough to be able to lock it safely away in your memory until you can pass it on to the next person to share this cell. Or, if you get out of here, take it with you."

I stayed silent, almost fearing to breathe.

Old Gao continued, "It's a good story. Perhaps the day will come when it will be safe for you to tell it to the whole Chinese people, maybe even the world. Do you want to do it?"

I had to say what was in my mind. "This is exactly the reason why I was arrested. I could gain my freedom, but..." I smiled, "… what a delicious irony it would be, if, by arresting me without just cause, they gave you the opportunity to get your story out of here. Yes, I want to do it. It is a perfect way to get revenge for both of us."

Old Gao whispered, "The year is 1939…

CHAPTER 1.

Spy School, 1939

1.

Early one October morning in 1939, in China's Xinjiang Province, close to the Sino-Soviet border, Andriev, a liaison officer attached to the Soviet Embassy in China, led a group of twenty young Chinese Communist Party members, including Gao Qing, onto a canvas covered military truck. None were volunteers. They had been carefully chosen and transported to this place. Before the truck moved off, a high ranking Chinese Party member instructed them to obey every Andriev's orders… they would soon know why.

A few kilometres inside Russian territory the truck stopped. The group de-trucked at a small railway station to en-train, said Andriev, for the Soviet capital.

"Comrades" he informed them. "You are going back to school."

Five days later they were in a cleared area deep inside a forest on the outskirts of Moscow. It was cleverly laid out and camouflaged so that from both the ground and the air it looked like a large holiday park. An outer brick wall encircled the whole area, broken by one well-guarded entrance blocked by a pair of heavy iron gates.

Several architecturally superb houses, originally built for the Russian royal family, ringed the clearing. Farther away, hidden under tall pine trees and encircled by a high dry-stone wall with one guarded gate, was a huge complex comprising modern buildings disguised as holiday homes. Many more structures were buried deep underground.

The only road ran from north to south through the park. There was plenty of evidence of holiday life. Football and hockey pitches, tennis courts, a running track, outdoor swimming pool, a large lake with rowboats and a picnic area.

The complex was guarded around the clock by troops. Some dressed in local peasant clothes and posing as workers. Others playing at being on holiday.

The truck taking the group of Chinese from the railhead to the school had passed a large military establishment. Gao saw several bombers and many fighters. Large hangars housed more aircraft. Troops were drilling on a big square and to one side of it, dogs were being exercised. All this was open to view in order to draw attention away from the school and give a reason for the number of personnel in the area.

One of the houses, a three storied beauty, housed the school headquarters. Everything inside was of high quality. The snow-white walls, shining red wooden floors, elegantly decorated offices, library and mess hall reeked of luxury. The Chinese were shown the laboratories where they would learn the forensics related to the craft of information gathering. There was also a cinema, a card room and badminton courts. Their living quarters and classrooms were all underground.

Training began the day following their arrival. For six mornings of every week they were expected to be up, dressed and ready to be marched into breakfast by five-thirty and at their desks by six-fifteen. From Mondays to Fridays, they had twelve hours of intensive training broken by a fifteen-minute morning break, forty-five minutes for lunch and a second mid-afternoon fifteen minutes. Evenings began with one hour of compulsory revision. On Saturdays they worked until mid-day, leaving the remainder of the weekend free.

There were other classes there, but they rarely mixed. The twenty Chinese were given the title "Far East Group" and as the longest serving Chinese Red Army officer, Gao was appointed "Senior Student".

Their Soviet Army teacher, speaking in Mandarin, began his lecture by telling them the rules, which were strictly enforced. First came the expected - time of reveille and lights out, keep themselves, their kit and living area clean, obey all orders, no going outside the school perimeters without a pass, bring nobody in. No alcohol or loose talk… blah… blah… blah. Then the teacher stunned his new students with "…You are now in a Soviet spy-school. From this moment onwards, each and every one of you is forbidden to contact your own Party in China. You are no longer Chinese Communist Party members, you now belong to the Communist International Group, always referred to as Comintern. You will obey their orders and no other authority. You will never reveal anything relating to Comintern to a third party, no matter how important that person might be. To break this rule means severe punishment."

They couldn't believe their ears. It was unreasonable! Why had the Chinese agreed to such a thing?

The Russian teacher was obviously expecting their response and said with a little smile, "Don't worry, we have been teaching students from around the world for a long time. They too had problems with this rule. You will quickly get used to it."

That day after class, the twenty Chinese students gathered in Gao's room. All were unhappy. Huang Chi, face red with indignation, started them off.

"I don't understand this rule" said he. "Why can't we contact our own Party? Do our people know about this? Are we no longer Chinese?"

Being the group leader, Gao quickly used the "hush" gesture. This was a spy school. There was every chance that their words were being monitored. Gao liked the look of this earnest young man. He was from a poor peasant family living in Sichuan Province. From childhood he had accompanied his father to the mountains to cut wood and gather herbs for sale in the local market. His mother had taught him basic literacy and had chosen his wife, to whom he was devoted. In due time he had an adored son. After joining the Red Army he continued his education and excelled in mathematics. He was of medium height, squarely built, sturdy, tough, honest, direct and down to earth. Because of his woodcutting background, he was given the nickname Chopper. As time passed, Gao and Chopper became the closest of friends.

The discussion raged in hushed tones without getting anywhere. It was pointless anyway. The rule existed and they did not have the necessary answers to argue against it. Eventually, as the Senior Student, Gao felt obliged to bring the meeting to a close.

"Our number one discipline has always been to obey all orders without question," he stated, not expecting an argument. "Don't ask if it is right or wrong and don't talk about it anymore. It is time for lights out, so the meeting is over."

All quietly departed for their respective rooms. Chopper shared with Gao. In silence, they went to bed.

2.

Every day, Gao suffered student grumbles.

From one, "I'll never pass the Russian language test, I can't roll my tongue around the words."

Quickly followed by another, "Please don't talk about chemistry. I'll fail for sure."

"How do they expect us to remember all those strange foreign names? I hate geography." complained a third.

Whilst a fourth whined, "Philosophy and psychology are my undoing, I don't understand any of it."

Gao too had problems keeping up. It was hard work. They lost five Chinese in the first two months. By the end of six months only four were left. Huang Chi (Chopper), top grades in mathematics and martial arts. Zhou Shao-fei, nicknamed "Sparks" because of his telegraphic and telecommunications skills. Yang Tian-yun (Hunter), an excellent horseman, and Gao Qing, referred to as Big Brother. Gao was top in pistol shooting and languages.

After every sudden departure, their class tutor told them that so-and-so had been sent home. Not one was ever seen, or heard of, again.

Every Saturday evening, a dance was held in the ballroom. At the beginning of their seventh month, the four Chinese were invited to attend, but by then they had got into the habit of relaxing in their quarters, usually playing cards. In addition, none of them had learned to dance, so they didn't go. Suddenly the door to the room banged open and in strode their class tutor. His name was Feilibov, a tall, lean, forty-something Russian with a pronounced hooked nose, looking very smart in his dress uniform.

He snatched the cards from Gao's hand and shouted, "All of you must go to the dance. How dare you disobey!"

The four Chinese hurriedly dressed in their best uniforms, without managing to look anywhere near as impressive as Feilibov, and followed him. Up the stairs, out of their building into the floodlit night, across the compound, passes checked, inner gate opened, over the threshold of a Tsar house and into the ballroom.

It was brightly lit by many hanging chandeliers with, in the centre, one of those revolving mirror-balls that reflected little squares of light as it turned. Down both sides of the large oblong-shaped room there were lines of chairs with a few already occupied. At the end nearest to the entrance, a specially cordoned off area held comfortable looking wingback chairs with tables in front of them. On every table sat a small lamp, an ashtray, a telephone and half-a-dozen gleaming glasses. To the side of every chair stood an ice bucket, complete with bottle. This area was reserved for senior officers and high-ranking guests. Only a few of the chairs were being used. At regular intervals around the room fresh flowers erupted out of large vases on small tables, perfuming the air and pleasing the eyes. Small groups of men and women talked animatedly. Couples danced, dipping and swirling in time to the music coming from a balcony where the Russian military orchestra played. There was every colour of skin, facial contour, uniform and civilian dress on display. One of the tutors had told them that recruits from every country in the world were daily graduating from the spy school.

Surrounded by waltzing couples, Feilibov strode down the middle of the room with his Chinese students following along behind like embarrassed schoolboys. He stopped at the far end, underneath the balcony, and indicated where the Chinese should sit. Gao was quite happy to watch but after just a few minutes a pretty girl dressed in a beautifully fitting blue creation that emphasized her slim roundness came up and asked,

"Please, could I dance with you?"

After months of severance from the opposite sex, to him she had the loveliest blue eyes, the warmest smile, the blondest hair and the sexiest shape he had ever seen. He was on his feet and into her arms before his brain reminded him that he couldn't dance. He didn't care. He was not about to let this beauty go. Somehow they circumnavigated the room. Gao's eyes were on hers for most of the time. He did drag them away to smile stupidly and apologise for every blunder into another couple. He noticed that all four of them were on their feet and stumbling their way around the floor.

This first encounter with a European girl, *and she had chosen him*, made Gao feel rather splendid. At one point he noticed Feilibov standing to one side, a satisfied, almost cunning smile on his face.

"My name is Natasha." Her voice was soft and musical, making Gao forget Feilibov.

"Mine is Gao Qing," he replied.

She smiled and asked, "Do you like the Soviet Union?"

"Yes, I do...especially now...tonight." Gao said, in stumbling tongue-tied Russian.

"Can you come to dance every weekend?"

"Oh yes!" A breathless Gao managed to say.

"Ahhh, Comrade Gao Qing, I am so pleased to be dancing with you," sighed Natasha.

Gao felt her soft body press into his chest as her head rested on his shoulder. Her fragrant hair took all sense out of him. He was dancing on air in the hand of the Buddha!

Her voice, muffled by his uniform said, "I am tall with blue eyes. I chose you because you are the tallest man in your group and you have such intensely alive brown eyes."

It was past five in the morning when Gao returned to quarters. To his surprise his three friends were waiting.

"You must be tired," said Chopper scornfully, by way of a greeting.

Gao began to undress, wondering what was wrong. Chopper was glaring at him. Hunter had turned towards the window. Something on the floor held Spark's interest.

"Is something the matter?" Gao asked, alarmed.

"You!" Chopper cried out. "With that Russian girl. Have you forgotten where we are? Do you want to be thrown out like all the others?"

"No, I haven't forgotten." Gao replied quietly. "I enjoyed myself tonight, but one night of dancing doesn't mean a betrayal of everything I have worked for. And I hope to see her next week too." He shrugged his shoulders and joked, "When in Russia, do as the Russians do. It *was* Feilibov's idea."

Chopper was not to be denied. "When you took that Russian girl in your arms, did you forget that our motherland is engaged in a bitter war against Japan?"

Gao smiled as he replied, "Oh yes indeed! For a while I forgot everything except being so close to… her name, by the way, is not 'that Russian girl', it is Natasha." He looked at the three of them then continued, "I think it is important to strike a balance between work and play. Tonight I was playing, and if Natasha or some other girl wants to play some more and it doesn't clash with my work, then I will…and so should you."

Chopper stopped glaring, relaxed, and smiled. " You are shameless Big Brother, but I cannot fault your logic. By the way, did you notice the strange look on Feilibov's face? I did and it puzzled me until I realised that he had sent the girls. That is why I was worried when I saw you clinging on to Natasha and blundering around like a drunken oaf. It is a relief to know that you were in control of yourself. So go and fuck every girl in Russia, just as long as you remember that when we finish here, we go back to China."

"Yes, you are right. I will only fuck when Feilibov tells me to." Gao countered, setting them all off into gales of laughter. Later in his bed and just before he fell asleep, his brain reminded him how good it felt to have these young men as his friends. However, it was beautiful Natasha who shared his dreams.

3.

The next Saturday morning, in a line around the classroom, Feilibov had hung about a hundred and fifty black-and-white photographs. The subjects were men and women, no two the same, different in age and dress. Speaking Russian, Feilibov commanded, "Comrades, I want you to memorize the names and details of at least one hundred of the people in these photographs. Of course, it would be better if you can remember more. One hundred is the target and the minimum I will accept."

Using a short stick he pointed to the first picture. "This is someone we all recognize, Chiang Kai-shek. He is President of the Kuomintang Government and speaks Mandarin with a Zhejiang dialect. Next comes Mao Zedong, Communist Leader from Hunan Province. Adolf Hitler…" He spoke for about an hour-and-a-half without resorting to notes, reciting the name and details of the person in every photograph. All were VIP's, whether Chinese Communist, Chinese Nationalist, Japanese, Russian, American, French, German or British.

Suddenly he called, "Comrade Huang Chi, tell me something about these four people," he pointed at random.

Chopper was caught completely by surprise. "You went too fast Comrade Feilibov, I cannot remember."

"All right Comrade." Feilibov pointed to four different photographs. "These are all Chinese. Tell me about them."

Poor Chopper, acutely embarrassed, had to admit to not remembering.

Feilibov turned to Sparks and asked him to name the same four Chinese. He did, correctly and in full.

Feilibov turned back to Chopper, "You should feel ashamed of yourself. Do you think martial arts can save your country? A strong body will not make you into a good intelligence gathering operative if your brain is empty."

This was a reminder that Chopper, during the last martial arts training session, had beaten all four of his Russian instructors. Now Feilibov was taking Russian revenge by belittling Chopper.

Silence.

The students had learned that there was usually a trick hidden behind such behaviour. Silence was their only defence.

"Comrade Huang Chi, you must memorize seventy names today and the rest by Monday," commanded Feilibov.

"Yes, Comrade," replied Chopper. "Please let me use this classroom for the rest of today and tomorrow. I promise to commit all these names to memory."

Feilibov nodded and said he would report the request to the authorities. Satisfied for the moment, he advised Chopper that the details to be memorized were to be found on the reverse of the photographs. The class was dismissed until Monday.

After lunch, Chopper returned to the classroom. His three friends went with him. He protested at first until Gao admitted that he too needed to work. They toiled all afternoon and slowly at least half of the information was committed to their memories. They stopped only because they had to eat and prepare for the dance. The next day, Sunday, they again worked all day, except for meals, steadily memorising the rest. On Monday morning, Chopper reeled off every name and detail. So did

Hunter, Sparks and Gao.

Feilibov was satisfied but just so that he had the last word on the subject, in a voice awash with sarcasm, he scolded, "With information a Russian child could absorb with ease, it takes three adult Chinese to stuff the brain of one."

This was to let them know that he knew how the four had spent the weekend.

*

It was a particularly difficult period. Their ability to remember was stretched to the limit as their tutors forced information into them. For example, an elderly Russian told them to use the huge maps pinned to a wall and learn, in one day, the locations of every major river, mountain range, country and capital cities of the world.

Their compulsory hour of evening revision was no longer enough. As day followed day, they revised for longer and longer periods. Work ate into their sleeping time as they struggled to keep up. Random testing was commonplace. No mistake, however small, was allowed to pass without some form of punishment.

One summer Sunday afternoon, the only day of the week when they could relax, the four friends decided to take a walk. They could speak freely in the open air. As they emerged from underground, they sniffed the flower-scented air and filled their lungs. As was usual, Chopper started them off.

"The work is too heavy. I wake up tired after losing so much sleep and cannot concentrate on the lessons."

All four acknowledged that it was hard - too hard sometimes. Their tutors were merciless when punishing their lapses. After a good moan they agreed that failure definitely wasn't an option, therefore they only had one course of action, to support each other through to graduation. Decision made, they enjoyed the rest of their walk.

4.

A year flashed past. They were now fluent in Russian, English and Japanese. They had quick minds, excellent memories and strong bodies. Educationally they had progressed beyond their wildest expectations and their confidence in themselves was growing by the day. As a bonus, they had each other.

Winter came early that year. Moscow was covered with layers of heavy snow and thick ice but it made little difference to the four friends buried deep underground. Typically, Feilibov chose this time to allow their Russian girlfriends join them on their Sunday afternoon walks. Also, they were given turns to be taken to the city, sightseeing with their particular girl.

A subtle influence had crept into them. Even honest and straightforward Chopper was more restrained. Their fiery Chinese temperaments had faded, to be replaced by a quieter, more positive introversion. From bluff and bluster to quiet dangerousness. All of them now felt entirely comfortable to be seen with their Russian girlfriends.

Gao was always happy when Natasha was by his side. She wanted to know everything about China and asked Gao to teach her Chinese. She stated that her parents knew all about Gao and had given their approval, which was a puzzle to him. How could her parents approve without meeting him? Gao said nothing about that, but he did ask why she wanted to learn Chinese.

"My secret." she replied.

*

Six more months went by. By now the four Chinese students were experts in all forms of killing, espionage, surveillance, cat burglary, safe cracking, codes and ciphers and other spy skills. They could run fast, jump high or long, climb up the side of a building and abseil down, squeeze into small places and stay quiet and still for hours if necessary. If, after spy school, any one of them had chosen a life of crime, they would have been nothing less than master criminals.

They had been thoroughly tutored in the art of self-control. To an outsider, if they wished it to be so, they could appear cold, or calculating, or emotionless, or without feeling. They could also act exactly the opposite. Only Gao had a weakness. He was in love. That was something beyond his control.

A sunny early summer Sunday of 1941, when they and girls were walking as usual, Gao noticed that Natasha was allowing a gap to grow between the others and them. He felt good. The meadows were awash with wild-flower colours, bees buzzed, birds were singing and so was his heart. By now Natasha was the most important person in his life.

She wore a white semi-transparent dress over a pink lace-fringed slip, and her golden hair hung in a ponytail, tied with a pink silk ribbon. She looked stunning. As they chatted she slipped her tiny delicate hand into Gao's big rough mitt.

Softly she breathed, "I have dreams about you. One day I want to visit you in China."

Gao was pleased to hear this, and confided, "I dream of you too. In my dreams we are close…very, very close." He couldn't have made his meaning plainer. She seemed not to mind. Smiling contentedly, she walked on for a while, then, with a serious look on her face, she inhaled deeply and said in one long breath, "Comrade Gao Qing, I know your time here is almost up. There are things I can only say to you in private, so, before you bid farewell to me and return to China, I want to take you to my home. Will you come?"

Gao nodded without speaking, and a month later it was over. Each of them had excelled at something. Sparks set a new spy school speed record for tapping out Morse-coded signals and receiving messages as fast as the fastest tutor could send them. Chopper defeated his martial arts instructors for the last time and Gao Qing's pistol shooting was excellent whilst Hunter was a superb horseman.

5.

Their last Sunday dawned warm and mellow. At noon as arranged, Natasha arrived by limousine to take Gao to her home. She drove with expert efficiency into the city, around Red Square and down a side street to stop in front of an iron gate. Through a side window Gao saw the famous onion-shaped domes. The gate opened, allowing Natasha to drive to the front entrance of a huge house. A butler came to the car and opened the door to let Gao out. He gaped in surprise and wonder.

"It belonged to a general of the Tsar," explained Natasha. "When the Communists took power, this house passed to my father. He commands the army of the Ukraine and is garrisoned in Odessa. Mother is with him. I live here by myself cared for by a few servants."

They climbed the front steps and reached the beautifully carved wooden front door held open by a black-and-white uniformed servant girl. Natasha took Gao's arm and guided him inside and to the left into a huge, sumptuously furnished drawing room.

Natasha gave a gentle tug on a bell-pull before sitting beside Gao on a leather settee. Almost immediately the same butler entered, closely followed by the door-girl carrying tea on a tray. She set the tray on a side-table then stood back to allow the butler to serve them. At the conclusion of this little ceremony, the butler and maid left the room.

"Not exactly what Marx had in mind when he wrote his Communist Manifesto," remarked Gao, "but don't mind me, I am enjoying myself."

They laughed together as they munched on small sandwiches.

She swallowed delicately before asking, "Do you have a similar house in China?"

He laughed. "No, not at all. I come from a poor peasant family. My parents worked for the local landlord. I left home and joined the Red Army at the age of twelve and never went back. I don't even know if my parents are still alive."

Poor Natasha! Gao noticed a small sliver of cucumber stuck to a tooth as she stared at him open-mouthed. Her facial expression showed that she was not sure if what she had just heard was the truth.

She found her voice. "I thought you were rich because you are a senior army officer. All Russian high ranking officers are rich. Is it not the same in China?"

"Yes for the Nationalists. No for the Communists."

Natasha bowed her head and sat quietly for a while. The butler and maid reappeared, this time carrying a tray containing small silver spoons, crystal glasses, ice cream on gold-rimmed plates and a bottle of red wine. They retreated with the tea tray.

Natasha handed Gao a spoon and a plate of ice cream. She placed a glass of wine where he could reach it. He could see that she had something on her mind.

"What is it?" he asked.

She gave him a long look before saying; "Did you know that we girls were chosen especially to dance with you?"

"We guessed."

"Do you know why?"

He shook his head.

"Speaking honestly, nobody in Russia is free. We obey orders. Your tutor, Comrade Feilibov, is an expert on Chinese affairs. Although he doesn't look it, he is half Chinese. The other half is a Russian father who is a family friend, so Feilibov has seen me grow up. After I had chosen you to be my dancing partner, it was he who told my parents.

"He was following instructions issued by Comintern. I think he has learned to respect you because he particularly wants you to know that I had to report everything I could find out about you to him. He forwarded my reports together with his own observations directly to Stalin…'

"Stalin!" Gao interjected, almost dropping the half-empty plate. He couldn't take it in. His mind raced as fast as his pulse. "What does Stalin want with me?" he croaked.

"Don't be afraid," she said softly, stretching out her hand to cover his. "Feilibov told me to tell you that Stalin is entirely satisfied with your progress. When the time comes for you to be presented to him, Feilibov wants you to be ready. And in my heart I thank him for bringing you and me together, because with you I have found love. True, honest, natural love that turns my blood to warm sweet honey every time I see you."

Big tears filled her eyes and ran down her cheeks. Gao felt his last shreds of resistance melt away as love, held in check since their first dance, swept over him.

"I love you too." He said in hushed tones. It was not enough. "I LOVE YOU TOO!" he shouted, pulling her to him.

Some time later their urgent kissing eased to gentle caresses.

"I am leaving shortly to wherever I am sent." Gao said to her.

"I know. And when you leave, I will never be able to get in touch with you again. Feilibov has explained it all. You will go and that will be the end."

More tears.

Gao hated to see her so unhappy so he searched for words to give her hope.

"It need not be the end. As soon as the war against Japan is over I will be able to pass a message through Comintern to Feilibov. He can tell you where I am and pass messages between us."

He knew it was a forlorn hope but better than nothing at all.

They clung to each other for a long time until, all too soon, daylight disappeared.

"Darling," he murmured, "it's dark. I must return to the school."

"No, I won't let you go. Not yet. Even under Communism real love does not need anybody's approval."

She took his hand, stood up and led him upstairs.

That night Gao discovered a new Natasha who really was warm and honey sweet.

*

Hunter was the first to leave, knowing only that he was on his way to the mountains of China's Xinjiang Province. Five days later Sparks received his orders and left, not knowing his final destination. Gao Qing was appointed the head of the Far East Intelligence Network and to his surprise and joy, Chopper was made his deputy.

At about eleven in the morning, Feilibov ordered him to change into his best uniform, and because Natasha had warned him, he guessed the reason. An hour later, Stalin, making one of his rare visits to the spy school, rose as Gao entered the classroom.

It was Stalin's eyes that Gao most remembered. Constantly moving and alert, they sparkled like black sapphires. Stalin held out his hand. After shaking hands, Stalin sat on a plain chair whilst Gao remained standing.

Stalin, speaking Russian with a marked Georgian accent, boomed, "Comrade Gao Qing. I am happy to meet you. I understand that you and your three classmates have proved to be excellent pupils and now you are returning to China."

"Yes, Comrade General Secretary. I await my orders."

"I am looking forward to hearing great things about you. This experiment to set up a class exclusively for hand-picked Chinese Party members has so far proved to be a success. Please remember that everything you do will be for the people. I will be reading all the reports. If you do well, I will authorise the school to repeat the experiment. Comrade Gao, do not let me down."

"I will do my best to live up to your expectations, Comrade General Secretary. My time here has given me all the tools I need to do well. Now it is up to me."

Stalin stood and held out his hand. Gao Qing shook it before saluting. Then he was ushered out.

*

Gao and Chopper left together, heading for their Motherland. Their destination was the big city of Lanzhou situated in northwest China. On arrival, someone would meet them and they must obey his every order. Who was this man, and what was his name? They were not told, nor could they ask.

CHAPTER 2.

Northwest China, June 1941

1.

At dusk, the Russian transport aircraft bumped down and slowly taxied to a stop. Andriev led Gao and Chopper off the plane and onto a waiting truck displaying the white star of Chiang Kai-shek's Kuomintang Government. Which was a worry to Gao and Chopper, dressed as they were in their Communist Army uniforms. China was still at war, not only against the Japanese invaders but also against itself. The Kuomintang no longer had orders to kill any suspected Chinese Communists, but unofficially they continued to do so. This time they were safe. At every checkpoint, after Andriev showed his papers to the Kuomintang sentries, the truck was allowed to proceed without incident.

The truck stopped in front of a large building. Lights came on as Gao and Chopper climbed over the tailboard and dropped to the ground. They quickly read a board saying, in both Russian and Chinese, "The Lanzhou Liaison Office of the Union of Soviet Socialist Republics." To their total astonishment, they saw Feilibov standing by the door!

Andriev saluted. With a little smile he said, "Meet your Controller. From now on you will follow his orders without question." Again saluting, he climbed back into the truck and was gone.

Feilibov had his supercilious "I tricked you again" smile as he led his two best students into the building. In his office, cups of Chinese green tea and bowls of rice with pickled vegetables were laid out. As Gao and Chopper ate, Feilibov briefed them.

"Everything has been arranged. You must get to your safe house before the curfew begins at 2200 hours. Take off those uniforms and put these on."

He passed over two sets of nicely cut navy-blue silk gowns and round skullcaps that have, for centuries, been worn by middle-class Chinese businessmen. Gao was to pose as a rich silk merchant named Chen-ye. Chopper, as Long-wu, was his associate. Their task was to get into the city of Chongqing, eleven hundred kilometres away, without having their names noted.

Feilibov handed over their forged identity papers and finished his brief.

"Someone is waiting for you outside. All you need to do is follow him. Good luck."

As they left the building, a shadowy figure wearing a black gown and a distinctive top hat appeared a few metres ahead of them and began to walk fast. They followed the hat until, ten minutes later, the shadow silently stretched out his right arm and pointed to the front before disappearing into a side alley. They continued to walk forward. A young man carrying a newspaper stepped out from a doorway and asked, "Are you from Mr. Fee?"

Gao gave the pre-arranged response. "Yes, we are they."

"Come."

2.

Inside an old, but very beautiful traditionally built house, another man introduced himself. "I am Comrade Fu-zhi, Kuomintang Governor of Xiahe County. I live here in Lanzhou, and yes, I am a Communist." He was of the opinion that when the Japanese had first invaded China, the Communists and the Kuomintang armies should have immediately united. "...and when Chiang Kai-shek refused to unite, showing himself to be a dishonourable man, Communism seemed to be the only way forward for the Chinese people." The house was now a Communist place of safety inside the Kuomintang controlled city.

Madam Fu-zhi was used to having strangers suddenly arrive at her home and asked no questions. She welcomed Gao and Chopper, then quickly arranged for the servants to prepare accommodation and food. When they had eaten their fill, she led the way across the courtyard to a side-wing of the house into a comfortable room. Tired from the long journey, the two men were soon fast asleep.

*

Gao shook Chopper awake and gestured with his hand behind his ear, as if listening for a sound. There was movement outside the door. They silently crossed the room. Chopper stood with his back against the wall on one side of the closed door and Gao did the same on the other. Chopper grasped the handle. On Gao's nod, he abruptly pulled the door open to reveal a crouching man, listening.

Chopper pulled him into the room and quickly shut the door. An expertly placed karate stroke from Gao stunned the eavesdropper. It had taken five silent seconds.

To the letter they had followed their training. "Be vigilant at all times. Deal with any suspect who appears to be a threat to your mission. Be merciless. Cover your tracks."

They searched the man - no identification, just a vicious looking knife.

Gao whispered, "I'll get our host, you keep watch."

Comrade Fu-zhi, in response to Gao's persistent knocking, called, "Who is there?"

"Chen-ye. Please come, I have something to show you."

The Governor, with a black silk dressing gown carelessly draped over his thin frame, followed Gao back to the room. When the door was firmly closed with Chopper standing with his back to it, Gao quickly whispered an explanation as to why they were speaking across an unconscious man lying on the floor. The Governor responded with the information that the man was a well-known local bully and paid informant who had long deserved death.

Not long afterwards, Gao and Chopper watched the young bodyguard drop the body down a deep dry well in the garden of the house and replace the heavy wooden lid.

"He has been paid in full," murmured the Governor.

The next morning, the Governor, Gao and Chopper had a long conversation about security. How did the dead man hear about them so quickly? Who had let him into the house? How did he know what room they had been given?

There was only one answer. An informer.

The Governor decided that he needed help and summoned his close friend, Mr. Zhong-xi, a fellow Communist sympathizer and the richest landlord in the area.

Zhong-xi arrived in an ornate carriage pulled by a matching pair of black mares. Aged about forty, he was dressed in a dark blue gown made from the very best quality silk. In addition to the liveried driver, four bodyguards and four servants accompanied him.

Without revealing any secrets or mentioning the dead man, the Governor told his friend about the security problem and asked for help.

"Of course!" said Zhong-xi, turning to the two guests. "I have a large estate not far from here. You can stay with me for as long as you wish."

The Governor showed his gratitude in the traditional Chinese way. He bowed to his visitor whilst holding his hands in a praying position. So did Gao and Chopper. After a chat and refreshments, Zhong-xi led the way to his carriage and bowed the two men in. They waved farewell to the Governor as the horses moved off.

Gao's peasant background did not prepare him for such opulence. The estate covered thousands of acres of the very best agricultural land. It included many houses clustered together like a village. Every house had its own piece of land to allow those that worked on the estate to feed themselves. Unlike most landlords, Zhong-xi treated his workers with respect. In return, they willingly worked hard in his fields. He told us that many of the workers were Communist Comrades hiding from the Kuomintang. Neither Gao nor Chopper had ever seen such a place. Everything was out of the ordinary.

Mr. Zhong-xi told his family and servants that his two guests were rich businessmen friends who must be treated with the utmost respect. Money was no problem, Zhong-xi threw it away like dirt. Every day the cooks had orders to prepare a grand feast. No less than sixteen dishes every evening, eight hot and eight cold, just for them. This was on top of a superb breakfast, huge lunch and several dishes of delicious nibbles in between.

For the second night of their visit, Mr. Zhong-xi engaged a local theatrical troupe to give a show in the open-air theatre. It was an excellent way to spend an evening. The show was programmed to begin with a short drama, followed by half-an-hour of circus acts, then singers and dancers. After a refreshment interlude, the main event was to be Peking Opera.

Gao and Chopper decided that they quite liked their generous host, but they were worried. He was not to know that they didn't like the idea of being on display as honoured guests, and as expected, the booking of the theatrical troupe caused the Lanzhou City Kuomintang Intelligence Department to take an interest. It was their job to investigate anything unusual, no matter how innocent or trivial.

Shortly before the show was due to begin, an army colonel and two soldiers arrived on horseback, ostensibly to pay a friendly visit. The guests were introduced.

"Colonel Yuan, may I please introduce two business friends, Mr. Chen-ye and Mr. Long-wu."

When the show began, the colonel showed little interest. He left after fifteen minutes.

Mr. Zhong-xi hurried over and whispered to Gao.

"He came with ill intent, not goodwill."

Gao agreed and said that he and Chopper should move on.

Mr. Zhong-xi, with many people to protect, was quick to suggest that instead of waiting for the train, they could travel to Chongqing by bus. There was a scheduled departure the next day. "However," he warned. "It is a difficult journey over poor roads, with many delays".

Gao and Chopper said yes, they would take it. The quicker they got out of Lanzhou, the better.

3.

For many years during and after the anti-Japanese war, the long-distance "bus" between the two cities was a dilapidated American-made ten-wheel flatbed truck with a makeshift olive green canvas covering. About thirty adults, a few children and sundry birds and animals crowded in. Gao and Chopper paid extra to be allocated two spaces on the wooden benches that ran down both sides between the wheel arches. Most of the passengers sat on the wooden floor.

The long journey across the mountains was slow, bumpy and uncomfortable. The bus stopped at all the villages to drop off and pick up passengers. Every village had two checkpoints, one in, one out. Gao noted that a junior officer and two soldiers manned every checkpoint. Usually, the bus was waved through without inspection.

In low voices, Gao and Chopper decided on their next move. To avoid having their names noted, they decided that instead of staying on the bus to the terminus in Chongqing, they would alight outside the city limits and look for an unguarded pedestrian-only path into the city.

The bus continued to pass through the checkpoints without hindrance. They had crossed the border between Gansu and Sichuan Provinces after a cursory glance at their papers. All had been smooth, until, with about fifty kilometres left to go, the bus was stopped at a checkpoint. A young Kuomintang officer, full of aggressive arrogance, boarded.

"Papers!" he barked.

Sauntering down the bus, he kicked passengers, livestock and luggage out of his way as he randomly checked papers and travel permits. Then he spotted the girl. She was aged about twenty and by her dress, a student. She sat on a side-bench reading a left-wing newspaper, showing no interest in the officer. He stopped and stared at her, she ignored him.

He leaned over and shouted, "Why are you reading that disgusting rubbish?"

She looked up and into his eyes. In a clear, cool voice she replied, "This is my choice. It is not a banned publication so I am breaking no law."

She returned to her reading. The young officer, in danger of losing face, snatched the newspaper out of her hands.

"You are under arrest as a suspected Communist," he shouted. "Pick up your belongings and come with me."

The girl paled. She knew that as soon as he said "Communist" her life was in danger. Her accuser, if he decided, could immediately shoot her. Bravely, she stood straight and resolute. Eyes boring into his, she stated, "I am studying law in Chongqing University. My papers are in order and I have done nothing wrong."

"I think you are a Communist." He turned to the two soldiers. "Handcuff her. I will take her to headquarters."

Chopper looked at Gao. Gao nodded and gestured with a slight side movement of his head, meaning, "Let's go with her."

His thinking process told him, "If the girl is a Comrade, we must help. If she isn't, she is innocent. If we don't stop him, this jackass will first rape, and then kill the girl. It is almost time for us to leave the bus anyway". They stood up.

Chopper bowing respectfully said, "Mistress, how can you go alone? I have instructions to see you safely home. I must come with you."

Utterly confused, the girl looked at Chopper. His servile posture made him appear to be exactly like a family servant. She quickly realized that he was prepared to help her, and replied, "This officer is taking me from the bus. Please tell the General."

Gao spoke up. "I must come too. The General will want to know exactly what has happened to you."

Chopper bowed to the officer. "Sir, we serve the General and his family. We have orders to never leave the side of our Mistress. Please may we go with you?"

The young officer, caught by surprise at this intervention, turned pale when he heard "General". His confusion was clearly evident. If he released the girl he would lose much face with his soldiers and be the laughing stock of the barracks. To continue with the arrest risked big trouble. Deciding that his loss of face was too much to bear, he dropped off the back of the bus and beckoned the soldiers to bring the girl. Gao and Chopper quickly gathered their things and jumped down too. The bus driver, glad to be away, crunched the gears and drove off.

Leaving one soldier to manage the checkpoint, the officer ordered the girl, Gao and Chopper to sit in the back seat of an American-made Jeep. The officer occupied the front passenger seat, telling the second soldier to drive. Gao was behind the driver. Chopper sat behind the officer, with the girl in the middle. When the engine fired into life, out of the corner of his mouth Gao muttered in Russian, "Don't damage the uniforms". Chopper turned up his right thumb to indicate his understanding. They headed towards Chongqing.

Gao let the jeep travel two or three kilometres, all the while checking for possible witnesses. When there were none, he turned his thumb down. Chopper's iron fist crashed into the base of the head in front of him, snapping the spinal cord. Gao put his pistol to the temple of the driver. "Stop!" he ordered. The Jeep skidded to a halt.

Gao had no conscience about killing the officer. The driver was a different matter. After all, he was just an ordinary Chinese doing his job. What to do with him?

The driver solved the problem. "Is he dead?" he asked.

"Yes," confirmed Chopper. Despite the pistol still at his temple, the driver relaxed.

"Good," he said. "I have had enough of him. He was the worst kind of man." He spat to emphasize his feelings.

Gao moved the gun away from the driver's head. "Get out and undress," he ordered.

The driver didn't seem at all upset to take off the uniform. Well trained, he lay the tunic jacket and trousers carefully on the front seat of the jeep, cap on top, shoes and socks on the floor.

Barefoot and standing in his undergarments, he said in resigned voice, "I suppose you are going to kill me too." He knelt and waited for the bullet. No plea for mercy, nor any sign of fear.

"Do you have a family?" Gao asked.

"A wife and two kids. I have a picture in my wallet."

Gao picked up the wallet. Inside, he found a little money and a photograph of a peasant wife with arms around two smiling kids. He didn't want to shoot this man, but needed a good reason.

"What would you do if I let you go?" he asked.

"Join the Communists!" The driver laughed at his own joke, but this was deadly serious.

"Why would you do that?"

"Because I joined the army to kill Japanese, not mess about on a checkpoint. Mao Zedong needs trained men. I would find his army and join the Communists."

"On your feet soldier," Gao ordered. The driver stood up. Gao passed him his wallet.

"Give me your identity tag," said Gao. "And if you swear not to say anything about what has happened here, you can go."

"I swear." The driver took the identity tag from around his neck and passed it to Gao then held out the little finger of his right hand. Gao curled the little finger of his right hand around his. They had used the ancient sign of absolute fidelity. To break it meant committing suicide.

Gao was satisfied.

"China needs men like you," said Gao. "It is good to send you away without clothes. You have a clean beginning."

Gao took off his own shoes and passed them to the driver. Pulling on the shoes, the driver turned and ran away across the fields.

The girl was a bundle of nerves. She had seen Chopper kill a man with one blow. When Gao turned towards her still holding his pistol, she shrank back, her handcuffed hands covering her face. Realizing his mistake, Gao quickly holstered it.

As softly as he could, Gao said to her, "Don't be afraid. When we got involved, our only intention was to save you from him." He tilted his head towards the body. Naked, it no longer looked like an officer. Gao found the key and unlocked the handcuffs on the wrists of the girl. Returning to the body, he removed the identity tag from around its neck and replaced it with the soldier's. When the body was found, the soldier would be reported dead, with the officer listed as a deserter.

Dressed in army uniforms, with their civilian clothes tied into bundles, they drove towards the city. Chopper did the driving with Gao as the officer beside him and the girl in the back. Now that she was sure they weren't about to kill her, or worse, she began to talk, and talk, and talk.

From her constant stream of words the two men learned that she was studying law at university. Her father was a silk merchant and there was plenty of money. She was aged twenty-one and when in Chongqing, she lived with her family. Her elder siblings had already graduated as lawyers. She was glad that they had let the soldier go. She wasn't a Communist. A previous passenger must have discarded the newspaper she had been reading. She had found it on a seat... and on... and on... and on...

On the road, they saw several military vehicles going the other way. Chopper and the other drivers waved to each other, whilst Gao saluted. They stopped beside the first bus stop they came to and let the girl out.

She made a small bow and said, "Thank you for saving me. I know

I talk a lot but this is one secret I must keep, because, if I say anything, I will condemn myself to death. My family must know, but nobody else. If I ever see you again, please let me say hello."

In the fading light, Chopper turned the jeep around and drove some seven or eight kilometers before seeing a suitable side road. They went up it for about two kilometres before stopping. It was now completely dark so they made camp.

4.

At first light they took stock of their situation. The sudden disappearance of a jeep filled with two army personnel and three prisoners would have been circulated. The jeep had its own identity code painted on the side so they had to dump it. Their descriptions, when last seen by the soldier left on checkpoint duty, meant a change of appearance, but how?

Their map showed an ancient horse-trail that meandered through the hills towards Chongqing. They decided to stay in uniform and drive the jeep until they could hide it somewhere, then wear their gowns. If they got the chance they would change into other clothes.

At mid-morning, they found a long-ago abandoned clay quarry, now full of dirty water. Except for the shoes Gao was wearing, they watched everything belonging to the army sink without trace. Wearing their gowns and carrying hand luggage, they followed a winding path that headed upwards into the hills.

It was well past noon when the path led them to an old temple hidden deep in a forest of tall, ancient trees. The gate was open, allowing entry into a tidy courtyard. In the high-ceilinged praying hall, under a large statue of Buddha sitting cross-legged on a raised platform, knelt an old man dressed in a Kasaya (an orange and red patchwork outer vestment worn by senior Buddhist monks).

They waited in silence until the old monk completed his chanting of the prescribed scriptures as his hands counted the long row of beads hanging like an oversized necklace from around his neck. As Communists, Gao and Chopper were non-believers, but that didn't stop them from respecting the need of others to believe.

When the monk eventually turned to look at the visitors, he was surprised to see two well-dressed, but dusty men standing before him. Gao stepped forward with his hands across his chest in a praying position. He gave a small respectful bow and murmured, "Most eminent Abbot, we are so sorry to disturb you."

The Abbot blessed them. "Amitabha, Amitayus," (Buddha be merciful). He too had his hands in a praying position. Bowing low, he said, "Come sirs, you are always welcome to rest here awhile. Have you eaten?"

Such gentle courtesy and flowery language was a leftover from the ancient Chinese civilization when the people were renowned for their politeness, warm hospitality, good manners and strict rules of etiquette.

Gao replied, "Your eminence, before answering your question, if it pleases you, may I humbly ask a question of my own?"

A nod from the monk allowed Gao to continue, "how many people stay here?"

"I have six young probationers, two tutors and me, your humble servant."

It was safe for them to stay awhile.

"We would be pleased to accept your kind invitation to eat with you," confirmed Gao.

The Abbot led them through the main section of the temple to the dining area and invited them to sit at a table. When they were settled, the Abbot clapped his hands once. Two shaven-headed young men appeared as if from nowhere and bowed.

The Abbot ordered food and cups of green tea be brought for his guests. One of the young monks returned to the kitchen, the other went to an open fire over which a large cauldron was hanging. The lid was removed and a ladle used to fill two bowls with rice porridge. The bowls and tea arrived at the same time and were quickly consumed. More tea and porridge were served together with a selection of pickled vegetables. This time Gao and Chopper took longer over each mouthful. Such plain food is standard fare for the devoted followers of Buddhism. To these two hungry men, on that day, it was a banquet!

After they had eaten, the Abbot led them into a side chamber he used as his living area and office. They thanked the old man for his hospitality. He shrugged as though it was nothing.

But it wasn't "nothing" it was an essential part of their chosen way of life. In temples all over China the monks toiled in the fields to provide for themselves and water had to be carried a long way from the nearest source. Gao pulled a 20-yuan banknote from his pocket and asked, "Please your eminence, if I may impose upon your good will one more time. To travel these hills we need suitable clothes. If you can spare a few rags, this money is to help with your charity work and we will leave our gowns here."

The Abbot disappeared into the depths of the temple, to reappear after a few minutes with two white Kung fu tops, two pairs of black trousers and four rice-buns.

"These clothes are old," he said. "If you don't mind wearing them, they are yours. The buns are for your journey…Amitabha."

With these words the Abbot knelt down on a prayer mat and closed his eyes. It was his way of saying goodbye.

A young monk entered and silently bowed them out to the courtyard. They changed clothes, pushing their pistols inside the waistband of their trousers and covering them with the loose tops. Leaving their neatly folded gowns and caps, with the banknote on top, they continued on their way.

*

They crested the high ground and began their descent. The path they had been following all day ended in a small clearing as it joined another more travelled path. They stopped, wondering which way to go. The map wasn't any help. Gao's instincts told him that they should turn left. They heard voices. Not knowing who owned them, Gao and Chopper tucked themselves out of sight in the undergrowth.

A shoulder-pole team appeared, surrounded by heavily armed scoundrels.

For many centuries, the most common way to transport essential goods from one part of China to another has been by shoulder pole. It is a straight bamboo pole about three metres in length and, with a large basket or bundle attached to each end, balanced across the shoulders of a porter. In this way, by using the strong shoulders of the young monks, many of the religious orders help support their temples by earning money transporting other people's goods.

At their head will be their leader. From years of pole carrying, he will have knowledge of thousands of kilometres of ancient footpaths and trails that criss-cross the length and breadth of China. And where you find the porters, there will be bandits waiting to steal their loads. Gao and Chopper had walked into a shoulder-pole team versus bandit-gang confrontation.

There were nine unarmed porters being harassed by over twenty bandits. This group of porters was identically dressed in black shoes, white trousers and white arm-less vests with extra padding across the shoulders. Their heads were shaved. Around their waists all wore the same shade of blue sash. This was their team identification.

The bandits were a motley collection of ruffians dressed mainly in animal skins. All carried rifles, machetes, knives and a few also had pistols. Robbery was their way of life and they could be unimaginably cruel.

From the shouting, Gao gathered that the bandits wanted all the goods and the leader of the shoulder-pole team was trying to negotiate.

"I can only give you two loads. You know very well that we earn our living by carrying goods. If you take everything, we are out of business. That will mean no more for you either. With the loss of two loads we will not earn any money this time."

The bandit leader, a fierce looking bewhiskered individual aged somewhere in his forties bellowed back, "Stop! Leave everything on the ground, then go. I don't care if you live, die or starve. If you don't obey me, my men will shoot you in mid-stride."

The head porter stopped moving and made a signal. As one, his followers halted, laid down their loads, unravelled the sashes from around their waists and released the poles from the bundles. They then moved into an ancient tried and tested defensive formation. Three surrounded the old man and the bundles whilst the other five formed a small outer circle around them. They held the poles in one hand and the sashes in the other. If the bandits wanted to take the bundles, then they were going to have to fight for them.

Chopper whispered in Gao's ear, "These porters are experienced martial arts experts, they won't be intimidated by the guns."

The two groups silently stared at each other.

One of the bandits raised his rifle and pointed it at the old man. Before he could pull the trigger, the porter nearest to him flicked his sash. Gao realized that the sashes were weighted at one end, perhaps with a stone. It snaked out almost three metres, wrapped itself around the rifle and took it out of the grasp of the bandit and into the possession of the porter.

The other bandits raised their rifles. Again they were too slow. All five of the outer circle of porters, moving extraordinarily fast, used their poles and sashes to smash robber heads, arms and legs. The seemingly innocuous bits of wood and cloth were lethal weapons in the hands of these experts. Just two shots were fired, each hitting a porter, before the robbers retreated into the trees to fire from cover.

From where they were hiding, Gao and Chopper could see some of the bandits crouching in the undergrowth, firing their weapons. Another porter went down. They looked at each other. Should they get involved? Of course they must.

Firing their pistols, they caught the bandits completely by surprise, picking off a number of them before the rest ran away. One of the dead was the bewhiskered bandit leader.

The flashing poles and sashes had killed two bandits and wounded several others. Gao and Chopper had killed five. Depleted in numbers and leaderless, it would be a long time before that particular bandit group would again try to rob a shoulder-pole team.

Gao and Chopper stepped out from their hiding place. Like striking cobras two sashes uncurled and wrapped themselves around their wrists. A split second later, strong fingers forced their hands to drop the pistols. The old man, aged about sixty, barked an order and their hands were freed.

Chopper grinned and said in a perfect Sichuan dialect, "I have never seen such incredible skill. Well done!"

His grin and dialect eased the tension. The porters stepped back, their bodies as tight as springs, ready for any emergency.

Chopper continued, "We are on our way to Chongqing. We didn't want any trouble so we hid when you appeared. We saw the bandits try to rob you and decided to help."

At that moment, Gao spotted a bandit taking aim with a rifle. In one motion, Gao pushed the old man aside and knelt to retrieve his pistol.

He was too slow.

Like bullets, three stones smashed into the forehead of the bandit. Gao clearly saw blood spurting. Gao and Chopper were dumbstruck. These shoulder-pole carriers were so fast, like lightning!

Every Chinese boy listens to the local storyteller painting mental word-pictures of the exploits of ancient chivalrous swordsmen and martial arts experts. Now they were seeing it with their own eyes. Gao watched Chopper, the number one spy school kung-fu expert, look at these men with eyes filled with hero worship.

"It is wise for travellers to be prepared," observed the old man. "You have your pistols. We use our skill. Fate decreed that men must die here today. It was not our time. Why else were you brought here with your pistols at exactly the right moment to help us? We lost two of our number and one is wounded. Without you, all of us might have perished, so we thank you."

He called his men together. The damage to the wounded porter was not serious. The bullet had passed through the muscled flesh between his neck and his right shoulder. The old man sprinkled a bright yellow herbal powder over the "in" and the "out" holes then used a clean cloth as a bandage.

"I will carry your load my son," he said to the young man.

Gao introduced Chopper and himself, using two failed spy school student names. There was no reason to take chances. The old man pointed at each porter in turn.

"We come from a temple in the mountains where we follow the Shaolin code of honourable conduct. Each of us has a religious name. On the road we use work names. Pole One is the eldest, Pole Two is next eldest, Pole Three next…, and so on. On the road I am known as the Old Man. In the temple these men call me Master. I have taught them everything they know."

That explained their martial arts expertise. For thousands of years the Shaolin Monks have been celebrated throughout China for their fighting skills and bravery. They never attack, they respond to being attacked. Normally they follow a deeply religious monastic life dedicated to hard work, peace and respect for all living things. Emperors have used monks trained within the walled boundaries of the Shaolin Temple as trusted bodyguards. Gao and Chopper felt deeply honoured to be in their company.

The shoulder-pole team was heading for the city. Gao thought how useful it would be to help these new friends and at the same time get into Chongqing unnoticed.

"Master, if you do not have any objections," Gao said, "we will accompany you to the city. We can replace the two dead men and carry their loads."

The old man agreed.

After burying the dead porters, the team lined up alongside the loads. Chopper was at number five and Gao Qing was number seven. The old man took the lead. He bent and lifted a pole. The rest did the same. Gao found his load to be much heavier than he expected and realized just how strong a shoulder-pole carrier had to be. The old man began a singsong chant. "Hei Hoo! Lifting our loads, Hei Hoo! Towards our goal, Hei Hoo!" The team followed his lead and off they went, chanting to the movement of their legs. The wounded man brought up the rear, able to travel at his own speed.

At dusk, they made camp. After a meal of boiled rice and vegetables, they settled to sleep. Both men admitted to painful shoulder blisters but were happy. Tomorrow, all being well, they would arrive in Chongqing, safe and sound.

And that was how it turned out. They were just two more anonymous workers entering the city through a pedestrian-only gap in the city wall. At the delivery address they said goodbye to the team and parted as friends. The old man prophesied, "Our paths will cross again." He was right.

CHAPTER 3.

Chongqing – the Mountain City, 1941

1.

The mighty Yangtze River has a number of major cities sitting beside it. One of the biggest is Chongqing. Through five thousand years, Chongqing has steadily grown from a family hut into the most important city in the region, with, in 1941, a population exceeding two million. All Chinese call Chongqing the Mountain City. Westerners called it Chungking.

At the foot of the city, running for several kilometres alongside the river, are the docks. Vessels of all shapes and sizes fetch and carry goods up and down the Yangtze, making the dock area the second busiest place on the river. Only Shanghai is busier.

Rising steeply upwards, there are rows over rows of one or two storied dwellings, interspersed with retail and business premises. Sadly, after a prolonged Japanese bombing campaign, much of the city was in ruins. But it never stopped humming with vibrant life as the resolute Chinese inhabitants went about their business. Ships still arrived and left on schedule, shoulder-pole teams carried goods in and out of the interior and road traffic was, if anything, heavier.

As they weaved their way through the busy streets, Gao thought that the Chongqing bus and truck drivers must be the best in the world. They had no straight, flat roads to enjoy. All thoroughfares went up, down or tiltingly sideways. There was a constant cacophony of vehicle horns, bicycle bells and bellowing tradesmen, which often made it impossible for people to converse.

Newspaper boys ran after rickshaws, thrusting the latest news under high-class noses. Alongside the main roads, outdoor food vendors sold cooked rice, vegetables, dumplings, boiled sweet corn, spiced meats, noodles or fish.

While the central section of China was the war front, the big battles were taking place in the coastal areas of eastern China, making Chongqing an important link in the supply line. When Nanking, the Capital City of all China fell to the Japanese in December 1937, Generalissimo Chiang Kai-shek set up his provisional government in the city of Hankow. Just prior to the fall of Hankow on 25th October 1938, Chiang was forced to move to the Mountain City. Chongqing became known as the Far East Political and Military Headquarters.

After the Japanese invasion, Chiang Kai-shek ordered an enlargement of his information-gathering network, causing the Japanese to follow suit. All over China, paid informers took every opportunity to uncover and sell secrets. The various interested communities most active in China included the Nationalists, Soviets, Japanese, British and Americans. All used information-gathering operatives. Strangely, the Chinese Communists had few informers. Mao Zedong had other priorities.

By the time Gao and Chopper entered Chongqing, the city was a hotbed of intrigue and betrayal. Not only were the Allies conducting spying activities against the Japanese, Chiang's Nationalists were spying on the Chinese Communists. Germany too had a spy network, whilst Britain, as well as spying on the Germans and the Japanese, kept an eye on the rest. So who to trust? The answer to that was nobody.

Their first priority was new clothes. Their next need was a suitable hide-away. They found the "Good Luck Hotel". Alone in their twin-bedded room, they bathed and shaved. When they ventured back onto the streets in their new black silk gowns and skull caps, cotton socks and shiny shoes. With eyes covered by the latest fashion-fad, sunglasses, and carrying leather attaché-cases, they looked like successful businessmen again.

*

Yellow Corner Village, part of the western suburbs of the city, is to be found by following the only vehicle route to the Yellow Mountain. In 1941, the village boasted the modern Kai-xuan hotel. Built in the ancient Chinese style, the hotel was a popular meeting place for locals and foreigners. Gao and Chopper were on their way there too, to join Feilibov for lunch in the hotel restaurant.

They alighted outside the hotel, walked in, chose a table and sat down. Almost immediately a young waitress placed glasses and a carafe of freshly boiled water in the centre of the table. Another girl brought each of them a hot flannel-sized towel impregnated with lemon juice for them to wipe their hands and face. As soon as they put the used towels down, they were replaced. Two leather-bound folders, one detailing the substantial menu, the other containing the wine list, were handed to them. Gao asked for a pot of Jasmine tea.

Right on time, through a window, Gao watched Feilibov arrive in a huge black limousine. The liveried chauffeur hurried round to open the door and hand him out. He in turn gave his hand to an extraordinarily stunning, extremely sexy, long-legged blonde western woman wearing a knee-length red silk dress. Arm in arm, Feilibov and the girl headed towards the hotel entrance. Chopper, as direct as always, nodded in the general direction of the window and echoed Gao's thoughts.

"Only the best for Comrade Feilibov."

They were beside them. "Hello gentlemen," greeted Feilibov. "It's good to meet you again."

Gao and Chopper stood to shake hands with him and be introduced to the woman. She turned out to be Russian and was there for a particular purpose. When Gao invited them to sit down, the woman insisted upon taking the chair that faced the room, making the three men fade into the background.

They ordered lunch, washed down with beer. The girl ate and drank little. Instead, she filled her eyes and ears with everything that was going on around them. The men talked quietly about nothing in particular, using both Russian and Chinese. At regular intervals Feilibov made a joke and they all laughed. Every so often he added one extra Chinese or Russian word to a sentence, then raced on with his joke. For over an hour, word by word, Gao picked up his message. "Bashan (Palm Hill) is your code-name. Use it only when you contact Moscow. Chopper's nickname is now his code-name."

2.

A week later Gao was told to return to the hotel without Chopper. The unusually clement early autumn weather had brought out what tourists there were, so the restaurant was busy. Gao was directed to a corner table, which, he suspected, had been kept vacant especially for him. He sat down with his back to the room with a view through the window to look at. It was a good idea to have the hotel manager as his contact. He could visit or telephone anytime without arousing curiosity.

Not far from the hotel, set in its own grounds on the slopes of the beautiful Yellow Mountain, sat Cloud Chambers, a huge mansion owned by Chiang Kai-shek. Before the war, the house had been Chiang's favourite country retreat. After relocating his government from Hankow to Chongqing, he used it as his official residence.

Gao was finishing off the last mouthfuls of a delicious lunch when he heard the distinctive tap of high heels. He turned and saw a woman wearing a simple black dress, standing with her back to him, talking to other diners. Soon it was his turn. When she arrived, he looked up and into a pair of beautiful smoky-black eyes. Feilibov had given him a real Chinese beauty to be his contact.

He had been briefed. She was in her mid-thirties, but as he had just discovered, looked ten years younger. A soft voice bubbled out of her small lipsticked mouth and gently caressed his ears.

"I hope you enjoyed your meal. Can I get you anything else?"

"No, thank you," replied Gao, quietly. "I would like to send a message to the kitchen. The food here is excellent."

Again his ears were caressed. "My name is Zhao Ying. I own this hotel. I will make sure your message is delivered. You speak with a familiar dialect, where are you from?"

"Hubei Province. I am here to visit my cousin."

They both smiled. Recognition phrases satisfactorily completed, they could proceed.

She turned to a nearby waitress and said, "This is my cousin. Everything he consumes is on my account." To Gao she offered her hand. "Let's go to my rooms."

Her large apartment was tastefully decorated and expensively furnished. Gao could only describe it as being Chinese with a distinctive western influence. A picture window facing the street was framed by heavy maroon velvet drapes. Patterned carpet runners lay on polished redwood parquet flooring, and around the room, original Chinese paintings and handwritten scrolls hung on the walls.

Zhao Ying gestured for Gao to sit in one of a matching pair of maroon leather fireside chairs facing each other across the hearth of an open fireplace, laid but not lit. By the side of each chair, waiting to be used by the occupant, was a small table. Other furniture included a beautifully carved wooden sideboard, a desk and a leather-bound swivel office chair. On the desk sat the very latest design in telephones. Zhou Ying handed Gao a newspaper and walked towards an inner room.

"Please wait for a few minutes while I freshen up," she called back over her shoulder.

When next he saw her, she was wearing a pretty western-style knee-length white dress embroidered with lace flowers. On her feet she wore white back-less mules which drew attention to her shapely legs. She had released her thick wavy black hair, allowing it to cascade down to her waist. She looked superb.

Gao watched her placing a tray containing a bowl of assorted candies, a pot of jasmine tea, cups and saucers, on the sideboard and began to pour the tea.

"What do I call you?" she asked.

"Well, you're older than I, begging your pardon, I suggest Xiao-Di (Little Brother)."

"If I am going to obey your orders, I prefer Da-Ge (Big Brother)." She handed him his cup. "Have you been briefed about me?"

"Yes."

Zhao Ying had been born into a family of well-to-do intellectuals. At puberty, she blossomed into a beautiful young maiden. In 1921, a Peking-based warlord, General Xiao Yao-nan visited the area and decided that he must have Zhao Ying as his fifth concubine. Her parents, given the choice between a large dowry or vile torture, chose the money and signed the consent forms.

Her new "husband" was the Commander of Infantry in the Government of the Warlord Alliance. He often went away, either to attend political meetings or to direct his troops to fight a bloody civil war against the Kuomintang. When travelling, he always took a wife or a concubine to keep him company.

Despite hating her new life, Zhao Ying quickly established herself within the household. She became the General's favourite nighttime companion by learning how to please him. Before her sixteenth birthday, rumours of her beauty had spread far and wide, giving much face to her husband. He took every opportunity to show her off, and in almost no time, Zhao Ying had become his number one companion and hostess at his innumerable parties, gatherings and political get-togethers.

She was targeted by the Soviets, who were, at that time, working closely with the fledgling Chinese Communist Party. They had expert psychologists able to accurately interpret behavioural characteristics constantly looking for possible converts to Communism.

After months of surveillance, they began having secret talks with

ZhaoYing. Eventually, she admitted hating her marriage and the Warlord Government. With the co-operation of Comrade Dong Bi-wu, one of the founders of Chinese Communism, the Soviets persuaded Zhao Ying to join their information-gathering network.

Her main motivation for joining the Communists was the hope that she would one day escape her life as a concubine.

She was in her early twenties when her husband died. Over the years she had amassed a small fortune, so she left his house, and assisted by her network controller, bought the Kai-xuan hotel. She was told to behave exactly like the sort of greedy businessperson the Communists professed to despise by making the hotel a success. She did. And in the process of getting richer, she provided an excellent meeting place for undercover Soviets.

3.

Feilibov leased a luxury apartment in the best part of the city for Gao and Chopper. In their role as rich businessmen, such accommodation was part of their disguise. When they were ready to move in, Zhao Ying offered her car to transport their belongings. Later, she arrived carrying a large leather suitcase and said to Gao, "This is yours, a present from Feilibov."

Gao watched Zhou Ying's departing rear, admiring her splendid figure and fluid movement before he turned his attention to the suitcase. Nestling among silk off-cuts was the very latest radio transmitter/receiver, usually referred to as a transceiver. Also included was a code-book to be used when encrypting/decoding messages, a vial of invisible ink with special pens, two browning pistols, ammunition and shoulder-holsters, two hand-grenades and other bits and pieces.

Feilibov had made some modifications to the apartment by creating several hidden cavities where Gao and Chopper could store their stuff. The transceiver equipment disappeared into a false bottom built into the main bedroom's fitted wardrobe. Chopper secreted his bits and pieces under the floorboards of his room and Gao's went behind a skirting board in the lounge.

At 2100 hours that first night in their new accommodation, Gao connected the transceiver, tuned to his wavelength and began transmitting to Moscow by the Russian equivalent of the Morse code.

"Bashan calling, Bashan calling, come back." His message was quickly acknowledged.

Every operator has his or her style, such as the length of the dashes, the shortness of the dots, the speed of transmission and the way a message flows. It is as distinct as a voice and as individual as a signature, enabling an experienced operator to recognize the hand of the person sending the message. From his time in spy-school, Moscow already knew Gao's style. Any deviation would quickly arouse suspicion.

This fact destroys completely the myth created by writers and film-makers that an enemy can be tricked into accepting false information sent by a replacement Morse code operator, even if the correct call sign and code-name is used. This could happen only if the receiving operator is new and unsupervised - *not* a likely scenario.

As soon as contact was established with Moscow, Gao followed the instructions contained within the pages of the code-book and transmitted his first encrypted message. Usually what needed to be said was hidden within groups of five letters, or five numbers between one and nought, set out in lines of eight groups running from left to right.

For example, if the instructions in the code-book told him to use ABCDE ZYXWV or 12345 09876 to contain a small part of a message, that would be just two of the hundreds of groups transmitted. He also used the code-book to decipher messages received.

That first night was a busy one. Moscow sent Gao the details of operators situated all over the Orient. After decoding the Moscow message, he contacted everyone in his network in turn by tuning to each individual's radio frequency and transmitting his or her call sign followed by his own. From each he received a coded status report and any information they thought Moscow should know about. Before signing off, he introduced Chopper and let them hear his style, then told each operator to expect to be contacted at about the same time every night. When the last operator had signed off, he re-contacted Moscow and relayed everything to them.

From that night onwards, Gao and Chopper took charge of the network. On the second night, Chopper was the operator whilst Gao did the encrypting and decoding.

Three weeks went by. The network settled into a smoothly regulated routine. Long periods of sleeping time were a thing of the past. The two men learned to cat-nap, because, during the day, they had to venture out and appear to be going about their business.

One morning Feilibov, dressed in smart and fashionable western attire, introduced Chen, a young Chinese man dressed as a servant. But he wasn't a servant. He was a fully trained telegraphist.

Code-named Blackbird, Chen was a welcome addition. Good company, hardworking and an excellent operator. A week after his arrival, he was on duty when Moscow sent Gao a special message. Gao was instructed to locate the hideout of a Communist turncoat named Dong Jian-yun. Her details said that she was an attractive, mid-thirties female member of Comintern. She had been recruited whilst studying in Moscow and had graduated from the same spy-school two years before Gao and Chopper.

Years later, Gao heard the reason why Moscow wanted her found. During a routine inspection trip around her territory, she chose to follow the old Silk Road through northwest China to get to her destination. It was an unlucky decision. For some men, an attractive woman travelling alone is a magnet. A local Kuomintang officer accused Dong of being a Communist and arrested her. He brutally beat, raped and sodomised her before sending her on to the Central Intelligence Unit in Chongqing.

The man put in charge of her case, named Meng, was a clever and ruthless interrogator. He had broken many suspected Communists. His long list of confessions followed by execution resulted in early promotion and the trust of Chiang Kai-shek.

When Dong was brought before him for the first time, despite her injuries, he was struck by her good looks. He was no rapist. He wanted her to voluntarily submit, so how to get her? After a few cursory questions, he sent Dong back to her cell. Two days later he had a plan.

He ordered her injuries be attended to. When she had fully recovered, he began a programme of "hard and soft" interrogating techniques, coupling threats with promises. One of Meng's oft-used tactics was to force Dong to witness the extreme agonies of his torture victims, all the while reminding Dong that he was the only barrier between her present sweet life and the bitter death she was witnessing. His breakthrough came when Dong fainted after being forced to watch a woman have her face cut to shreds and her eyes gouged out. When she came to, she was his.

Dong was not taken back to her cell. Meng installed her in a luxurious apartment with two servants to care for her. That night, in the large comfortable bed, Meng and Dong became lovers. The next morning, Dong was caught between two evils. Severe punishment by the Communists if they discovered that she had shared a bed with a Kuomintang high official, or being tortured to a slow death.

She couldn't face the idea of suicide, so she took the only avenue open to her. After extracting a promise from Meng that he would protect her, Dong divulged everything she knew, including the details of the people in her network.

Meng kept his promise. He visited several different cities and towns within his jurisdiction and found suitable accommodation in each. As he moved about his area, Dong moved too, never staying longer than a month in one place.

Meanwhile, her disappearance had been reported. When, months later, her network began to be systematically destroyed by the Kuomintang, Comintern was convinced that she must have broken under torture before being executed. However, rumours about Meng and his new mistress began to circulate, and it wasn't long before they reached

Moscow. Then a routine report included the information that three men and one woman had been seen boarding a small military aircraft bound for Xi'an. Two of the descriptions fitted Meng and Dong. Gao's orders said he was to travel to Xi'an as inconspicuously as possible, find out the truth and report back.

He used a map to plot his course, then telephoned Zhao Ying. The autumnal weather was turning cold and would soon be colder. He needed warm underwear, worn but serviceable peasant jacket, trousers, hat, gloves, socks and shoes. He also instructed her to purchase a ticket on the first passenger ship going to the city of Yichang in Hubei Province, some three hundred kilometres down-river.

The following morning, Zhao Ying arrived, carrying a well-used suitcase containing everything Gao needed. He added his bits and pieces, such as several sets of identity papers in different names, a camera and his pistol.

It was necessary for him to be dressed in his usual business clothes for the first part of his journey. After one last check that nothing had been overlooked, he shook hands with Chopper, left the flat and climbed into Zhao Ying's car. Blackbird, posing as a servant, placed the suitcase in the boot and stood back as the car pulled away.

He was very conscious of Zhao Ying sitting beside him. She reached forward and turned a handle that raised a glass partition isolating them from the driver. He could smell her, hear her quiet breathing and the gentle zinging sound her silk stockings made as she moved her legs. She turned herself so that they were almost facing each other and looked at him with her glorious sexually charged eyes.

"Please take care of yourself, Big Brother," she murmured.

He looked at her for a long time before answering: "You will be in my thoughts as the ship leaves the jetty, and I will still be thinking of you when I return."

Caressing him with her eyes, she reached out and slid her hand into his.

"Hurry back. I will be waiting."

4.

The ship safely reached Yichang. The area around the city was under the control of General Li Zong-ren, the most senior General in the Kuomintang Army. His one million well-trained and well-armed loyal troops patrolled every mountain, river and road, keeping the Japanese at bay. Therefore, compared to the chaos caused by the anti-Japanese war in other parts of China, life in Yichang was relatively peaceful.

Dong had been born in the poor eastern area of the city. Gao deposited his suitcase in the Left Luggage Office at the port and still dressed in his business silks hailed a passing rickshaw. It didn't take long for him to find the Dong family home and arrange a meeting with Dong's father. He used the information Moscow had supplied about Dong to convince the father that he was an old schoolmate of hers.

He was a kind old man who had made good. The inside of his little house was clean and well furnished. The ultimate status symbol, a huge radiogram with several stacks of records standing on a table beside it, was playing the last bars of the tuneful "Old Shanghai', sung by the famous female star, Zhou Xuan.

Gao accepted an invitation to sit and eat whilst Ma and Pa Dong gossiped about their daughter. It had been many months since her last letter. They thought she was somewhere far away fighting the Japanese. Gao gently bade them farewell, and left.

Another rickshaw returned him to the dockside. He retrieved the suitcase and in a nearby public toilet changed into the warm underwear and peasant clothes. Zhao Ying had thoughtfully included a large square of homespun cotton cloth. He placed his essentials on it, then tied the four corners together to fashion a bag he could carry on the crook of one arm or on a short shoulder pole. This was the normal way peasants carried their belongings.

He re-deposited the case, now containing everything he had just taken off, back into the Left Luggage Office. After rubbing some dirt on his hands and face, he was ready to proceed. Until his return, he was a peasant. That meant plenty of walking. Under normal circumstances a peasant would not use a rickshaw. The air temperature at river level was still quite high, making him sweat inside his winter clothes. Good. He would soon begin to smell like a peasant too.

He crossed the city, heading inland towards the hills. On his way he purchased some chunks of dried meat and a jar of preserved vegetables. By late afternoon he was safely through a gate in the city wall and on his way to Xi'an, a distance of at least a thousand kilometres.

He found what he thought must be the correct trail chosen in advance by Chopper and himself and was soon climbing steeply upwards. There was not another soul in sight as the sky darkened, forcing him to stop for the night.

The next morning he breakfasted on dried meat and vinegary vegetable chunks washed down with water from a nearby stream, then continued his journey upwards, over the top of the high hills and down the other side, heading towards a village with a railway station.

Many trails began to link together, then separate again, making it difficult, even with the help of the map, to be sure which was the right one. Suddenly he heard a familiar sound.

"Hei Hoo, Hei Hoo!"

As a precaution, despite knowing the voice, he hid in the undergrowth. As it got closer, he recognised the familiar shaved heads, white trousers, padded vests and dark blue sashes. It was the shoulder-pole team. Knowing how fast the monks could react to danger, he held his hands in the air as he stepped out of hiding.

"Hey!" he shouted. "Remember me?"

They were as surprised to see him as he had been to see them. After handshakes all round, they stopped for the mid-day meal.

"I'm on my way to visit an old friend of mine," Gao lied. "From what I have been told, there is a railway station up ahead."

The Old Man looked at him… no, not *at* him, he looked *through* him.

Gao suspected that the Old Man knew exactly what he was about, but being bound by the Shaolin code of chivalry, said nothing except, "Once again it is written that we must meet. You are heading away from the railway. It is over there." The Old Man pointed in a right-angled direction. "Come, walk with us, I can show you the correct path."

The Old Man was tough, able to set a fast pace, making his men sweat profusely under the unusually warm sun. There was no cooling breeze and because the trail had widened considerably, very little shade. After a couple of hours Gao heard Pole Four, the Old Man's favourite, shout, "There's the Temple. Let's rest awhile."

To Gao's great relief, the Old Man nodded his agreement.

In the shade of the building, they sat with their backs against the cool stone wall. The Old Man adopted the usual meditation crossed-legs-straight-back position and closed his eyes. Two porters stayed on guard whilst the rest of them dozed.

A good snooze later they were awakened by the sound of approaching vehicles. An American-made jeep led a line of military trucks crammed with Kuomintang troops into the clearing and stopped.

Immediately a squad of soldiers jumped off the rear of the leading truck and surrounded the shoulder pole team, pointing their rifles directly at the porters. The rest of the troops jumped down. Facing outwards, they quickly arranged themselves into two neat lines, making an inverted "V" to create an area of safety within the protective shield.

"Well trained." thought Gao.

The driver of the jeep jumped out, ran around to the passenger door and opened it. Out came a polished American cavalry-style boot followed by the body of a Kuomintang three-star general.

The driver opened a rear door of the jeep to free two one-star generals from the cramped wooden rear bench seat. It was cramped because the machine-gunner was also sharing the back seat. He had to stand on it to man his gun.

The three-star general looked like a fighter. Aged about fifty, of medium height, he was wide and powerfully built, with a square head and jutting jaw. "Definitely not a man to disobey." silently opined Gao, but of course he knew who he was. From the photographs Feilibov had forced them to memorise in spy school, he recognised none other than the anti-Japanese war hero himself, General Li Zong-ren.

The General walked towards the porters. Although he didn't actually strut, his body language suggested that he was in full command and proud to be so. When he saw the Old Man, a look of surprise crossed his face. With a wide smile of delight, the General placed his hands in front of his chest as if he was praying, and respectfully exclaimed, "Old Master! What a great pleasure to see you looking so well. What are you doing here?"

The squad stopped pointing their rifles and stood to attention.

"Your Highness, I have followed your progress with interest and pleasure," said the Old Man, beginning a respectful bow.

General Li reached out and raised the Old Man back to a standing position, then turned and told everybody within earshot.

"This is my Master and my Mentor. He taught me everything I needed to become the man you see today. Please treat him and his men with respect."

Then came a sight that Gao would forever remember - the second most important man in China bowing to a monk. When upright, the General said, "The weather is uncommonly warm. You must be tired."

The Old Man nodded. "Quite tired."

"What business do you have here?"

"As usual, earning some money for the temple by portering goods."

"Ah yes," responded the General. With a rueful grin he continued, "I remember it well." He pointed at Gao. "What about him?"

"He is my friend. During a previous trip, at great risk to himself, he helped us fight off a murdering bandit gang. I am showing him the way to the railway station."

The General changed the subject.

"I am here to pray. Please rest awhile, then we can talk."

And that is what happened. Soldiers made a pile of the fallen leaves for the two men to sit and talk in a friendly way, perfectly at ease with each other.

Before parting, the General gently pleaded, "Please go carefully, Master. The mountains can be dangerous, with the war and everything."

The Old Man responded, "I have no worries, Your Highness. My men can protect themselves and your army is out there keeping the Japanese away. I am most proud to have helped in your development into such a hero of the people. It is I who should be asking you to be careful. My death will change nothing. Yours would break the will of the Chinese people to resist."

The General smiled as he asked, "Am I so important?"

The Old Man was *very* serious. "Almost everybody has a good opinion of you and the people are rarely wrong. You can trust their judgement. Nothing the Japanese can do will break the spirit of the Chinese people as long as we have you to lead us. Yes, Your Highness. You *are* that important!"

The General, hero of the people, removed his cap and made a second bow to the Old Man. "I am so glad to have met you again today. You have helped me enormously."

The Old Man also bowed. "Goodbye Your Highness. I will continue to include you in my prayers."

The two men parted as equals. The tough General to command his troops and the wise old monk to lead his shoulder-pole team. For Gao, it was a lesson in respect and equality that, for the rest of his life, he tried to follow.

The shoulder-pole team went on their way until the Old Man stopped and told Gao to follow the trail going east to the village and the railway station. As it was near to sunset, Gao was tempted to stay with the group overnight. He had learned to respect the Old Man and enjoyed his company, but he had to go. And it was a good thing he did. A train going his way arrived before dawn the next morning.

5.

Gao had two problems to solve. Discover the exact address where Meng's new mistress was staying, and find out if the mistress was Dong. But how?

Fortunately he had plenty of time to think. In his guise as a peasant, he had to travel in the cheapest section, which meant hard wooden seats running the length of the carriage, overcrowding, noise, animals, dirt and stink. Because of possible disease, all water in China has to be boiled before drinking. Chinese trains of those days had a water boiler fitted at each end of every carriage. By using the tap, passengers could draw off boiled water as and when they wanted it. Most of the travellers, especially families, brought their own food with them. Others, like Gao, could purchase food from vendors plying their trade on the station platforms.

In general, the passengers were a friendly bunch. Grubby kids came to play or sit on Gao's knee, and he wanted for nothing. Food and boiled water regularly came his way. So did newspapers and magazines, which he read from front to back, absorbing every item of useful information. But all the time his mind was grappling with how to complete his mission, or rather, how to begin.

The answer was right there in the newspapers. *Journalists.* China was full of them. The newspapers of the world had people constantly searching for something new to report. And when journalists relax, what do they do? They gather in their favourite hotel bar to drink too much and brag about the stories they have uncovered. He thought about it. He could speak their common language, English, and he *was* after a big story. Yes, he could be a journalist.

He arrived in Xi'an at the same time as the shops opened. He bought a serviceable second-hand lockable leather bag of the kind commonly used by doctors. He then found a shop that sold western style clothes worn by middle-class Chinese. In a stationery shop he purchased a notepad and pencils and ordered a box of printed name-cards introducing him as, "Weiming Hu – Journalist". From there, following the directions given by a helpful store employee, he entered the public bath building and had a haircut, shave and a good soak. He emerged looking like a newly arrived freelance reporter anxious to make his mark.

More questions led him to a small hotel near to the bar of the Xi'an Hotel, a favourite place for journalists. As soon as he was alone in his hotel room, not needing his pistol, he wrapped it in his peasant clothes. Locking the bundle in the leather bag, he placed the bag inside a wardrobe.

That evening, after eating in a small restaurant, he collected his newly printed name-cards and made his first appearance in the bar of the Xi'an Hotel. Nothing interesting happened, and nothing for the next two nights. His daytime ferreting didn't dig up any clues either.

On the fourth evening, he arrived early as usual. Other early customers, mostly foreigners, were straddling stools along the length of the bar, drinking and chatting. Like the previous three nights, he sat at a table situated as close to the middle of the long bar area as possible. From where he sat, he could hear some or all of almost every conversation. He placed a newspaper in front of him, ordered a glass of beer, bowed his head as if reading the paper, and began to listen. There was plenty of talk but nothing about the one subject he was interested in.

The bar slowly filled. A few Chinese "good time girls" joined the men. Steadily, the noise level went up in direct proportion to the amount of alcohol going down. Nothing was said that interested Gao until a tall "Clark Gable" type arrived. Gao hadn't seen him before.

"Hey Jugs, over here," called someone.

"Jugs?" Gao wondered, "what kind of name is that? "

"How did your exclusive go?"

"It didn't. It's been put back a week."

"Bad luck. I was hoping to get the lowdown on his new lady friend. I hear she's a real cutie."

That interested Gao. He quickly swallowed the beer in his glass and moved towards the bar as though wanting a refill, positioning himself behind the two men.

"Me too. It would make a nice change from looking at your ugly mug!" Jugs even spoke like Clark Gable. "But I probably won't get to see her. I hear he keeps her away from the spotlight. Hey Barman, my usual."

That was all.

Gao decided to try and get to know Jugs, or the friend, or both. Best to wait and see what happens. If one of them left the bar, he would try his luck with the other. If they left together, he would have to wait for another opportunity. Two hours later Jugs staggered out. Gao went to the bar. He stood beside the friend and waved his arm, earnestly trying to attract the attention of the barman. As the friend was about to drink, Gao's elbow "accidentally" nudged the friend's arm, causing the drink to spill.

"I am so sorry," Gao said, using his handkerchief to mop up the spilled alcohol. "Please let me buy you another."

The friend looked at Gao rather dubiously until the mention of a free drink. "Okay," he agreed. "I'll have a scotch and water. No ice."

Gao's new drinking partner was Roger from Washington DC. Jugs was Roger's friend. "Jugs" was a nickname made up from the initials of his four given names, John Ulysses George Stanley. Jugs had just missed an exclusive interview with someone important but it wasn't Meng.

Roger and Jugs lived in the same apartment block and both freelanced for American newspapers. Gao, handing over one of his newly printed name-cards, said he too was freelancing until he could get a job with a newspaper. Roger kept forgetting Gao's false name of Weiming, so he renamed him William. Shortening it to Bill, Roger introduced Gao around as "my pal Bill," making Gao an accepted member of the Xi'an journalistic fraternity.

Roger told Gao, "The Chinese Secret Services here are piss poor. On the one hand you have the Military Investigation and Statistics Bureau set up by Chiang Kai-shek, and on the other there is the Central Intelligence Service he inherited from Doctor Sun. The two organisations do collaborate on some cases but in general they don't. Each has its own system and wants to control the other, so they have more quarrels than cooperation. If you want to know something about the military, you can exploit the situation to your advantage. The best person to talk to is a half-Chinese, half-Scottish lady, Brenda Fang. She loves hearing any new gossip and knows everything that goes on in this city. You can find her most weekdays in the office of the Foreign Press Bureau. Tell her Roger sent you."

Roger prepared to leave. Gao said thanks for his help. As Roger zigzagged his way out, he shouted, "Happy to help a rookie. Welcome to the club."

*

Aged about forty, Brenda Fang was short and squat with big breasts, but what made her stand out from the Chinese crowds was bright ginger hair framing her pale oriental face. A warm friendly smile was her best feature.

Gao introduced himself by speaking English and handing over one of his name-cards. "Hello, my name is Bill Hu. I'm a freelance reporter trying to get onto the staff of the *News*." All Japanese-free Chinese cities had a *Daily News* newspaper. "Roger said that if anyone can help with a big story, you can."

Brenda waved Gao to a chair and left, to return with two mugs of green tea. Placing one in front of him, she sat behind a rickety desk covered with bits of paper stuck onto spikes. Near to her right hand stood a black candlestick telephone. Speaking English with a Scottish flavoured accent, she asked, "Hello Billy Hu. How can I help you?"

Gao sipped his tea, wondering if he could trust her. Deciding that he had no option, he leaned forward and murmured conspiratorially, "This is big. I need you to promise not to say anything to anyone for at least two weeks until I've got my scoop and sent it in."

Her dark eyes glistened with interest.

"...and that's why I'm here. I need to confirm that Dong is alive and living with Meng. An address and a photograph would be the best way." Gao spread his arms expansively. "Just imagine the fuss it will cause. A top female Communist Spy shacked up with the Kuomintang's Central

Intelligence Service's famous persecutor of Communists. With a scoop like this, I'd be taken seriously by any newspaper editor."

Brenda looked out of the grubby window, wondering if *she* could trust *him*. Gao knew she was hooked on his story. Her eyes had widened with interest and she had listened attentively until he had finished.

Gao sipped his tea, saying nothing. In spy school he had been taught that such a moment required time for thinking. In such circumstances, the thinker has three options. One, to agree. Two, to ask a question. Three, to refuse. Options two and three provided an opportunity for further persuasive argument.

At last Brenda turned back to him. "Meng arrested a good friend of mine who was not remotely interested in politics and tortured him until he confessed to being a Communist, then he shot him. I would love to see Meng get his comeuppance."

Despite not knowing the word comeuppance, Gao knew what she meant.

She continued, "I have a contact in Military Intelligence who would enjoy getting one over Central Intelligence and at the same time see Meng brought down. Leave this with me, I'll get back to you."

On the back of the card, he jotted down the telephone number of his hotel.

Three days later Gao was back in her office. Brenda slid a photograph across her desk. On the reverse was written an address.

She explained, "My contact said he met the woman in this picture during a courtesy visit to Meng's new house. Meng introduced her as his personal secretary. It's a bit dark and hazy. He snatched a shot of her without using a flash, but you can see her features clearly enough. That's as far as we can go on this one. I hope it helps."

That evening when Gao telephoned Chopper, he had good news.

"I think I have located exactly what our customer is looking for. You can tell him that I will be returning as fast as possible with a sample of the goods and the address of the stockist."

Back in Chongqing, Gao handed over the address and photograph to Feilibov. A month later, he received a coded message from Moscow.

"The Dong file is closed. Well done."

Gao's first solo assignment had been successfully completed. Later, just as he had said it to Brenda Fang, when the Soviets let it be known to the newspapers that Dong was Meng's mistress, there was a big fuss resulting in both parties being executed by the Kuomintang. Sad but inevitable for Dong, good for Communism to get Meng.

6.

On June 22 1941, just two weeks after Gao and Chopper had left Moscow, Germany broke the August 1939 Russo-German non-aggression pact by launching "Operation Barbarossa', Hitler's long-planned invasion of the Soviet Union.

The battle-hardened German divisions quickly advanced, placing Leningrad under siege in October and taking the major Russian industrial cities of Kharkov and Rostov soon afterwards. This resulted in more Soviet agents being deployed throughout the Far East and linked into Gao's network. Dong's old network was revived and they too were assigned to Gao. Orders came that they were to be operational for 24 hours a day. Chopper and Blackbird were happy to have Gao back helping with the ever-increasing workload.

Zhao Ying telephoned to welcome Gao back. She said she had a "cousin" staying in her hotel. Could she bring him over? When she arrived and hit Gao with one of her sexy looks, his breath stopped in his throat. He still loved Natasha and one day wanted to marry her, but how could any red-blooded, sex-starved young fellow not notice such temptation?

He shook hands with his new "relative" Chong-min. He had been carefully chosen. When he and Gao stood together, they were approximately the same height, weight, colouring and looks. That made four of them living in the apartment. Not long afterwards they became five when a lady cook who, in real life couldn't boil water, arrived.

Of course Gao's cousin and the cook were operational helpers. The group organised themselves to give the impression to any nosy outsider that they were just a normal household. Gao and Chopper kept up the pretence of being busy businessmen, Blackbird was the servant, "Clockface", the so-called cousin, was a houseguest, and "Rainbow" was the cook and did the shopping. In fact, Clockface and Blackbird did most of the cooking, Chopper maintained the radio equipment, Rainbow was the administrator and Gao dealt with everything else. When needed, Clockface took the place of Gao during "business" outings.

They were a busy little unit able to keep the channels open around the clock by operating an overlapping shift system. However, there was one problem they couldn't solve.

By mid-December, with the Germans just 40 Kilometres away from Moscow, the Russians rallied and halted the German advance. Slowly, under the brilliant leadership of Marshal Konstantinovich Georgi Zhukov, they began to drive the Germans back.

Gao's worries about the safety of his beloved Natasha began to subside. Some weeks previously, Feilibov had brought him one letter from her that had managed to get to him via Comintern. In it she told him that she had volunteered to serve as a nurse in a military hospital attached to the Soviet Sixteenth Army. She had also promised herself to him for their lifetime by writing, "...no other man will ever touch my body until we are united. It is my wish to be the mother of your children. If it does not happen, I will forever remain single and celibate."

Gao handed his reply to Feilibov but had no idea if Natasha ever received it.

Their problem was finance. Moscow had stopped sending them any money. At first, it was simply a matter of the odd missed payment of their regular monthly allowance paid directly into Gao's Swiss bank account. The nearer the Germans got to Moscow, the more erratic the payments until they stopped altogether. When they raised the matter with Feilibov, he just shrugged his shoulders in a useless gesture of helplessness.

Thank goodness for Zhao Ying. She began to finance their operation but was unable to pay them any wages. Chopper, who had worked for so long without a break, and now with no pay, was very indignant.

"Bloody Tortoise Eggs!" he cursed.

In China, "Tortoise Eggs" is not only the highest form of scold and curse, it is the supreme insult. It clearly showed a tired and discontented Chopper.

Gao needed a time when he could give Chopper a break, and found it during a lull in the fighting in Russia during the 1941 Christian festival of Christmas and the 1942 New Year celebrations. Gao sent Chopper home to his wife and son. When a refreshed Chopper returned, it was Gao's turn to go away, but not on holiday. His absence was in the line of duty.

Now that he had command of a large network with agents as far afield as Japan, Vietnam, Korea, Hong Kong, India and Siam, Moscow ordered him to set up a support unit in case their apartment in Chongqing was ever discovered. Gao absolutely refused to carry out this order until Feilibov handed over sufficient cash to finance the operation. Feilibov did.

"Silkworm" appeared and took Gao away to visit "family".

*

The Yangtze River flows through very contrasting terrain. Chongqing is a mountain city, whereas the opposite north side of the wide river is flat and fertile with just one hill. That hill was their destination. A perfect position for wireless reception and only a day away from their city apartment.

Gao had so many bags, boxes and crates to take with him, including a spare transceiver and a diesel-fueled generator, they needed a horse and carriage to convey everything. However, that wasn't in any way suspicious. For rich men on the move, lots of luggage was normal.

To get to Beipei, Silkworm's home village nestling around and on the hill, they crossed the river on a flat-bottomed ferry wide enough to accommodate the horse and carriage. Silkworm owned and published a magazine with a small but loyal customer base. It gave him sufficient income to provide a better than average lifestyle for his family.

His house had been built on top of the hill. A few months previously, Silkworm had been ordered by Moscow to add a two-storied annex to the main house. Three rooms at ground floor level for guests. Three rooms underground. Gao was billeted in the annex. By day he worked for Silkworm as an assistant editor, by night, in the three rooms underneath, Silkworm assisted him to set up the reserve communications centre.

Suddenly Gao's life changed dramatically. He became so ill, he had to take to his bed. He could eat nothing, drink little and had a high fever. Despite the special care given to him by Silkworm, Gao's weight loss was dramatic. With no sign of an improvement, Silkworm was forced to telephone Chopper. That same day, Zhao Ying and a doctor turned up at Silkworm's home. The doctor diagnosed severe inflammation of the kidneys coupled with a secondary glandular infection.

Zhao Ying had brought Gao a letter. On the envelope was written, "Please forward to the Assistant Editor - Feilibov." She waited until the doctor had completed his examination before handing the letter to Gao. He was so weak he hadn't the strength to open the envelope so Zhao Ying did it for him. There was just one page bearing the crest of the Soviet Embassy. She handed it to Gao.

General Ivanovich has instructed me to pass the following message to Comrade Gao Qing: "It is my great sorrow to inform you that my beloved daughter Natasha was killed on the battlefield when carrying out her duty to save lives. Please turn your grief into strength to fight against the forces of evil. I know that would be her wish. " signed by…

Gao couldn't remember the name of the writer. He felt his body smash into tiny pieces a split-second before his brain exploded.

7.

Because of his already weakened condition, the news of Natasha's demise brought Gao to death's door. For days he lay in bed, trance-like and incommunicative. His brain hadn't exploded but it wasn't functioning properly. All it wanted to do was repeat the words, "Natasha was killed on the battlefield...Natasha is dead."

His tortured imagination gave him a continuing graphic picture-show of her being blown to pieces or being decapitated by shrapnel - her beautiful face smashed and bloody, or her soft warm honey-sweet body lying broken and twisted into one grotesque position after another. The worst vision was seeing her kneeling beside a fallen hero when a nearby exploding shell caused earth to bury her alive and her body being eaten by ants, maggots and worms. Zhou Ying, watching Gao's strength steadily decline to a dangerously low level, took matters into her own hands.

"Big Brother," she said quietly into Gao's seemingly deaf ear. "The doctor has said that it is impossible for him to treat you properly under these conditions. If we don't get you into hospital, you will die. I have booked you into a private ward. My car is waiting to take us across the river...and no arguments!"

In the hospital, Gao was hooked up to a drip and other medical equipment. Not that he cared. All he really wanted was to be with his Natasha. However, the doctors and nurses had other ideas, and despite Gao's indifference, they began to get the better of his ailments.

During the latter stage of his illness, he had improved sufficiently to be allowed to frequent the recreation room where patients could read newspapers and magazines, play chess and cards, or write letters home.

One morning, a familiar face appeared. In hospital for tests was an old Red Army friend of Gao's named Kong Yuan, a chatty fellow who enjoyed playing a card game called Throwing Old K. So did Gao. For his last three days in hospital, Gao and Kong spent many hours competing for points and sharing jokes and gossip. There was a one dangerous moment. When they first met, there was confusion with Chen-Ye - Gao's assumed name. Kong, an experienced undercover operator for the Communists, quickly understood the reason. Gao's real name remained hidden.

To everyone in the hospital Gao appeared to be a successful silk merchant. Kong was known simply as the Head of Administration in the Communist Liaison Office. Gao was not as he appeared, nor was Kong. Behind closed doors, Kong was privy to everything handled by Comrade Zhou En-lai. It had been Zhou En-lai who had ordered Kong to create the "coincidental" meeting with Gao.

Before the Japanese invaded China, there were two main political parties. The Kuomintang, also known as the Nationalists, and the Communists. The Kuomintang, headed by Chiang Kai-shek was the party in power. Mao Zedong was the revolutionary Communist leader. Chiang hated Mao and feared his growing Communist influence, so he issued orders that all Communists must be rooted out and executed.

Following on from the Japanese invasion, Chiang was forced by his own generals to stop persecuting the Communists and form a united Kuomontang/Communist alliance that held, albeit uneasily, by the need to defeat the Japanese.

However, despite the alliance, Communists were still in danger. The Kuomintang took every opportunity to bring false charges against any suspected Communist. Such arrests almost always ended in execution, but there were exceptions. One safe haven for Communists was the Communist Liaison Office, (CLO). The site had been carefully chosen. It was situated on the edge of the city as close as possible to Chiang's official residence "Cloud Chambers". Inside the walled-off CLO compound, Communist guards patrolled. Around the outer fence, Kuomintang soldiers kept a round-the-clock vigil. There were two gates. The wide main gate that all visitors must use and a rear smaller gate used by compound staff. At both gates, Communist and Kuomintang army personnel stood side by side. Those working and living inside the compound enjoyed a sort of Diplomatic Immunity.

Comrade Zhou En-lai and his wife lived in rooms above the CLO. Five more important Communist families, including Zhou's most trusted deputy, Dong Bi-wu, and Gao's friend, Kong Yuan, also lived in apartments within the compound. Zhou En-lai, the most respected of all the Communists, stayed there from 1940 to the end of World War Two.

Because Mao Zedong and Chiang Kai-shek hated each other, it was Zhou and Chiang who met to discuss any inter-party business and to run the war. Comrade Mao Zedong, the Communist leader, stayed safely out of harm's way in Yan'an, northwest China.

A month after Gao's admittance to the hospital, the doctors allowed Zhao Ying to take him away to convalesce in her hotel. Although he was physically close to a full recovery, he never completely got over the shock of reading that letter.

He bade farewell to the medical staff and wished Kong good health.

"I'll be in touch," replied Kong. "I can send a bit of interesting business your way."

He spent three weeks with Zhao Ying. She was soft, caring sweetness, exactly what he needed, and, of course, they became lovers. Although he couldn't love her as he loved Natasha, he found her to be stimulating company, both in and out of bed.

During this time together they learned to trust each other sufficiently to exchange many of their secret thoughts. In answer to a question from Gao, Zhao Ying admitted having little interest in politics. She had joined Comintern simply to get away from her old life. Nevertheless, she was totally committed and completely loyal.

Gao told Zhao Ying that he was a committed Communist. He had bad memories of a feudal system that enslaved the peasants, including all of his family, to the landlord. It was a hateful system, cruel and unjust. Communism offered a chance to sweep it all away. Twelve-year-old Gao Qing, full of youthful fire and enthusiasm, joined the Communists. As an adult, the fire was still there, burning as fiercely as ever.

They found that they had a similar attitude towards the demand that they belonged only to Comintern. It was Zhao Ying who first admitted to being most distressed about having to set aside her natural patriotism for her own country. To her surprise and delight, Gao agreed. She then admitted to having an important contact within the CLO to whom she passed information that might help China defeat the Japanese…

… She took a deep breath before dropping her bombshell. "The day following your admission into hospital, I feared for your life. You are the first man I have loved, so you can imagine my distress at the thought of losing you. I told my contact all about you. I also told him that Moscow has stopped sending you money and my funds are low. Could he make sure that you had the very best medical attention the hospital had to offer?

"He said that you were too valuable to lose and promised to do everything within his power to keep you alive, including paying your hospital bills. Now that you are well, he has asked for something in return. He wants you to agree to a meeting with Comrade Zhou En-lai."

Of course Gao agreed. Zhou En-lai was his childhood hero! Although Gao had once seen Zhou from a distance, he had wanted to meet with him for almost all of his life. Now, thanks to Zhao Ying… he kissed her. That must have been the meaning behind Kong's words when he said he had something interesting for Gao.

Gao first had to return to Beipei and complete his assignment. When it was time to leave, the reserve communications centre was working perfectly and Silkworm had been trained to use and maintain the equipment. Silkworm was a good man. The new centre would be safe with him.

*

It was now April 1942. The five people continued to work long hours. Feilibov came and went and Zhao Ying supported the unit from the hotel profits, which, with no indication as to when Moscow might resume the payments, was a constant source of irritation. Chopper summed it up thus. "The people running the Moscow end don't value us, or our work."

Of course they had sympathy for the Russians, that is why they continued to do their jobs despite their steadily deteriorating situation. Something had to change, but what? The answer, when it came, was disguised as an invitation.

The telephone rang. Chopper answered to hear Zhao Ying say, "Is he there?"

"No. Can I help?"

"Tell him to expect an important telephone call in one hour."

*

The telephone rang exactly on time. Gao answered.

"Master Chen Ye?"

"Speaking."

"This is Madam Zeng. I am a fashion designer needing silk urgently. Sorry to cause you any inconvenience. Can we meet at seven this evening in the Kai-xuan Hotel? (Zhao Ying's Hotel) …Excellent. I will be waiting."

"Curious," thought Gao. Of course he intended to keep the appointment, but he was not about to be caught unprepared. He told Chopper to accompany him and to carry his pistol.

At five-fifteen, Chopper hailed a rickshaw to take him to Yellow Corner Village. At five-thirty, Gao did the same. It was six-fifteen when Gao stopped his rickshaw a hundred metres before it reached the hotel main entrance. Chopper was sitting in his rickshaw a hundred metres away from the other side of the main entrance. Chopper nodded that all was well. With a perfect view of everything happening around the hotel main entrance, they sat in their respective rickshaws and waited.

It was a fine spring evening with perfect visibility. Dusk was not due for at least an hour. Plenty of shoppers and traffic provided cover whilst Gao and Chopper waited patiently, checking everyone coming and going through the hotel entrance. At six-fifty, a large black car passed Gao and stopped outside the hotel. The front windows were clear glass, allowing Gao to see the driver. Black curtains on all the rear windows hid the passengers. This was normal. A large man and a small woman alighted and went into the hotel.

At seven, Gao waved Chopper to join him. Apart from the car, which looked innocent enough, neither of them had seen anything sinister, unusual or dangerous.

Still on their guard, they walked into the hotel. Zhao Ying was waiting to signal them to follow her to a back room she reserved for her more important customers. She guided them through the door then quietly shut it behind them.

A well-dressed woman of some fifty years was sitting on one of the brown leather dining chairs. Behind her stood a giant of a man, bald-headed, dressed in a black western-style suit, stiff-collared shirt, black tie and waistcoat. A black trilby hat and a pair of black leather gloves were on a nearby table. He was at ease, with his legs slightly apart and his hands loosely clasped in front of tight belly.

Gao bowed respectfully and asked, "Madam Zeng?"

The lady nodded then invited Gao to sit opposite her. Chopper took up a position behind Gao. The two men swiftly weighed their chances of beating the other in a fight, then looked away.

Madam Zeng delivered her opening sentence as though she had rehearsed it.

"Master Chen Ye, I need you to trust me. If I invite you to take a drive with me, with just my driver for company, would you accept?"

"Begging your pardon, Madam, why should I?"

"Is not I that wishes to speak with you."

Ahhh, now Gao understood. This was not about silk.

"Please pardon me for a few moments," he murmured, leaving the room to check with Zhao Ying. She had no doubts about Madam Zeng. That settled it. If Zhao Ying was content, so was he. He returned to the room to reply, "Of course I will go with you. We will leave our companions here to enjoy a good meal."

Chopper nodded, and smiled at his opposite number. The smile was reciprocated and the two men shook hands.

"We are on the same side," said Madam Zeng. "We do not need guns. Please hand your revolver to your friend. I will leave mine with my companion."

She pulled a small calibre pistol out of her handbag and passed it to the giant.

"How did she know I was armed?" Gao asked himself as he passed his pistol to Chopper, then let the matter go.

By the time Madam Zeng and Gao climbed into the big black car, dusk was well advanced into night. It was a quick ride to their destination. The car stopped in front of a gate. The driver wound down the window on his side and showed his pass. A torch was flashed onto the faces of those sitting in the car. The torch was withdrawn and the car moved forward into the grounds of the Communist Liaison Office. It drew up in front of a small door where a waiting servant bowed them into an office. Standing behind a desk was someone Gao immediately recognised as Comrade Dong Bi-wu. Madam Zeng left the room through the door they had just used.

Dong Bi-wu was senior to Gao in age and status. Like every other Communist, Gao held this man in high esteem. He was a founder member of the Chinese Communist Party and was renowned for his noble character and good virtue.

He had a kind face, warm brown eyes, sported a goatee beard and was dressed in the standard Communist non-combatant uniform of high-necked grey jacket and trousers similar to the style made famous by Doctor Sun and also favoured by Mao Zedong. He waved Gao to a chair. Almost immediately tea was brought in and served.

When they were alone, Dong Bi-wu was all warmth and friendship.

"Comrade..." He leaned forward and asked, "Is it all right to call you Gao?" At Gao's nod, he continued, "At last we meet. I have heard so many good things about you."

"Comrade Dong Bi-wu," Gao replied. "I feel honoured to have

come to your notice. Since childhood you have been a hero of mine. When I was less than ten years old, a speech I heard you make in our small village gave me the ambition to join our Party. Two-and-a-half years later, in the spring of 1929, I did."

Dong Bi-wu looked pleased. "I undertook to spread the message of Communism all over China during those early years, and now you provide proof that my hard work was worth while." He smiled delightedly and for a brief moment looked young again.

"And later," he continued, "I had the pleasure of selecting you, together with nineteen others, to go to Moscow. It was highly experimental. Four of you graduated, turning the experiment into a success."

The door opened and in walked the man Gao most admired in the whole world, Zhou En-lai. With him was Gao's old friend, Kong.

"Comrade…?" Zhou raised his eyebrows questioningly.

"Gao."

"Comrade Gao. I apologise for not being here to greet you," said Zhou. "I hope you will forgive my apparent lack of respect. I had something important to attend to."

Gao was greatly touched. It was this kind of openness and consideration for others that had made Zhou the most treasured man in China. The Chinese comrades respected Mao Zedong. They loved Zhou En-lai.

"When did you return from Moscow?" asked Zhou.

"Last June. The Russians flew my Lieutenant and me to Lanzhou in a military aircraft and told us to make our own way to Chongqing."

Zhou, with a quizzical look, exclaimed, "It is now April. Why didn't you report your arrival to us?"

Gao was stunned by his question. Didn't they know that Stalin insisted upon absolute control over all spy school graduates?" He decided to ask. It was their turn to be surprised. They didn't know, so Gao explained it to them.

"From the moment we were handed over to the Soviets, it was forbidden for any one of us to make contact with our own Party. We argued long and hard against it but in the end we had to obey. Since then I have felt like a traitor. I know I am working for the good of Communism, but my heart and loyalty is to my Chinese Comrades, not the Soviets. Therefore, by speaking out this evening, I have broken Soviet discipline. Whilst I am here, I will also speak for my Deputy, Comrade Huang Chi. He hates that rule."

Zhou looked serious. When he spoke again, Gao was pleasantly surprised to be asked to stay for dinner.

"I have a few questions for you," said Zhou to Gao.

They moved from the office into a small dining room where a meal was already waiting. Simple food perfectly cooked. Gao refused to drink the strong rice wine and settled for a glass of beer. His three companions began to question him. He answered as truthfully as possible. He told them about his secret mission to Xi'an to find Madam Dong, the setting up of the reserve communications centre, and his meeting with the Old Man and General Li. He also admitted to killing the officer and letting one man live. And finally, he had a little moan about Moscow's failure to send operating money.

Nothing was said for several minutes. They had finished eating. The table had been cleared except for a pot of jasmine tea and four cups. Zhou broke the silence.

"Comrade Gao, I understand from all you have told us that you are prepared to inform us of anything of interest to China as well as continuing to report everything to Moscow. Is that correct?"

Gao nodded.

Zhou continued, "If I agree to secretly fund your operation in return for doing some work for us, are you in a position to accept?"

Again Gao nodded. He couldn't think of anything to say. Zhou was giving him exactly what he wanted, operating money, a return to his Chinese roots, self-respect and to be a useful member of the Chinese Communist Party. He found his voice.

"Comrade Zhou, this is exactly what I had in mind. Since spy school I have wanted to put the interests of China above those of the USSR, but I couldn't. If I stopped working for Comintern I would be found and killed, therefore my work for the Russians must continue."

A long conversation followed as they worked out their strategy. Eventually Zhou asked Gao to memorise three contact names together with their telephone numbers, radio wavelengths, callsigns and personal identification codes. If number one wasn't available, he could call number two. Only if he could not connect with the first two should he contact number three as a last resort. Using techniques learned in spy school, it wasn't long before Gao had everything committed to memory.

All three men shook hands with Gao. Madam Zeng was summoned to escort him back to the hotel. He almost burst into happy song! Zhou En-lai had agreed to classify his dual involvement as "Top Secret - on a need to know basis". Gao no longer cared about Stalin and his silly rule - he was back with his own people. From now on he could work for both sides. Of his colleagues, only Chopper would know the truth.

* * *

Yu Tianming.

West Hill Dictatorship Team, February 1967.

It was a cold winter. Our living conditions were so poor, both of us contracted a nasty skin disorder. And chilblains on our hands and feet drove us crazy with the pain and itching. But, for me, nothing could spoil the wonderful story that was unfolding as Old Gao went over every detail, making sure I would forever remember.

Natasha, Sparks, Hunter, Chopper, the rich landlord, the shoulder pole team led by the wise Old Man, Feilibov and the sexy Zhao Ying became as close to me as old friends. I awoke every morning impatient to know more, but on this day I was disappointed. At the point in his story when Old Gao was being driven back to the hotel after his meeting with Zhou En-lai, we were interrupted.

The door to our cell was unlocked and pulled open. Soldiers entered, carrying things. A long trestle table was erected and covered by a white bed-sheet. Six chairs were arranged along one side of the table. A notepad, ashtray and a mug was placed on the table in front of each chair, and a huge metal teapot was put down in the centre of the table. On a wall, one of the soldiers hung a large portrait of Chairman Mao.

Old Gao and I had risen to our feet. A soldier placed Old Gao's arms behind his back and handcuffed him before putting shackles on his ankles.

The soldiers marched out to be replaced by five officers and one soldier. The outer door clanged shut and we heard it being locked. One of the officers shouted,

"Gao Qing, this is a very serious moment. We are going to interrogate you, and we want you," he pointed at me, "to be present."

Then something unexpected happened. The six men turned to face the picture of Mao. Individually they held aloft a copy of Mao's "Little Red Book of Quotations" and collectively they shouted, "Endless Life To Chairman Mao! Endless Life To Chairman Mao! Endless Life To Chairman Mao!"

Still holding their Little Red Books up high, they performed a variation of the Loyalty Dance - a kind of shuffling movement of the feet.

Throughout China, every individual had to daily demonstrate his or her loyalty to Chairman Mao. The ritual was always the same. One. Hold the Little Red Book high in the air and shout three times, Endless life to Chairman Mao. Two. Perform the Loyalty Dance. To be caught not doing this daily ritual meant severe punishment, even death.

We prisoners were not expected to perform the ritual. However, before being incarcerated, I had done it religiously every evening before retiring for the night, not realizing, until that moment, just how ridiculous it was.

In the cell, I was struggling to stifle a sudden urge to laugh when a pair of feet got straw-entangled and the owner almost lost his balance. Ritual over, the five officers sat in a line along the table, poured tea and lit cigarettes. The soldier sat at the end, ready to take notes.

The senior officer, sitting in the middle of the five, looked sternly at Old Gao and spoke loudly, "Gao Qing, only a confession can lead to leniency. Do you understand?"

I looked at each officer in turn. Compared to Old Gao these five seemed so… nothing very much. Of course they had the power of life and death over us prisoners but all I could think was, "They are rabbit droppings trying to be elephant turds."

Old Gao stared at them without a reply.

"Are you Yu Tianming?" shouted Big Cheese to me.

"No." I answered, as firmly as I could. "I am number 74."

"So you are," glared Big Cheese. "Listen and learn." His gaze returned to Old Gao.

"I want the truth from you so I will tell you the truth. The investigation into your case began in 1952. In 1959, at our request, the Soviet Union forwarded some of the information contained in their files. They seemed to know all about you. If you are a loyal and committed Chinese Communist Party member, you should tell us everything because we represent the Party." He paused before continuing, "What were you doing in Moscow?"

Old Gao answered in a low but clear voice, free of fear. "I was given orders signed by Comrade Deng Fa, the Director of the Central Party Committee Security Bureau."

"Who countersigned your orders?"

"Comrade Zhou En-lai."

"Why didn't you make contact with your own Party?"

"It was the discipline. I followed orders."

Big Cheese rose to his feet and leaned forward. Shouting loudly, as though expecting Old Gao to be intimidated, he bellowed, "What discipline? What orders? You must tell us everything!"

It didn't work. The quiet, level voice of Old Gao asked, "Does Premier Zhou En-lai know you are here today asking me these questions? You do realise that you are in danger of forcing me to reveal top secret information to…" he pointed with his nose at the rest of us, "men who are not entitled to know."

The officer frowned. He knew from previous encounters that this was Old Gao's strongest defensive weapon. He resettled himself on the chair, thought for a while, then spat out, "You are a cunning, lying, traitor! How dare you use the name of our respected Premier to avoid answering my questions. If you do not answer fully, it will be the worse for you. I remind you once more that only a full confession can result in leniency."

"Are you prepared to accept the consequences of your actions?" asked Old Gao. "If you sign a paper saying that you are, I will tell you everything. But be warned. When I do, you will seal the fate of everyone here."

Silence. Big Cheese lit a cigarette and I distinctly heard a tremble in his breath as he exhaled. He was not comfortable with himself. He chewed on his lip, closed one eye and weighed up his options. Old Gao had won that round.

Big Cheese tried again. "I will report this conversation to Premier Zhou En-lai. We will soon have the proof of your lies. In the meantime I want you to tell us everything you know about the Marshals and Generals who were in command of the Red Army before 1937. We must dig out their crimes."

Old Gao stood stony-faced before his interrogators.

I was highly disturbed. Was nobody safe in Mao's Cultural Revolution? A big net had been cast in an attempt to disgrace the heroes of the revolution. Why did Mao want to punish those who had commanded the Communist armies thirty years previously? It made no sense.

Old Gao, fully in control of himself asked quietly, but forcefully, "What crimes? On whose authority do you follow this line of questioning?"

Big Cheese again jumped to his feet. "Damn you, you filthy turncoat!" he shouted, running around the table in his hurry to repeatedly punch Old Gao in the face.

Only I could see Old Gao using his spy-school training. He stood stiff and solid, silently taking the punches. When they stopped, he spat out a mouthful of blood.

"You are wrong," he mumbled, "I am neither a turncoat nor a traitor. My political ideals have never changed. I still follow the teachings of Lenin and Marx. For a turncoat, you must look to yourself. It is..."

"What?" roared Big Cheese. "You dare to accuse me?"

"I do. It is you and your kind who have turned away from true Communist principles. You are Fascists. Every last one of you. How else can the persecution of loyal and honest freedom fighters be explained?"

Big Cheese was almost beside himself with rage. He pulled his revolver from its holster and raised it to Old Gao's temple. Without a thought for my own safety, I lunged forward to protect my friend. With both hands, I grabbed the wrist of Big Cheese, forcing the pistol barrel to point skywards.

"No!" I shouted. "You must not kill him. If you do, you will disgrace the uniform of our army. Let him be!"

I continued to hold the wrist. Big Cheese lashed out with his calf-length leather boot, kicking Old Gao in the groin.

This was too much, even for Old Gao. He doubled over. I released my hold on the wrist and bent down to help him. A fist, still holding the pistol, crashed down on Old Gao's head. I got between the attacker and the attacked and shouted, "If you kill him, how will you get his confession?"

Old Gao, doubled up in pain and not far from unconsciousness, looked at me and gasped, "Let him kill me. I will never help them to persecute innocent comrades."

His cold gaze went to Big Cheese. In a firmer voice, he said, "In the old days, a Comrade was a friend and Communism meant a free society with all the people being equal. Today, China is drowning in hatred and so-called "Comrades" are betraying each other. If you cannot see what you are doing is wrong, then *you* are the turncoat. As for me, you can call me a turned coat because I have turned away from everything that you, *Comrade,* represent."

Big Cheese stared at Old Gao. I spotted a shadow of respect flash in his eyes before he gained control and hatred returned. "You are a dead man," he growled at Old Gao. To me he threatened, "You too will be punished."

He returned to his seat. None of the other officers had got involved. From their expressions I concluded that they were as disgusted as I at the treatment given to a helpless prisoner.

Big Cheese decided to stop the interrogation. The door was banged with a fist and opened. The six men filed out. Soldiers entered to remove everything brought in earlier and to release Old Gao from the handcuffs and shackles.

Still curled up on the ground, Old Gao spat out a mouthful of blood to mumble,

"Today I condemned myself to death."

"Damn *them* to death." I growled. In reality, however, I felt helpless against the evil that was consuming China. It was a fact that nobody could go up against Mao Zedong but fate had given me the chance to strike my small blow. Before that day I had only *wanted* to do it. After witnessing the violent attack on Old Gao, I absolutely *had* to take his story out of that cell.

* * *

Gao Qing's story continues.

CHAPTER 4.

Moles in High Places, Spring 1943

1.

Although Mao Zedong was in charge of his provincial section of the Red Army in 1931 when the Japanese first invaded China, he was a long way down the list of possible candidates for Party Chairman. Wang Ming was the Communist number one at that time and Chiang Kai-shek headed the governing Nationalist (Kuomintang) Party.

Whilst the Japanese forces marched northwards into Manchuria almost unopposed, the civil war between the Communists and the Kuomintang continued without pause. Chiang Kai-shek declared, "If we are to fight against the foreign invaders effectively, we must first settle our internal differences. Forget the Japanese. We have an even worse enemy in Chinese Communism. Our number one task is the total annihilation of these traitors in our midst."

For the next few years, Chiang threw his well-equipped, better-trained and much larger army against the ragtag peasant militia, pushing the Reds ever backwards. Communist casualties were huge, forcing the high command to demote Wang to a lower position and take the vastly depleted Red Army on the renowned Long March to the northwest of China. There, the survivors set up their base camp in Yan'an.

Those same years had been good to Mao. He had steadily risen up the Communist ranks. During the Long March, he was made leader.

For the Communists, facing almost certain defeat at the hands of the Kuomintang in 1937, the second Japanese invasion of China was considered a blessing in disguise. The Kuomintang had no option but to stop chasing the Communists and face the Japanese.

Mao stayed in Yan'an, well away from the fighting, consolidating and expanding his forces. His only ambition was to re-ignite the civil war, defeat the Kuomintang, and take power in China. He more or less ignored the Japanese, preferring to bide his time. And anyway, he needed to build up his army. To do that, he needed good propaganda.

The Communists constantly claimed that Mao's military brilliance was the guiding force behind every victory against the Japanese, whilst always blaming Chiang Kai-shek for the setbacks. Communist propaganda got most peasants to believe that the Red Army was an all-conquering war machine whilst the Nationalist Army barely got involved. But in fact the reverse was true. It was Chiang Kai-shek's Kuomintang forces that did the bulk of the fighting. Up to 1943, the Red Army had been involved in one big battle and a few skirmishes against the Japanese and precious little else.

Mao was not much interested in espionage and spying but Chiang Kai-shek was. He had a wide intelligence gathering net. From the peasant informer to the high level diplomat willing to sell information, the Kuomintang constantly searched for more and more secrets. But, as Roger from Washington had correctly informed Gao, the two primary intelligence organisations were "piss poor".

Apart from the low-grade intelligence gained from torturing Communists, most of the information stored in the Kuomintang files had come from the Americans under a "need to know" agreement. Following on from Pearl Harbor, America was China's strongest ally.

The men in charge of the two Kuomintang intelligence-gathering agencies in 1943 were a Mr. Chen Li-fu, Head of the Central Intelligence Service (CIS), and Lieutenant-General Dai Li, who headed up the Military Investigation and Statistics Bureau (MISB).

Both departments were under the direct leadership of Chiang Kai-shek. When the Kuomintang Government fled to Hankow and then to

Chongqing, the CIS moved with him, leaving the bulk of the MISB operating under cover in Nanking.

Both agencies had offices spread all over China. Wherever one agency opened an office, the other did too. In Chongqing, the CIS was the dominant information gatherer and the MISB controlled telecommunications, mail and media.

2.

The loathing between Mao and Chiang put huge strains upon the so-called "United Front" against the Japanese. Both sides were guilty of turning a blind eye to assassination. Communist killing Kuomintang and Kuomintang executing Communist was never officially admitted nor denied. Hatred between the two sides was so intense, such killings often led to a reward for the perpetrator. Even worse, although the Japanese were daily publicly proclaimed to be China's number one enemy, both the Communists and the Kuomintang privately considered each other to be their natural adversary. This resulted in the Kuomintang wasting huge amounts of resources and manpower chasing Communists instead of fighting the Japanese.

A good example of Chiang's pathological hatred of Mao and the Communists was his expansion of the CIS. He created a whole new department dedicated to "Red Busting".

The activities of this branch of the CIS were kept very secret. The long-term objective of the hand-picked CIS agents was the total destruction of the Chinese Communist Party. Some were trained to harass and hinder the Communists at every turn, others were ordered to penetrate deep inside the Communist organization and quietly, sometimes successfully, instigated rebellion within the Communist ranks. They also created situations specifically designed to falsely implicate high-ranking Communists in some kind of traitorous activity then agitate for their execution. A fair number of top Communists lost their lives this way.

Of course Chairman Mao was the number one target but he always wriggled free of danger.

When the Japanese attacked in huge numbers in 1937, Chiang had been forced to accept the United Front and allow the Communists to set up their Liaison Office in Chongqing. He immediately gave orders to the CIS to check on everyone known to have any contact with those inside, and from time to time to kidnap, interrogate and execute CLO officers. That is why Gao had been taken to and from the compound during the hours of darkness in a limousine fitted with black curtains.

The CIS also kept surveillance on all the embassies, with the Soviets getting extra attention, particularly the Military Attaché's Office. Anyone going in who was not known, or not an employee, was followed when leaving and whenever possible, secretly arrested, interrogated and murdered.

Moscow had no interest in Chinese internal affairs. Nevertheless, Feilibov was very aware that CIS activities represented the greatest threat to the Chinese arm of Comintern. One arrest or defection of anyone connected to the organisation could jeopardise the whole network. Using this as a lever, he persuaded his superiors in Moscow to recommence payments into the Swiss Bank Account. Comintern retaliated by ordering Feilibov to expand the number of safe houses from where Gao's group could transmit. He leased several penthouse apartments around the city and equipped them. Gao split up his operators and set up a rota and shift system, moving them to a different flat every week. Each operator had a special frequency and was allocated a number of contacts to control. It was a kind of espionage merry-go-round, designed, as far as possible, to confuse any interested outsiders. When it was running efficiently, Feilibov moved Gao out of his expensive luxury apartment.

*

During the night of the move, Gao stayed with Zhao Ying in her hotel. In Chinese eyes, there is nothing unusual in same-family members spending time together. Gao's and Chopper's bags, papers and equipment were spirited out of the apartment.

The next morning, Gao, following Feilibov's instructions, walked out of the hotel wearing his usual rich silk Chinese-style gown and skull-cap. A rickshaw dropped him near to the north gate of the city. He walked the last hundred metres or so until he spotted a sign saying, "Northwest Woollen Mill". He continued his walk along the front of the two-storey building to the corner and turned left. The building was long. As he walked, from several air extractors, sounds of machinery leaked out. He reached the end of the building and stopped. A wide alleyway had a lorry being loaded with bales of merchandise.

He retraced his steps and walked into the lobby. His first impression was clean marble and glass with concealed lighting. Under an old-fashioned sign shouting "Northwest Woollen Mill", an old, wizened, bald headed man dressed entirely in black peasant clothes sat beside an equally old mahogany desk pushed up against a wall. The man politely creaked to his feet and shakily bowed an ancient Chinese welcome.

"Please advise the manager of my arrival," Gao instructed.

The old man replaced himself in his cushioned wooden chair and reached under the desk. From somewhere high above, a bell sounded, followed by footsteps hurrying downwards. Seconds later a tall, thin, dignified looking man, aged around fifty, appeared. He was dressed in a dark grey pin-stripe western style suit, snowy white shirt with starched wing collars and black bow tie. Shiny black leather shoes, a gold-banded wristwatch and a gemstone ring on his little finger completed his attire. He had long, thick grey hair, and from the look in his dark brown intelligent eyes, was a mischievous boy at heart. He looked at Gao enquiringly. Gao made the pre-arranged signal. With his back to the old man, he placed his left hand on his abdomen with the index finger curled underneath, hiding the top two sections. The man made an almost imperceptible nod of his head and said, "Please come with me."

Gao noted the non-use of names at this stage. He followed the man up a marble staircase, through a white-painted wooden door into an apartment fit for an Emperor! The man turned to watch Gao's reaction and was not disappointed. "It's quite a contrast, isn't it," he chuckled.

Gao had walked into an ancient Chinese apartment. Everything, from floor to ceiling, had to be hundreds of years old, with the only exceptions being the modern equipment in the office he was taken to. They remained standing, the man behind a desk and Gao in front of it. The man waited.

Gao counted to twenty before asking, "Have you got it?"

The man bent to retrieve a folded page of red paper from the waste-paper bin. From his pocket Gao pulled out a blue folded page and handed it over. His host opened up both pages and laid them one over the other exactly. He checked the top left-hand corner before holding the pages up for Gao to see. Gao nodded as the two pin-holes in each paper matched perfectly. Laying the two pages side by side on the desk, he motioned Gao to check that the creases also matched. They smiled and relaxed.

"I am the owner here and my name is Yan Bao-hang," said the man, sticking out his hand.

"I am Chen-Ye," replied Gao, taking it.

They sat down.

Gao, in a friendly voice, said, "I have read your file. I know that your codename is Ma-que (Sparrow)."

"That's fine with me," responded Sparrow. "To the public I own this place and the old man works for me. But in fact he is my senior. With him downstairs, we are safe here."

"Where is my stuff?" Gao asked.

"There," Sparrow pointed out of the window to the building opposite. Gao saw an elegant English style house. Lace curtains at the windows hid whatever was going on inside. From where he stood, it seemed as if a multicolour explosion was taking place on the two balconies overlooking the street. Large pots erupted with flowers of different beautiful hues, protected from the hot sun by miniature palms.

"Don't worry Comrade," said Sparrow. "Everything is arranged. Your equipment and personal belongings are already installed and your new partner is waiting for you. Feilibov has done you proud, she is an excellent housekeeper."

Gao knew about the woman but had not yet met her. Feilibov had explained it all to him. For security reasons he and Chopper had to be separated. Chopper was now living in a cheap hostel and working as a porter in the nearby docks. It was a perfect cover.

Feilibov had driven Gao to the docks to see Chopper at work. Gao stood beside the car, waiting. Chopper, dressed in black, with a sack draped over his head, carried boxes past the car, not five metres in front of Gao. Only when Chopper wanted him to, did Gao see his cheeky grin. Nobody would suspect Chopper of being anything other than an illiterate labourer. Gao already missed him.

That night, under the light of a full moon, Gao walked to his new home. The house had been particularly selected for him. It stood on a corner with the main road running along the front, an alley to each side and a rear lane, giving him plenty of emergency exits. Most usually he would use the front entrance. He remembered how pleased Feilibov had been with himself as he described it. And Gao had to admit to being entirely satisfied. He pushed the bell. A woman in her late twenties, wearing a leaf-green silk qipao, opened the door. He knew he was expected. What he didn't expect to see was her big welcoming smile.

"Please come in, my Master." He heard her low voice and liked it.

She closed and bolted the heavy wooden door before leading him up a wide staircase to the first floor. Turning right, she opened the first door to the left. As he entered the room, she turned a dimmer switch. From the high ceiling a huge centrally located chandelier and many pairs of wall-lights slowly lit up until every corner of the large room was illuminated. Gao instantly knew that he would use this room a lot.

The old shiny-black wooden floorboards had seen plenty of service, but that was their charm. They said "hello" the moment Gao walked in. The comfortable-looking high-backed red leather settee and matching armchair begged him to relax, perhaps to snooze awhile. Around the room, bookcases bursting with English and Chinese language books invited him to spend his life reading the literary treasures they held. At the end of the room, a superb, beautifully carved chair and matching writing table awaited his need to correspond.

Occasional tables stood strategically, willing him to place things on them. Gold-framed paintings of traditional English country scenes and one of a speedy-looking sailing ship hung on the walls, lit by their own individual lights.

Gao walked around the room, touching things. As he passed the ship painting, he peered at the little brass plaque pinned to the frame and read "Cutty Sark".

"Master," the soft harmony of her voice floated into his ears. "Let me show you the rest of the house."

Two more reception rooms, a dining room with drawing room attached but separated by a pair of sliding doors, four en-suite bedrooms, a family bathroom and a well fitted kitchen with a huge scrubbed pine table surrounded by a dozen chairs. In every room he sensed a quietly confident dignity that was altogether English, and very decadent. As a Communist, he should have disapproved, but he couldn't. He just loved it.

"And finally, your study."

He stood beside the swivel chair behind the leather-topped desk and looked around.

"Where is my equipment?" he asked.

The woman nodded towards a huge varnished door to his right.

"Everything is in there."

He opened the door to another room equally as big as the study to find his things waiting, ready for use. He shut the door and invited the woman to sit and talk. He needed to confirm that everything he had read in her file was correct, and that she was the person he had read about.

Her full name was Mei Hua. She told him to simply call her "Hua" meaning Blossom. She was a widow. Her husband, a respected professor in the local university, had also been the underground member of the Communist Party responsible for local recruitment. He had recruited, then married, Blossom.

She was from a rich family. The house was part of her inheritance following the death of her father. He had purchased the house, almost exactly as it was now, from a Timothy Armstrong, who had made his fortune and returned to England.

Blossom had no children, she lived alone with a live-in maid. Two other servants came in daily. Just a week previously she had been instructed by Feilibov to "form a new family" with a male radio operator. Whatever she did in private was of no concern. In public, she must show herself to be his wife.

"Feilibov has been up to his old tricks again." Gao thought, with an inward chuckle. "He didn't tell me that I was about to gain a wife. I hope Zhao Ying will understand."

Actually it was perfect. A big house, a stylish wife and a supposedly successful business was exactly the opposite profile of a Communist. It was time for him to introduce himself.

"My name is Chen-Ye. By day I will be doing business with the Northwest Woollen Mill. By night I will use the radio. I am usually up and about by eight o'clock each morning. However, there will be times when I will need to work long into the night and sleep late. I have two cousins who will come to visit. One works at the nearby docks and another has her own hotel." He paused for a few seconds, then added, "One more thing. Please stop calling me your Master."

They talked some more, slowly getting acquainted. He advised her of his food and drink preferences and she told him some bits and pieces of her personal habits and routine. Then it was time for him to get to work. He asked her to show him which bedroom was his before bidding her goodnight. He took off his day clothes and put on something comfortable before returning to the study to start up the transceiver.

*

For Gao, married life began with the morning newspaper and breakfast. Perfect food served perfectly by a perfect woman. "Is there any better way to start the day?" he wondered.

Later, he walked to the woollen mill. The old man greeted him with a bow and pushed the bell. Sparrow clattered down to escort him upstairs, thus establishing his morning routine.

On Sundays the workforce rested whilst the machines were checked and serviced. Sparrow told him that in the fiercely competitive world of textile manufacture, time lost to machine breakdown could be the difference between profit and loss. By closing on Sundays, the company achieved two things. Contented workers and efficient machinery.

Zhao Ying visited him twice a week to make love and exchange information. She didn't seem to mind his conversion to a married man. And, in fact, she had nothing to worry about. Blossom was virtuous and dutiful. She looked after him in every possible way and every night she kept watch for anything unusual until he came down. Then she made them both a drink and they chatted until ready for bed. She to her room, he to his. Both parties did their jobs as best they could, including keeping their relationship on a strictly business footing.

3.

On a windy autumnal day, Gao followed Feilibov's instructions to meet his "third brother". Instead of his usual silk gown and skull-cap, he had been told to wear a smart western style suit and a flat cap. His destination was a city centre restaurant near to the post office. He hailed a rickshaw and arrived at the restaurant a few minutes early. A pretty receptionist guided him to his reserved corner table where he and his expected lunch companion could sit with their backs against a wall.

Summoning a hovering waiter, he ordered a pot of rice wine and two dishes. Not long afterwards, just as the waiter returned with his order, a man, tall for a Chinese, entered the restaurant. He seemed to be very much at his ease and wore his western style clothes as though born into them. Not fat or thin, he moved fluidly around the seated diners until he saw Gao.

"Ah, third brother, there you are." Gao said, smiling a greeting. The man made the same recognition hand gesture that Gao had given to Sparrow. Gao waved an invite for third brother to sit in the vacant chair.

"Only two dishes?" third brother queried. "Let me add one more." He turned to the hovering waiter. "Chilli chicken for my brother and the same three dishes and wine for me please." Once more he had proved his credentials.

Gao correctly replied by allowing his table napkin to drop to the floor and asking for a replacement. Both men relaxed.

Gao poured the strong rice alcohol into two egg-cup sized glasses and handed one to third brother.

"Gambei!" (Cheers!) He toasted.

They drank the contents in one go.

Third brother poured wine and said "Gambei".

They swallowed again. That was enough swallowing, they sipped from then on.

This so-called "third brother" had recently returned from the same spy-school that Gao had graduated from more than two years previously. His name was Lu Yu, with a codename "Serpent" because of his flexible body.

"I'll pay for this lunch," he said grinning hugely. "Today I am celebrating my twenty-fourth birthday."

His story was an interesting one. He was the middle of three sons from an important Kuomintang family, and had been sent to Paris at the age of twenty to complete his education. However, just days before the Germans invaded France, he had managed to fly out to Moscow where he was soon mixing with other Chinese elite, including Chiang Jin-guo, Chiang Kai-shek's eldest son, who was studying to be a Civil Engineer.

The Generalissimo had followed a tradition begun by Doctor Sun Yat-sen by sending Jin-guo abroad to complete his education.

Why Moscow, when Chiang hated Communists? Simple. Stalin had long ago recognised the Kuomintang as the rightful rulers of China. Also, the Soviet educational establishments were far superior to anything available in China.

The Russians welcomed all overseas students. Not only were their families willing to pay the high fees, it was a good opportunity to win foreign converts to Communism. In due time, both young men were contacted and Chiang Jin-guo was persuaded to join the Russian Communist Party.

When the Generalissimo heard, he was furious with his son for being so un-filial as to join the Communists. He threatened to disown the young man, forcing Chiang Jin-guo to terminate his Russian Communist Party membership and return to China with his Russian wife. Meanwhile, Lu Yu had been secretly recruited into Comintern.

As they ate, Gao was well aware of the looks given him by his companion. Serpent's careful observation said, "You look so young, only my age," (actually Gao was two years older) "and yet you are already an experienced old hand."

At the same time, as unobtrusively as possible, Gao was observing Serpent. His conclusion was, "He knows his business and will make a valuable team member."

For the remainder of the meal each of them sized up the other. They both knew they were doing it. Slowly, the beginnings of trust developed. At some point Gao brought the wine cup to his lips, leaned forward and said in a low voice, "As soon as you have something, go to the bookstore on Main Street. I will be there daily from one o'clock to one-thirty."

Gao already knew that the Soviets had given Serpent a complete set of papers saying he had just graduated from Moscow University. He also knew that he was a very valuable convert to Comintern because he had close relatives holding high ranking positions within Chiang's Kuomintang Government. This family connection was a double blessing. It made him much less likely to be a CIS suspect, and, after being introduced to Lieutenant-General Dai Li, known to all as Boss Dai - the head of the Military Investigation and Statistics Bureau, Serpent had been given an important position within the MISB.

Officially, Serpent's job was collating the information gleaned from mail, telephone and media intercepts. Unofficially, he was also responsible for intercepting and checking all mail sent to Chongqing Post Office Box number 92. This box had been especially set up for use by CIS operatives and was reputed to be secure. It wasn't. The MISB was secretly checking everything going in and out of Box 92 and Boss Dai had personally appointed Serpent into the job.

He was now above suspicion and perfectly placed to provide Gao with huge amounts of information. At last Comintern had a mole working at the heart of Chiang Kai-shek's MISB who was privy to CIS secrets.

4.

A week later Serpent appeared in the bookshop and began to wander around the shelves until spotting Gao riffling through a book on butterflies. Gao was inwardly yawning. It was not his preferred reading. He was pleased to hear Serpent's voice. "Ah, second brother, fancy meeting you here. This must be your lucky day. I have just bought a fine pair of crabs, a rare treat! Have you eaten?" Serpent opened a leather shopping bag to show Gao. A brown envelope rested on top of two large crabs.

Gao smiled. "Hello third brother. I will be happy to eat with you." He returned the butterfly book to the shelf and seconds later they were out of the shop. They crossed several streets and turned a couple of corners without speaking. Serpent followed Gao into a crowded department store and almost immediately thrust the bag into Gao's hand before disappearing into the lunchtime crush. Gao wandered around the store for more than an hour, all the while checking to see if he was being followed. He wasn't, so he went home.

He locked the door of his study, sat down and checked the envelope. It was addressed to P.O. Box 92, Chongqing. The sender's name was not given, just the number 215. He or she had glued a chicken feather to the top right-hand corner and had used the expensive but reliable and fast Air Courier Service. To the Chinese, a chicken feather means "extremely urgent". Rubber stamps used to confirm dispatch told Gao the letter had originated in northeast China.

He went to the kitchen and carefully steamed open the envelope. Back in the study, using tweezers, he pulled out a single sheet of paper and read, "I have to stay here. To move away would mean certain discovery. I am sending my trusted brother-in-law who will answer to the name of Midai. To avoid suspicion, he will travel by bus, train and boat. He is aged 37, of average height and clean-shaven. A small scar divides his left eyebrow. He will stay in the Jialing Hotel and is expecting to meet with your people there."

Gao thought there must be plenty of money available to the sender. The Jialing Hotel was the most expensive hotel in Chongqing. He continued reading.

"Contact words. You. Are you the Ginseng man?

Midai. I have some good quality Ginseng, are you interested?

You. Yes, but depends on your price and I don't want rubbish.

Midai. With such good quality as I have for sale, how can price matter?"

Gao read the letter again and again until he knew it by heart, then he burnt it. Blossom cooked the crabs that evening.

That night, his main item of news to Moscow was the letter. Three days later Moscow came back with an answer. One of their moles hidden deep inside the Kuomintang Northeastern Army Command, real name Jin Chan, was a suspected defector. Already his controller and radio operator had gone down fighting, causing seven others to flee the area. He had a brother-in-law, real name Dai Mi, who fitted the description of the man soon to arrive in Chongqing.

"This man must be intercepted," said Moscow. "Use all means at your disposal to get the information he is carrying. He must not, under any circumstances, contact the CIS. You have permission to use all methods of persuasion. He must not return home."

At that time, to travel the distance between the northeast of China to Chongqing required a long bus journey, three trains and a boat. Gao calculated that the journey would take at least two weeks, giving him plenty of time to prepare. His first requirement was Chopper.

Early the next evening, wearing old clothes borrowed from the woollen mill, he set out for the docks. It was a clear starlit night, making it a pleasure to be walking the city. Haunting sounds of industry wafted in and out of his hearing. A wood-saw whine here, a machine there, the hoot of a ship. The sounds brought on a fierce pride in the people. Nothing would ever stop the Chinese from getting on with life and to the average Chinese, that meant work, work, and more work.

Chopper had settled into the life of a dockside labourer and had fallen into their habits. Every evening he could be found with the other single porters. They played cards or gossiped the time away between eating and sleep.

Gao walked along the perimeter wall protecting the docks, turned into a narrow unlit pot-holed lane and shuffled slowly forward until he came to a ramshackle wooden structure. Above the door a sign said "Good Luck Restaurant". He quickly peered into the darkness around him, saw nothing, pushed the door open and stepped inside to immediately bang his head on a low beam. "THUD! " For several seconds he saw stars whilst a big lump grew out of his forehead. He staggered forward and fell down a short flight of wooden steps. Mocking laughter was his welcome into the free-time world of the coolie.

A sour smell of vomit mixed with cheap tobacco, strong liquor, bad cooking and stinking bodies was enough to turn the strongest stomach. Controlling his own desire to vomit, Gao peered through the smoke-filled dim light from a few oil lamps, trying to locate his friend. He knew where to look. They were trained to always sit with their backs against a wall near to an exit. And there he was, slouched over a table in the far corner.

"Hey cousin," Gao called out.

Chopper lifted his head and beckoned Gao to join him. Gao negotiated the tables and carefully stepped over a few drunks to sit facing Chopper on a rough, wooden bench made sticky from spilled alcohol and old food.

"Ah cousin," said Chopper, pouring wine into a tin cup and passing it to Gao. "It's good to see you. Come, drink with me."

Gao pulled out a paper wrap from inside his shirt and laid it on the mucky table. Chopper smiled broadly as his most favourite nibble, preserved chilli beef, was revealed.

"Sorry to see you here like this," Gao said in Russian, knowing his voice could not be heard above the general hubbub.

Chopper shrugged. "It isn't so bad. At least I work regular hours from dawn to dusk, and I sleep at nights." He shoved a chunk of beef into his mouth.

"I need you." Gao said.

"I'm listening."

"Tonight you sleep between clean sheets. Feilibov has fixed it for you to be missing for a while. When you're ready we'll go."

"Wait. As a coolie, I've learned to appreciate every little luxury."

He chewed the beef and gulped down the wine until all was gone. Patting his stomach, he said in the local Chinese dialect, "Now I'm ready."

*

Wrapped in a white bathrobe, Chopper emerged from a happy hour in the bathroom.

"That was good," he said. "I've left my coolie clothes in there. Don't wash them. When I return to the docks I will need them to be just as filthy as they are now."

Blossom took his dirty clothes and as carefully as newly laundered silks, folded and placed them on a shelf in a wardrobe.

After his nightly report to Moscow, Gao and Chopper worked on the details of their plan. The following morning, Chopper, still wrapped in the bathrobe, ate a huge breakfast before donning servant clothes. His mission was to collect three thousand yuan from Zhao Ying. From there he had to go to the Jialing Hotel to book two twin-bedded rooms for an indefinite period and await Gao's arrival.

Gao dressed in his usual Chinese business garb and walked to the mill to tell Sparrow not to expect him for a few days. He then took a rickshaw to the bookshop. Serpent didn't appear so there had been no change of plan. Midai must be on his way.

His next stop was a meeting with Feilibov at their pre-arranged rendezvous in the municipal gardens. There were no last minute instructions - the plan was progressing as expected.

He returned home for lunch and a change of clothes. He thanked Blossom for taking care of Chopper. "Don't be fooled by his appearance," he told her. "He is a loyal friend and an invaluable member of the team."

That afternoon, dressed in his very best finery, Gao stepped outside and hailed a rickshaw to take him to the Jialing Hotel.

5.

It was early November and unusually cold. Gao shoved his hands into the wide sleeves of his gown until the rickshaw stopped in front of the hotel. He paid his fare and alighted. A bowing porter took control of his case and a doorman opened the door with a smile and bowed him into the lobby.

"Master Gao." He heard Chopper's voice and turned toward it. Chopper was all subservience, exactly what a servant to the rich should be. He turned to the porter.

"Please take my master's luggage to room 209."

He turned back to Gao and bowed again before leading the way to the guest elevator. By the time they reached the room, Gao's case was on a stand, guarded by the porter. He bowed them a welcome into the room, palmed his tip and bowed himself out, closing the door behind him.

For the next five days, they waited. Gao left the hotel in the mornings as though doing business. Each lunchtime he went to the bookshop, but no Serpent. He returned to the hotel during the late afternoon.

Chopper stayed in the hotel, either in the lounge drinking tea or sitting at a desk in his room playing with an abacus. He often deliberately left the door to his room open so that the clack of the beads supposedly totting up the columns of figures in a large account book (borrowed from the woollen mill) could be heard, giving the impression of good business being done. They knew that the hotel staff had orders to report everything unusual to the management, who, in turn, told the police. Conducting business from such a prestigious location was part of the everyday life of the hotel and not at all suspicious.

Chopper kept his eyes open but didn't see Midai. What he did notice was the odd behaviour of two men staying in room 208, across the corridor from his. All day, everyday, a few minutes after one man entered the hotel, the other left, to return after a while, when the other man left. Chopper checked with his wristwatch. The "changeover", if that was what it was, happened at intervals of roughly ninety minutes. Also, the two men went into the dining room for breakfast and lunch at different times but ate dinner together. What were they up to? Did they have any connection to Midai? Gao and Chopper needed to know.

The next morning, their sixth in the hotel, Gao and Chopper were up early. Gao was in the lobby when the first man, they named him Blue because of his dark blue western-style suit, departed, carrying a briefcase. Gao followed at a discreet distance. Blue walked around just one corner then stopped and stood in the doorway of the bombed remains of what had once been a shop.

Almost immediately people began to talk to him. In quick succession Gao saw a teenage boy, some kind of rich trader, an old woman and a strange mix of city people. During the next hour and a half, Blue did good business, taking money before handing out small parcels from the briefcase. Then he returned to the hotel.

Chopper had used the time investigating the two doors to their rooms. They were made of a heavy solid wood hung on sturdy hinges. Only the turning of the lock could gain them entry into the room opposite. The locks were standard well-oiled mortises making no noise when the key was turned. He tried the key to Gao's room on his, and vice-versa. They were not interchangeable so he took the lock on his door apart. By the time Gao returned, chilled to the bone, Chopper understood the mechanism sufficiently to make a tool that should open all the doors.

Brown departed the hotel with Chopper in tow. They had a similar ninety minutes. Same place, same kind of business and back to the hotel. Now Gao knew why the men changed places so often, it was the cold. When Chopper returned to Gao's room he complained that his feet felt like blocks of ice. When he was warm, he went out again. He had a tool to make.

During Chopper's absence, Gao placed himself in the lounge area of the hotel from where he could see the entrance and the reception desk. Three men entered the hotel with porters in tow, carrying suitcases.

The face of the second man was familiar. Gao quickly drew a file from his memory. His name was Colonel Chen, the most successful of the CIS agents. Gao had seen his face many times on a photograph shown to them at spy-school. The other two were probably his assistants. Why was he walking into the hotel at this particular time? Gao needed to know.

He casually got up and went to fetch another newspaper from the rack standing to one side of reception. He overheard "Suite 302 is the very best in the hotel. Luxury lounge, sitting room and three en-suite double bedrooms overlooking the park. The hotel management want your stay to be a pleasant one and our staff are here to serve you." Lots of bowing.

Gao, in addition to the arrival of Colonel Chen, witnessed two Blue/Brown changeovers before Chopper returned. Whilst Gao kept watch, Chopper tried his new tool on the door-locks of both their rooms. It worked perfectly.

That evening Gao and Chopper had an early dinner served in Chopper's room. Later, as soon as Blue and Brown had gone to eat, Chopper's little tool opened the door to room 208. While Chopper stood guard, Gao made a quick visual check. Finding nothing of interest, he began searching.

With one sitting room and two en-suite bedrooms to check, it took him a few minutes to get to the closet where he immediately found something. Inside a large leather suitcase, to his surprise unlocked, he found eighteen cardboard containers about the size of a shoebox. He picked one out and opened it. It was full of paper money. The same with the others except for four that were stored on the right side of the case. They had something else in them, squares of a black doughy substance wrapped in greaseproof paper. Blue and Brown were opium dealers!

How could these two men live in the best and most expensive hotel in the city, and do business openly on the street without fear of arrest? Easy. It was an open secret and a sour joke among the ordinary people of China that although opium was officially banned, there were plenty of people making fortunes from it. The drug syndicates were well served by many layers of corrupt officials who earned extra money by giving protection to the traffickers. And business was brisk. Most street-prostitutes, sing-song brothel girls and the concubines confined to their lonely lives behind high walls, used opium. So did many millions of dysfunctional people throughout China. Blue and Brown had nothing to do with Midai.

Their next worry was Colonel Chen. Long ago, a visiting American had acknowledged Chen's rigid regard for law and order by giving him the title of "an honest cop". Other Americans had christened him "The Chinese Eliot Ness". He hated all wrongdoers and was good at catching them. Now aged over fifty, he was at the top of his profession. Respected by everyone and feared by many.

Chen headed up a special group set up by Chiang Kai-shek to root out corruption from within the ranks of the Kuomintang Security Services. He was also famous for taking every opportunity to arrest any common criminal that came his way. He was utterly ruthless, wringing out every last drop of information from them that might help him do his own job. When he was satisfied that there was nothing left to find, he passed on the wreckage to the civil police.

6.

The next morning Gao spotted Midai eating breakfast. He looked anxious. Chopper was all for going up to him there and then. In Russian, Gao whispered, "Have your breakfast and follow him when he leaves. See what room he is in but don't acknowledge him. Let him sweat while we check to see if anyone else approaches him."

For the rest of that day Chopper kept Midai under surveillance whilst Gao watched Colonel Chen. Midai was not approached by anyone and it seemed to Gao that Colonel Chen had no interest in the man. However, Gao's caution had given him the time needed to formulate a new plan. At dusk, he went out to meet Feilibov to report the arrival of Midai and to outline his new plan, making Feilibov smile.

"Good," he said. "Moscow will enjoy the irony."

Next, he went home to Blossom to collect some clothes and other bits and pieces. On his way back to the hotel he shopped for two bottles of strong rice liquor and two tumblers.

Chopper reported that Midai was in room 316. Looking worried, he had appeared at dinner. He had eaten almost nothing, all the while looking at the door as though expecting company.

Gao waited another hour then let Chopper go up a floor to room 316 to make the first contact. Chopper knocked and the door half opened.

Chopper asked, "Are you the Ginseng man?"

Midai opened the door fully and let Chopper enter, then closed it.

"I have some good quality Ginseng, are you interested?" replied Midai.

"Yes, but it depends on your price and I don't want rubbish."

"With such good quality as I have for sale, how can price matter?"

Chopper nodded his acceptance of Midai. "My Master has been waiting for you to arrive. I will return late tomorrow afternoon to take you to him. He will want to see what you are offering. Talk to no one and do not go out. This is a delicate business transaction. From now on use room service. Have you everything you need? Can I be of service?"

"No, thank you, I want for nothing. Please tell your Master that I will be ready."

Chopper reported that, as they talked, Midai visibly relaxed. He was clearly an amateur and must have been under a terrible strain. He had carried the precious package for thousands of kilometres, constantly fearing discovery. Now that he was about to be freed from the responsibility, it wouldn't be difficult to get it from him.

*

The following evening, after an early dinner in Chopper's room, Gao prepared for his meeting with Midai. As soon as Blue and Brown had gone down for dinner, Chopper let Gao into their room before going to fetch Midai. They had about an hour.

Chopper knocked politely on the door of Blue and Brown's room. Gao called "Come in!" Chopper, now wearing cotton gloves, as a servant should, ushered Midai in and motioned for him to sit in a straight-backed chair placed in the middle of the room. Chopper poured a full tumbler of spirit from one of the bottles Gao had bought earlier that day and handed it to their guest. He then stood behind Midai.

Gao, dressed in a western style blue pinstripe suit, white shirt and blue-patterned tie, sat on a straight-backed chair behind a desk. He had combed his artificially grayed hair differently, stuck on a small false mustache and wore horn-rimmed spectacles. He now looked like a totally different man aged over fifty.

Gao, using the Golden Silence technique learned in spy school, stared long and hard at Midai. The quietness slowly raised the tension. Midai began to sweat and squirm in his chair until he could no longer remain silent. He coughed and said, "Do you want to do business?"

Gao had established who was boss.

"My name is Colonel Chen," lied Gao. "You may have heard of me. Have you brought the package?"

He was hoping the name meant something to Midai. It did. He was also gambling that Midai had never seen a picture of Chen, but even if he had, would be too cowed to question his authority. Midai immediately reached in under his gown and pulled out a fat brown envelope. Then he surprised Gao.

"My orders are to not hand this over until I am offered money."

Behind Midai, Chopper had his fist in the air, ready to strike. A gesture of Gao's hand told him to lower his arm. Without realising it, Midai had played himself into Gao's plan.

"Of course," Gao said. "The money is here."

He stood, walked to the closet, pulled out the suitcase, carried it to the feet of Midai and opened it. Bending over, he took out a box from the left side of the case. The weight told him he had chosen correctly. He opened it to show the bank notes stuffed inside.

"There are seventeen more boxes like this," said Gao. "They are yours if the information you carry is of interest to me."

He dropped the box into the lap of Midai and held out his hand for the package. Eyes on the money, Midai handed it over. Gao opened the envelope and pulled out a bundle of papers. Hand-written notes, printed instructions and codes, a list of names, details of radio frequencies and transmitting locations. He saw all of that in twenty seconds.

"This is good information," said Gao in an all-pals-together voice. "I just need to confirm the source and authenticity. Where did you get it?"

Midai momentarily hesitated, then decided it was safe to talk.

"From my brother-in-law, Jin Chan. You know him as number 215."

Gao nodded his approval. With a voice full of friendship, he said, "We have a deal and you are now a rich man." He raised his glass and toasted "Gambei!"

Midai quickly swallowed all the liquor in his glass whilst Gao drank the water in his. Chopper refilled the glasses.

"Gambei" toasted Midai in return and drank deeply. Gao sipped, then nodded. With two fingers, Chopper sent Midai to sleep.

After taking all identification off Midai, they lifted him to a sitting position. From the bottle they poured a large drink down his throat and allowed more to soak into his clothes. The empty glass he had used had rolled across the floor. It had only his fingerprints on it so they left it there. They cleaned the glass Gao had used and put Midai's prints on it. Carefully they placed Midai stretched out over the case, money still clutched in his hand. They wiped off their prints and put his on the almost empty bottle they had used. They also put Midai's prints on the second bottle and all over the suitcase. They then cleaned the room of their presence.

In a small case, they carefully packed three of the shoeboxes, the second bottle and the glass Gao had used, now with Midai's fingerprints on it. Chopper carried the case. Gao carried Midai's envelope. They exited the room, locking the door.

Back in his own room, Gao wrote a note. "Colonel Chen, two opium dealers are staying in room 208 and one is in room 316." He gave it to Chopper.

While Gao cleaned up and returned himself to normal, Chopper, still wearing gloves, carried the small case to room 316 where he quickly cleared out all identity and checked that there was nothing left to connect Midai to anybody, anywhere.

From the second bottle, he half-filled the glass with Midai's prints on it and left it on a table. He then went to the bathroom. In the toilet, he poured away half of what was left in the second bottle and flushed all trace of it away. He placed the bottle, now about a quarter full, next to the glass. This, he hoped would give an impression that the occupant was a heavy drinker. Finally, to make it as easy as possible for a searcher, he hid the three boxes they had taken from room 208, two filled with money and one containing opium, in a drawer. When he exited the room, he used his little tool for the last time by locking the door. There was one last thing for him to do. On his way back to Gao's room, he pushed Gao's written note under the door of room 302 and hurried away.

Rejoining Gao, he transferred everything from the small case into a leather bag that already contained the envelope, Midai's personal papers, plus the clothes, mustache, glasses and make-up Gao had just used. The last thing to go in was the small tool that opened doors. After a huge sigh from both of them, Chopper returned to his room, leaving his door open as usual. He sat at the abacus, account book at his side, waiting for events to unfold.

Gao, dressed in his normal clothes and with his hair black and combed as usual, hurried from the Jialing to meet Feilibov in Zhao Ying's hotel to hand over the bag.

7.

Gao returned to the Jialing, and walked into the usual atmosphere of quiet efficiency. Chopper was waiting for him in the lounge area. As usual, to keep up the appearance of master and servant, he bowed deeply then led Gao to the elevator. When they got to Gao's room, he let out a silent "WHOOPEE!" Everything had gone as planned.

Not long after Gao's departure to meet Feilibov, the Hotel Manager had let Colonel Chen and his pistol-carrying assistants into room 208. Seconds later the guards had hurried downstairs and returned with Blue and Brown in handcuffs. From behind the closed door, Chopper had clearly heard thuds, pain-filled cries and shouting.

The drug dealers proved to be a good source of information that eventually led to the downfall of many corrupt officials and the arrest of a whole section of the drug network. Colonel Chen was publicly praised by Chiang Kai-shek and promoted to a one-star General. Midai was also arrested. Because he could not prove his identity and claimed he knew nothing about drugs, yet kept to his story of being tricked by Colonel Chen, he had a very bad time. Nobody knew what happened to him.

With Jin Chan still on the loose, there was a strong probability that he would betray the people working in his network. Moscow acted quickly, instructing the whole northeast network to disperse. When the CIS struck, they failed to catch a single suspect. Nor did they find one item of incriminating evidence. All papers and equipment had been spirited away, causing the CIS to doubt that Jin had told the truth. Chongqing CIS knew nothing about a letter to Box 92, or a courier. Unless Jin could prove his honesty, he was in danger of being most vilely tortured. He couldn't, so he was. Goodbye Jin Chan - Traitor.

*

During the time Gao Qing and Chopper were away dealing with Midai, Moscow made changes to the Soviet information gathering and espionage organisations. In order to keep the continued confidence and support of Britain and America, Stalin was forced to make concessions. He had to show the Western Allies that the Soviets had no interest in exporting Communism to other countries.

"On the contrary," Stalin is reported to have said to Churchill and Roosevelt, "my only ambition is to throw the German Fascists out of my country."

One of his changes was the supposed disbandment of the organisation known as Comintern but in fact nothing changed except the name. Control of the worldwide network of spies, agents and every member of Comintern was transferred to a special department within the NKVD (name later changed to the KGB). When Gao and Chopper returned to duty, they were told to bury themselves even deeper, keep quiet, and await orders.

Stalin's subterfuge was enough to keep the supply convoys sailing into Russian ports.

CHAPTER 5.

Hidden Among the People, 1943–1944

1.

By attacking Pearl Harbor on the 7th of December 1941, the Japanese signalled their entry into a war that had previously been viewed by most Americans as just another European conflict. And when the USA declared war on Japan, hostilities escalated into a truly global affair, with Burma, a British colony, being a key component.

Immediately after Pearl Harbor, the Americans joined forces with Britain and China against the Japanese, becoming Chiang Kai-shek's strongest ally. With the sea routes in and out of China blocked by Japanese warships, the Allies began to transport much needed men, machines and supplies up the Burma Road.

The end of 1941 and the early months of 1942 saw the Japanese swarm out over the Pacific and the Far East. By the end of May the Japanese were the new masters of Burma. Some 30,000 defending British and 95,000 Chinese troops sent to assist had been killed or severely wounded for a Japanese casualty total of only 7,000.

The loss of Burma deprived the Allies of their only important southwestern supply artery into China, forcing them to use a difficult and dangerous air route. Everything needed to wage war was flown from India, over the Himalayas, to the nearest Chinese city not controlled by the Japanese - Kunming.

The Allies could not allow this state of affairs to continue. Preparations for retaking Burma began. In China, American Lieutenant-

General Joseph Stilwell organized the retraining of the Chinese regiments under his command. In India, the British began to rebuild their forces. In the interim, allied engineers were instructed to plan and execute the difficult task of building a new road from Ledo in northern Assam to China.

In Chongqing, American Brigadier-General Claire Chennault was promoted to Major- General and given command of the newly formed 14th Air Force, China. The combined efforts of Chiang's defending forces and Chennault's "Flying Tigers" kept the Japanese from reaching the city.

2.

Back with Blossom, Gao was very busy. In the days following the German invasion of Russia, Stalin had ordered a huge recruitment drive to greatly enlarge and expand the activities of Comintern. If Fascist Germany was victorious, Communism might die in Russia but would survive worldwide.

By the end of 1943, Moscow had a worldwide web of agents buried deep inside the military and civil sectors of almost every country. The result was hundreds of extra field operatives passing on items of possible interest. And because Gao could send and receive Morse in the Japanese, English, Russian and Chinese languages, more and more of these new agents were assigned to him. Chopper was again at his side and they worked hard relaying information to and from Moscow. In November 1943, Gao was given Burma.

The night he first made contact with the Burma operator, he couldn't believe his ears - he knew this transmitting signature. As soon as Chopper was momentarily free, he waved him to listen in. Chopper too sat wide-eyed, a big smile on his face. There was no doubt. It just had to be Sparks, their spy school classmate. How to let Sparks know that he was transmitting to Gao and Chopper?

Actually it was simple. In spy school, the students had been given their own individual identification call signs for use during the telecommunications lessons. In his position as senior student, Gao had been given ABC. The next call sign was BCD, the next CDE and so on. Sparks's call sign had been HIJ. The next night, immediately before beginning his transmission, Gao prefixed his old classroom call sign of ABC and as his last flourish before finishing, he sent Sparks's old call sign HIJ. Gao was sure that Sparks, a superb radio operator, would notice the unauthorised extras and understand their meaning. He did.

From the next night, Gao, Chopper and Sparks added little bits to their normal transmissions, letting each other know how they were getting on. Sparks was hidden in deep jungle protected by Burmese Communists determined to fight against the British for an independent Burma. When the Japanese came, they temporarily joined the Allies. Independence could wait.

Sparks used his beautifully smooth, almost musical dots and dashes to tell Moscow, through Gao's relay, the information that must have delighted Stalin. The Japanese High Command had postponed their planned invasion of Russia to concentrate on Asia, with the subjugation of India and China being their primary objectives.

Gao made sure that the same message went secretly to Zhou En-lai. It was a vital piece of information that must have put a smile on the face of Mao Zedong. For once he knew something that Chiang Kai-shek didn't.

Gao and Chopper felt a strong bond with their old classmate. Nightly they wished him well and ended their transmissions with Churchill's famous "V for Victory" salute… dit-dit-dit-dah.

They couldn't begin to guess how many Comintern moles were active within the civilian and military headquarters of the warring nations. Night after night they relayed huge amounts of information that was so highly detailed, it made them think that it could only have come out of the mouths of the politicians or army commanders. There was no doubting the obvious. Comintern had penetrated to the heart of every major power, maybe as high as their governments.

3.

So far, Gao and Chopper had not been in any danger other than when they had calculated a reasonable chance of survival such as rescuing the girl on the bus. They could have easily grown lax and lazy about security, but at no time could they lower their guard. Their training and fear of discovery kept them vigilant.

About two months after they had dealt with Midai, in the same department store that Serpent had used to pass him the P.O. Box 92 letter, Gao was browsing away a little time before his lunchtime visit to the bookshop. He wouldn't have taken much notice of the man dressed in nondescript western clothes if it hadn't been for the multicoloured, predominantly yellow necktie he was wearing. It made Gao think of vomit.

Later Gao saw the tie in the street. He increased his walking speed, so did The Tie. He slowed down and looked in shop windows. The Tie dawdled too. There was no doubt. Gao was being followed. He cancelled his trip to the bookshop.

Back home, Gao discussed the matter with Chopper. Chopper took a walk and said that The Tie, exactly as described, was standing on a nearby corner. On the opposite corner, another very ordinary western-style suited man was loitering. Chopper thought they were a pair. Perhaps there were more. That night Gao told Moscow of his suspicions.

The next morning, Chopper, dressed as a servant, left the house by a back entrance and walked a short way towards the city before stopping at a newspaper stand. He bought a newspaper and leaned against a wall, reading.

Five minutes later Gao left the house by the front entrance and without looking anywhere but straight ahead, walked towards the city, passing Chopper on the way. He took Chopper and any followers on an hour-long walk before returning to the house. Chopper had hurried the last few hundred metres to wait for him.

Chopper reported, "I saw three men. One following you, another on the opposite pavement and a third in front. They're experts. They continually changed places, making it difficult to spot them. Only a choice of necktie let them down."

"How, and when, did they get on to me?" Gao asked nobody in particular.

His first thought was that a vigilant operator had picked up one of his nightly transmissions and reported it. Not that it mattered. They had to move fast. Gao needed to contact Feilibov, but how? He couldn't use the telephone. Every call had to go through a series of switchboard operators. Nor could he go next door to the woollen mill or take a rickshaw to Zhao Ying's hotel.

Once again he had to rely on his most trusted friend, Chopper.

*

With his dirty hands, feet and face, and dressed in his filthy coolie clothes, no one looked twice at Chopper. After dark, he went out through the back alley and into the street. Nobody around. He walked the area for an hour without seeing anything suspicious, returning just before curfew. It was only a daylight check. That meant that Gao's thoughts about the transmissions being traced were wrong. If it had been that, the house would, at the very least, have been put under twenty-four-hour surveillance. Something else must have put them on his trail, but what?

Actually, when it was safe to do so, Serpent found out for them. The CIS had put a tail on Feilibov, something they did from time to time. Gao met Feilibov. As a matter of routine, the CIS started to follow Gao. Only his rich appearance and the quality of the house he lived in stopped them from arresting him. A normal reaction. He could have had the ear of any number of important people.

Gao and Chopper didn't know this at the time, and it wouldn't have made any difference anyway. A quick move was their only choice. From a public telephone Chopper made a quick call to Zhao Ying. She passed on the message to Feilibov. An hour later, with the exception of some of Gao's outdoor clothes, everything connected to him and his work was silently loaded into a van. Gao thanked Blossom. He was sorry to leave, she had been a wonderful partner.

As Gao walked out of the house, Clockface walked in. Remember him from the old apartment? From a distance he could pass for Gao. Chopper stayed too, still acting the part of a servant, but his reason for staying was anything but servile. He had orders to protect Clockface and, if necessary, kill him and then commit suicide. Neither man could be taken alive, they knew too much.

Two days later, ten minutes after Clockface and Chopper had followed Gao's established morning routine by walking to the woollen mill, the CIS called at the house to conduct a thorough search. They found nothing. A few days later Clockface and Chopper made a midnight exit and Blossom returned to her solitary life.

4.

Two weeks later, Feilibov appeared at the hotel. Handing Gao a ticket, he said, "It's your lucky night. You have a front circle seat to the opening night of what will be the best show in town. During the evening someone will make contact with you."

Feilibov offered his hand to say goodbye. Moscow was not happy about him being followed so it was back to spy school for him. "Three hours from now, I will be on my way to Moscow. Twenty Chinese hopefuls await my presence." Andriev, whom Gao had met before, was his replacement. Then came his other news. "Comrade Gao Qing, you are now considered fully trustworthy and able to look after yourself. Congratulations, you are now an independent agent answerable only to Moscow. No more message relaying for you, just special operations. When you are settled in your new quarters, contact Moscow. They will tell you the rest."

*

The theatre was crowded to capacity. How Feilibov had managed to get the ticket Gao didn't know. Every seat was taken and the rear and side-aisles were crammed with people willing to stand. He found his seat, sat down, and looked around. The place was full of important people, including Chiang Kai-shek occupying his special box. The lights dimmed and the show began - Peking Opera.

It was such a good show, Gao completely forgot the reason why he was there until the lights went up. Whilst everybody was on their feet clapping and cheering, their attention fully occupied with the bowing actors, he felt a sharp elbow dig into his ribs.

The man was small, watchful, edgy. He spoke.

"Chen-Ye?"

Gao nodded. "I'm Jin Ze-ren. Mutual friend 'F' sent me."

He spoke quickly, in small, sharp sentences. Gao did the same.

"Thanks. Need accommodation. Quiet at night. No frills. No close or nosey neighbours. Not expensive."

" 'F' already done it. Perfect place waiting. Noon ferry, dock number one. Meet you by gate. Take you there." He disappeared into the crowd.

Gao joined the slow-moving human tide heading for an exit. From all around him voices talked about the show. The noisy buzz slowly lessened as people fanned out into the street. As he stepped outside, feeling relaxed and stress-free, he stopped to inflate his lungs with river-mist-laden air. The show had done him good. And Feilibov's last action on his behalf before flying to Moscow had proved his friendship and concern. Gao silently wished him well.

A distinctive female voice drew Gao's attention. It was light and giggly, as sweet as a nightingale and continuous. As two young women passed him, the voice suddenly stopped and a pair of big astonished eyes gazed at him.

"Oh," sang the nightingale, hand to face."Oh! It is you, isn't it? The man from the bus?"

He nodded. She reached out to grasp his hand. He recognised her and her non-stop chatter. Over two-and-half years previously, he and

Chopper had rescued this girl from the idiot Kuomintang officer. She pulled her friend to her side and introduced her.

"This is my little cousin. Dad arranged for her to live with me when my big sister got married and left home. Her name is Hui-wen (Clever) and mine," she looked meaningfully at him, because they had not exchanged names during their previous time together, "is Xiao-ge (Little Dove)."

He guessed that she wanted him to introduce himself.

He teased, "I bet you don't remember that my name is Chen-Ye."

She picked up his cue. "Of course not. Why should I?"

They laughed as though they had known each other for years, and why not? They had shared more in one day than most people do in a lifetime.

He made a little bow to tiny Clever and said, "Ni Hao?" ("You good?").

She shyly replied, "Ni Hao," the standard reply.

He hesitated when Little Dove invited him home to meet her parents.

"Please Master Chen-Ye. My home is near and I know my parents would be delighted to meet the man who saved my life."

Clever's eyes shone with admiration and she moved closer.

"Is Master Chen-Ye the one who saved you from the bad officer?" she asked, joining Little Dove in pulling at his arm.

"All right, little sisters," he laughed. "I will go with you."

With a girl on each arm, he let them guide him to their home.

Through iron railings he saw an elegant Chinese house with the traditionally beautiful sweeping gulls-wing roof. Many lights glowed in the thousands of lead-edged diamond-shaped panes that made up the dozens of windows. On each side of the imposing heavy iron gates stood a huge stone lion, symbol of strength. Inside the grounds a security man was patrolling. It was clearly a millionaire's mansion.

"How romantic," sang Little Dove. "A hero with two princesses about to enter the castle of the emperor. Into the lion's den we go!"

She pulled a lever on the gate. The security man hurried to open it.

Before they had reached the main entrance, half of the double wooden doors opened to reveal a lady aged about forty-five, dressed in a black qipao. Her hair was swept back into a bun with a large daisy-like flower pinned just above her left ear. She looked kind and graceful, exactly as he imagined the wife of a millionaire should look.

"Ah, my precious ones," said the woman in a loving tone, "you have brought a guest. How nice."

Little Dove held the hand of the older woman to make the introductions.

"This is Mother Wu, my personal maid. She has cared for me from the day I was born. She believes in Buddha and prays for me every day. I love her very much."

She surprised Mother Wu by saying, in a throwaway voice, "This is Master Chen-Ye. He saved my life."

The girls led him into a large square courtyard. Dozens of red lanterns, lights dancing erratically as the candle-flame inside each one flickered, showed their way to the house. At the door, Mother Wu bowed Gao in. He lifted his leg to step over the threshold and froze as a sudden screech came from above. "Come in please…Come in please."

Looking up, he saw a large parrot strutting along its perch. He greeted it with a wave and got two wings opened a little in return and a near-miss dollop.

In the brightly lit reception hall, ancient tables and chairs neatly stood around three sides, waiting to be used. Gao felt as though he would meet the Emperor at any moment, but there was no Emperor, just two old men playing Chinese Chess.

"Papa!" cried Little Dove. "I have brought you a very important guest."

The two men were dressed in ancient Chinese style long black silk gowns buttoned from neck to foot and gathered at the waist by a black silk cummerbund. On both gowns, perhaps a dozen beautifully embroidered white dragons breathed red fire. When the men looked at him, Gao saw two pairs of kind but curious eyes below heads of thick white hair and above two long white goatee beards. They stood and bowed. Gao felt as if he had stepped back a hundred years into the past.

One man said to the other, "I must not keep you from your guest. I will return to play another evening. Goodnight."

He bowed his way out through the door.

Little Dove could barely contain herself whilst waiting for the man to leave. When it was correct and good manners to do so, she gabbled, "Papa. I have pleasure in presenting Master Chen-Ye. It was this man and his friend who saved me at the checkpoint."

She turned to look at Gao, a huge smile on her face.

The old man also turned to face him. Eyes shining with gratitude, he stepped forward and grasped Gao's hand.

"Dear boy, my dear, dear boy, I can never thank you enough for what you did. You are indeed an important guest. Come, sit with me."

He waved Gao to the recently vacated chair. A handclap brought young servant girls carrying tea and nibbles. As they bent to serve Gao, they flirted with their eyes and smiled impishly. This house was obviously a happy home.

Little Dove and Clever sat on stools at Gao's feet, their eyes never leaving his face. A still beautiful lady aged about fifty, dressed in a simple blue Chinese qipao, white socks and black cotton shoes, entered. Gao stood and bowed when the old man introduced her as Madam Yun. She moved forward and took Gao's right hand in both of hers. Warmly welcoming Gao to her home, she softly murmured, "We are forever in your debt". She sat between the girls.

The impish girls returned and laid out dishes of savoury rice buns and bowls of different varieties of sweet candy. Again they flirted and he felt wonderful. He remembered that not since the day he had joined the

Red Army at the age of twelve had he had an evening he could genuinely call his own. And what an evening it had turned out to be!

Little Dove held a small plate whilst Clever and Mother placed some cake, a rice bun and other tidbits on it. She handed it to Gao, saying, "Please be at home." Then she asked after the gentleman who had helped him on that fateful day.

"He is away on business," Gao lied.

"What business is that?" asked Mother.

"Silk business." A second lie, deceit now as natural to him as breathing.

"When he returns, please pass on the thanks of my family."

In fact, Chopper had been very well situated. One of Feilibov's last acts on being ordered back to Moscow was to take care of Chopper. He recommended Chopper to an American contact looking for a personal valet.

That was nothing unusual. The Kuomintang, the Chinese Communists, the Russians and the Americans were allies, so there was a great deal of toing and froing between the various diplomatic and military establishments. Friendships were formed and favours done.

When Chopper departed Blossom's house he was under orders to go directly to the home of the Director of the American Liaison Office in Chongqing. Although the American had considered Feilibov a close friend, he would most definitely not have been aware that Feilibov was an important member of the Soviet NKVD. The American needed an honest servant, illiterate but capable, and because Feilibov was returning to Moscow, could he recommend his own valet? Feilibov recommended Chopper.

Feilibov had done the right thing. He had not only saved Chopper from another stint on the docks, he had placed one of his best men into a prime information gathering location. Chopper's new employer was in the habit of taking work home, and believing his new valet could not read or write, often left papers lying around. Chopper had daily opportunities to study and photograph anything of interest, using a tiny camera supplied by the Russians. He passed on his finds when he went shopping. His apparent devotion to his work and his honest dealings with money quickly gained the trust of the American. Chopper was never questioned, nor was his room searched.

Meanwhile, back in the house, the old man was speaking. "My name is Yun Pu. We are eternally grateful to you, Mister Chen-Ye. You and your companion witnessed an injustice about to be perpetrated and used your skill to help the victim, who happened to be my daughter. In these troubled times such bravery is rare."

Gao stood up. "Thank you so much for your kind reception and generous hospitality. Sadly, if I am to be safely home before the curfew, I must go."

"No, no," protested his hosts in unison.

Mother took control. "Come, Mister Chen-Ye, you must stay with us. The streets around here are cordoned off by this time of night. You will encounter trouble from the security patrols."

He nodded his agreement and thanked everyone for their concern.

Little Dove wriggled excitedly at hearing of his decision to stay, which was quickly noticed by the old man. Gao didn't miss anything either, so it came as no surprise when Father asked, "Mister Chen-Ye, can you tell me how old you are?"

"I shall be twenty-seven in a few months," he replied, for once able to give an honest answer.

"And your parents, how are they?"

Although the questions were kindly put, Gao knew exactly what was on Father's mind, the welfare of his daughter.

Gao again lied. "Sadly I lost both my parents before the age of twelve. As I had no other relatives, I left my village to seek fame and fortune and never returned."

Mother said, "This is now your home and we are your family. Your room is ready."

After Gao had wished everyone a good night, Mother led him away to a guestroom. He retired at once and slept so well that when he awoke it was already past nine o'clock.

He quickly washed and dressed then followed a waiting servant to the dining room. Mister Yun arrived at the same time as he, so they ate together and talked about the war. When they had eaten, a young male servant appeared carrying a suitcase.

Mister Yun explained, "Although nothing can ever repay you for saving our daughter, my family and I have prepared a few gifts for you. Please know that you will always be welcome in this house."

The servant carried the case to the street and summoned a rickshaw while the whole household, servants and family, gathered to wave him away.

"Be sure to visit us as much as possible!" yelled Little Dove.

Gao waved back then told the rickshaw boy to take him to dock number one.

5.

Jin Ze-ren was leaning against a post, enjoying the March sunshine. As Gao's rickshaw drew up, he moved ahead of it into the dockyard. Moored alongside the jetty was a small coastal ship used as a ferry and local freight transporter. Jin handed tickets to the reception officer and gestured to Gao. Immediately a porter was dispatched to the rickshaw to relieve him of his case. Waiting whilst Gao paid the rickshaw puller, the porter led Jin and Gao up the gangway, onto the deck, and into the sun lounge. After placing his case in a cubicle identified as a foot passenger luggage store, the porter bowed and left them to find seats.

The two men left the ship at Long Men (Dragon Gate) Town situated about six kilometres upriver. The town had developed along almost similar lines to Chongqing but was less than half the size. On one side of the Yangtze River, thousands of buildings perched on the mountainside. The other side was flat fertile agricultural land with just a few peasant huts dotted here and there.

They took separate rickshaws across town to a quiet area on the uppermost level and stopped in front of a two-storied building. On a weatherworn wooden board fixed to the wall Gao read, "Dragon Gate Garments Factory". Jin led Gao into a small workshop where six women were bent over treadle sewing machines. At the top end of the shop three men stood at a long table cutting out the bits to be sewn. All stopped work to look at Gao.

Jin announced, "This is Mister Chen-Ye, a close relative and my new book-keeper."

Everyone nodded and returned to their work. Jin led Gao upstairs.

The first room facing the street was Jin's office. Large framed pictures of Doctor Sun Yat-sen and Chiang Kai-shek hung on the wall. Jin shushed Gao with a forefinger raised to his mouth, then turned Chiang Kai-shek around to reveal a photograph of Mao Zedong on the reverse. He grinned and turned Mao back facing the wall. On his desk were an abacus, account books, black and red ink bottles, nibbed pens and a bamboo tube holding Chinese writing brushes.

Jin explained, "'F' wanted me to give you accommodation. And a cover story. No questions. That's it. You got it." He handed over a bunch of keys. "You come and go as you please. Wife and me lived here. Now we have a house. This place is a profitable sideline. In return for the accommodation and pocket-money, you'll learn how to do the books and run the place when I'm not here."

Jin opened the bedroom door and stepped aside. Gao's stuff had already been delivered and was piled in a corner. Gao walked to the window. He was not overlooked. Down below he saw a vegetable garden with a small stream running through it. The garden fence had a side gate leading to an alleyway. The rest of the upper floor consisted of a kitchen big enough to house a glass-topped round table and four chairs, a large storeroom, and a washroom containing a toilet, a shower and a washbasin.

"Thank you, Feilibov," thought Gao. To Jin, he nodded and said,

"Good. Very good."

*

The first thing Gao did when left alone was to see what the Yun family had gifted to him. Inside a leather wallet was a personal letter and a thousand yuan. A new navy-blue pinstriped western-style suit, shirts, socks and a brand new pair of brown leather shoes - almost impossible to get in wartime. A black silk gown embroidered with fire-breathing dragons similar to those worn by Mister Yun and his guest lay on the bottom of the case. The letter told him that the three women had chosen and packed the clothes and Mister Yun had donated the money.

Little Dove had added, "I hope these clothes and shoes fit you. Compared to my life, these things are of little value. Please remember that eternal friendship is also included."

Actually, the money was very important. It seemed to the Chinese members of Comintern that as far as the Moscow people were concerned, they were so tied into Communism they would work for nothing. And stupidly, they did. For the entire time since spy-school, they had received almost no personal salary. Whilst Chopper was now nicely settled into a well-paid job, Gao was almost broke. With a thousand yuan and Jin's pocket-money he could live comfortably for a long time.

That evening, Jin invited all of his workers to a welcome dinner in Gao's honour. In the old days this was the normal way to initiate a new employee. After work, everyone walked across the road to the conveniently placed "Fa-fu's Family Restaurant".

It had three large dining halls filled with tables. The food was excellent and the service first class, so business was brisk. It was a favourite eatery for important Chinese and American, British and Russian "Big Noses" or "Foreign Devils" as the Chinese call all Westerners.

Dressed in an American-style tuxedo, the owner, a well-known local celebrity, wandered around the tables cracking jokes and making small talk in English and Chinese. He was a huge man aged about fifty and named Fa-fu (Make Fortune). His bald head sat on a thick neck above wide shoulders but his most noticeable features were his big belly, round rosy smiley face and good-humour.

Most of his customers seemed to be regulars who were warmly welcomed with free Jasmine tea or an aperitif. Jin leaned across to Gao and advised, "Good man, Fa-fu. Looks like a smiling Buddha. Very generous. Talks a lot. Knows everybody. Get to know him."

Fa-fu arrived at their table at the same time they did. In a big joyous voice, he boomed, "Hello Jin. Got a guest eh? Let me take you into the private room."

They followed the bulky figure to a side room. It was much quieter and they had a waitress and a waiter all to themselves. As soon as they had settled themselves around a huge table, glasses of wine and cups of jasmine tea appeared.

"On the house," said Fa-fu. He turned to Gao, "To welcome you sir."

Jin made the introductions and Fa-fu's hand engulfed Gao's in a firm grip. Gao felt an instant liking for the big man.

"Mister Gao will need to eat somewhere," said Jin. "What discount will you give?"

A good-natured bout of bartering ensued until a deal was agreed. Fa-fu laughed delightedly and stepped to the door to bellow across the restaurant to his manager.

"Little-Boss Wang. The new man employed by Mister Jin is named Mister Chen-Ye. He will eat here three times a day and I have agreed a fifty percent discount. I couldn't resist. He's a handsome young fellow just like my son. You take good care of him!"

He beamed at Gao and affirmed, "There, that's settled."

He continued his tour of the tables.

Jin smiled at Gao. "Don't worry about him telling everybody. He is a good-hearted man who is well known for his loud mouth. We call him "Xiao Guang-bo" (The Little Broadcaster). Although he cannot read or write he is acknowledged to be the cleverest man in town. Every day he garners a fresh supply of gossip from his customers and using the restaurant loud speaker system, gives a show every evening when he makes jokes about the latest news. If he has heard something sad or serious, he simply tells everybody."

From Jin, Gao also learned that Fa-fu was loved and respected by the townspeople because of his ever-ready willingness to help those in distress without looking for any reward. The local Kuomintang Government had installed him as Mayor of Dragon Gate Town and he had proved himself to be up to the job. Everyone sitting around the table, and their two servers standing to one side, nodded their agreement.

When the table was laden with dishes filled with the different delicacies of the town, Jin proposed a toast to welcome Gao into the firm. He ended with "Gambei!" Everyone raised their glasses and returned with their own "Gambei!" before swallowing whatever was in their glass. Gao was now an accepted member of the team.

Glasses were refilled. Gao stood and thanked everyone for coming, with a special thanks to Mister Jin, his esteemed and generous "relative" for laying on such a wonderful meal. "Gambei!" he ended. "Gambei" shouted everybody. Glasses empty, chopsticks dived into the dishes as they began to eat.

Gao Qing's new life as an independent-agent-cum-book-keeper had begun.

6.

His bedroom was a reasonable size, with a bed, battered easy chair, chest of drawers and a small table with chair. It also had a huge wardrobe. Jin showed him its secrets. The entire back was false so that stuff could be hidden in the cavity. Perfect for him to hide his pistol, ammunition and other paraphernalia. Inside the wardrobe, rungs were let into the thick wooden right hand side panel, rather like a ladder. The seemingly solid top of the wardrobe slid to one side to allow access up the ladder and through a concealed ceiling trap door into the roof space. Jin explained that a previous owner of the property had run an illegal gambling den.

As soon as he was alone, Gao switched on the electric light in the roof space and carried up the transceiver. It sat perfectly on a wooden trestle table already there. A folding chair was up there too, enabling him to sit and work at the table. He was very satisfied.

The following morning he walked across the road to sample the restaurant breakfast. The previous evening he had enjoyed the skillfully cooked food they had been served. Breakfast, he was delighted to learn, was another culinary delight. Fa-fu came out from the back to talk.

"Is the food to your liking Mister Gao?" he asked.

Gao had a full mouth, so he just nodded.

Fa-fu placed a newspaper on the table and invited Gao to read while eating then bustled away to greet another seeker of good food. The newcomer was obviously a regular. Fa-fu sat with him, soaking up the latest news. Gao finished eating, walked to the cashier's desk and paid his bill.

He returned to eat an uneventful lunch and a solitary evening meal. That night he reported to Moscow and was told to call again the following night. The next day breakfast came around and again Fa-fu gave him a newspaper before greeting another customer, but this time he quickly returned to his table.

"Mister Chen-Ye, may I sit with you awhile? I have a little proposition for you."

Gao waved him to a chair. Plonking his bulk, he asked, "Would you like to eat breakfast here every morning for nothing?"

That made Gao stop eating and take notice. "How?" he replied.

"I know you are an educated man, Mister Chen-Ye, because I've seen you reading my newspaper. If you will agree to read the paper, then tell me everything of interest, I will pay for your breakfast."

He leaned back in his chair, a beaming smile on his face.

"That is very generous of you Mister Fa-fu. Of course I agree. When would you like us to start?"

"This morning would be good."

Gao started to read the front page. "Good news. A Chinese anti-aircraft battery in the Dabieshan Mountain Range shot down a twin-engined Japanese aeroplane. Eleven Japanese army officers were killed, including Lieutenant-General Takeda. So far he is the highest-ranking Japanese to be killed by our forces."

"Great news!" said Fa-fu. He rose and bellowed excitedly, "Chinese guns shot down a Japanese plane and Lieutenant-General Takeda has been killed. Hurrah!"

Later that night Fa-fu broadcast the news over the speaker system, adding a few embellishments of his own. Everyone enjoyed his show.

It was a very satisfactory arrangement. Every morning Gao got a free breakfast and a good read of the daily paper simply by telling Fa-fu the interesting bits. In the evening he ate the best food in town at a fraction of the menu price whilst listening to Fa-fu entertain his customers. It wasn't long before Fa-fu was calling him Little Chen and they were firm friends.

A month went peacefully by. After suffering heavy losses at the hands of General Chennault's Flying Tigers, the Japanese had stopped bombing the area. There was a distinct air of optimism in the town and rebuilding was already taking place. The myth of Japanese invincibility was cracking. The press and radio news changed from "bad but defiant" to "triumphantly good".

Every evening Gao was told by Moscow that he was not needed and to call again the next night. On some of his free days he took the ferry to Chongqing to visit to the Yun family, who treated him most royally. The two younger women always made a big fuss of him and when it was time for him to catch the last ferry back to Dragon Gate Town, the whole family urged him to stay longer. He had to decline. Moscow was waiting.

One morning, Fa-fu, eyes twinkling with good humour, stood in the entrance to the restaurant, waiting for Gao to cross the road for breakfast.

"I have another proposition for you," he purred.

When Gao was seated and filling his mouth with delicious vegetable buns, Fa-fu came over and sat in the seat opposite. This time there was no newspaper and despite there being no one within earshot, he leaned forward to speak quietly.

"You know that I am illiterate." It was a statement, not a question.

Gao nodded.

Fa-fu continued, "Yesterday, a delegation from the Town Government came to check up on the rebuilding programme. They were very satisfied. The recovery from years of Japanese bombing means that my workload is increasing so they have funded money for me to employ a part-time secretary. I immediately thought of you."

Jin and Gao had concocted a story just in case anyone asked why he wasn't away fighting the Japanese, and this was his opportunity to use it.

"Fa-fu," he confided. "Jin knows my problem. I am diabetic, requiring me to go to hospital every so often to collect my medication and have my blood-sugar balanced. I must have employment that is flexible enough for me to disappear every once in a while."

"Aaah, now I understand," replied Fa-fu. "We wondered why a young man like you was not in the army." Gao knew that his "affliction" would soon be public knowledge.

Fa-fu continued, "Little Chen, you have an easy manner and a good personality. I think you will be perfect in the job. It is a part-time position paying good wages for a few hours work a week. You will be earning two salaries at the same time and I will guarantee you the flexibility you need. How's that?"

"Let me talk to my doctor to make sure that the diabetes will not get worse if I work extra hours. If he says it is all right, then I accept. It will be my pleasure, with one added essential," it was Gao's turn to be mischievous, "I want free food too."

Fa-fu laughed heartily before nodding his head. "It is agreed. Let me know what your doctor says as soon as you can." He stood up and put his hands on Gao's shoulders, just like a father to a son. In a serious tone of voice, he said, "Little Chen, I will feel much better having you beside me during negotiations. It is the one time when my lack of learning makes me vulnerable to the vultures."

That night Gao's report to Moscow included an account of his conversation with Fa-fu. They immediately agreed. "It is to your credit that we can rely on you to support yourself whilst waiting for your next assignment. We like the idea of you hidden inside the local Government and yet retaining the right to be away when we need you. Well done, Comrade Bashan!"

The following morning Gao and Fa-fu agreed terms. For a generous salary and free food, Gao signed himself into the post of "Personal Secretary to the Mayor of Dragon Gate Town". Whenever Fa-fu attended a meeting or visited an important person, Gao was by his side. It wasn't long before they were seen as one unit instead of two people.

Fa-fu, by having Gao to guide him into understanding every contract, legislative document and administration directive, grew in stature and confidence. He was a magnificent orator with a brilliant memory and grasp of facts. Between them they usually managed to best his political and business opponents. Gao now had his own reserved table at the restaurant and had important people vying to be his friend.

Shortly after their first successful completion of a huge building contract, Fa-fu proposed Gao into his fraternal secret society called "The Dragon Gate Brotherhood".

The concept, he told Gao, had been brought to China by the British and was now popular among important Chinese. After initiation, a member was guaranteed protection from prosecution and hard times, no matter how bad the crime or financial situation.

When Gao told Andriev, he laughed and thought it a damn good joke to have a member of the NKVD protected by a capitalist inspired secret society. During a radio contact to Moscow, Gao was congratulated for showing "Brilliant Bolshevik Flexibility!"

CHAPTER 6.

Kogata, 1944

1.

In the late 1920's the Germans began using "Enigma" - a new concept encryption machine invented by a Dutchman. Similar in appearance to a typewriter, Enigma was capable of creating an electrically generated cipher, and so complex was the encoder, it was considered unbreakable.

During the 1930's, Polish engineers conscripted by the Germans to build Enigma, daily braved execution. Piece by piece, over many months, they managed to smuggle at least two of every Enigma component out of the factory. They then secretly reassembled the thousands of parts into two complete Enigma machines. One was offered to the French. Inexplicably they refused to take it, so it was passed to the British.

In 1939, Station X, a top-secret information-gathering centre, was set up in Bletchley Park, an English country estate. An important part the work done at Bletchley was in a department dedicated to cipher-breaking. From 1939 to long after the end of the Second World War, Station X gave much valuable information to the British and American intelligence gathering agencies.

Getting the Polish gift of Enigma turned out to be a huge stroke of luck for the Allies. Completely by chance, a full set of books giving the entire German Naval Enigma codes plus instructions on daily use was captured intact from a German U-boat. The submarine was allowed to sink, hiding this fact. Now the codebreakers at Bletchley Park were able to crack a large part of the Enigma code. In due time, all of the Enigma codes were broken.

For many years, the Japanese, believing that non-Japanese could not understand their language, sent many of their confidential radio messages in plain language without bothering to encode them. After Pearl Harbor, they rectified this mistake by encoding all their messages.

In 1941, four Americans arrived at Bletchley, bringing with them a Japanese diplomatic code processor nicknamed, "The Purple Machine". With this valuable addition to the Bletchley code-breaking family, the British set up a network of listening stations throughout their Empire. Around the clock, trained linguists scanned the radio frequencies of the world, paying particular attention to the German, Italian and Japanese (known collectively as the Axis) transmissions. Everything, no matter how insignificant, was passed to Bletchley. Coded transmissions were sent for deciphering and plain language messages went directly into the civil or military information pipelines.

Because the Soviets did not have Enigma or The Purple Machine, Churchill thought Stalin had to rely on the British for information. He didn't. Stalin had a mole, codenamed "Liszt', working at Bletchley.

During the early summer of 1943, the German High Command chose the town of Kursk, situated in the middle of the Russian Front, to deploy every piece of armour they had, totaling around 2,500 tanks and assault artillery. They were preparing to launch an attack they codenamed "Operation Citadel".

Liszt, sitting pretty in Bletchley Park, passed to Moscow everything he could get his hands on concerning Citadel, with the result that when the Germans attacked in early July, the Russians were ready and waiting. And so began the largest tank battle in history, involving more than five thousand guns and tanks and 2.2 million troops. By July 1943 the Germans had been well and truly defeated. In addition to huge tank, gun and troop losses, the Germans also lost 1000 aircraft. From that time onwards, Germany was forced onto the defensive. In the August of that same year, Liszt was posted away from Bletchley Park to St. Albans.

2.

For Gao, after weeks of operational inactivity, things began to happen. In June 1944, Zhao Ying telephoned, asking for an urgent meeting. Early the next morning he took the ferry to Chongqing and a rickshaw to Yellow Corner Village. Despite heavy rain, he walked the last couple of hundred metres to the hotel, all the while checking his back.

Zhao Ying was waiting and took him to her private apartment. As usual she had her personal priority, bed before business. Only afterwards did she tell him that the Chinese Communists wanted him to make a personal appearance before Mao Zedong in his northern stronghold of Yan'an. Could he accompany Zhou En-lai when he flew north for his regular meeting with Chairman Mao, returning the same day?

"Of course," he said. He wouldn't miss the chance to meet Mao.

The next day, after an uneventful flight, Gao was sitting in a room facing Zhou En-lai, Li Ke-nong - Head of the Communist Secret Police, and Mao Zedong. They were sitting in a cave dug into the hillside. For thousands of years the inhabitants of Yan'an had lived in caves. Outside the steel door, troops guarded the entrance. During the introductions, tough Li Ke-nong almost crushed Gao's hand. Zhou had a firm handshake whilst Mao, by far the tallest and most robust of the three, offered limp dough-like fingers. To his surprise, after touching the hand of Mao, Gao had to resist the impulse to wipe his own hand against his thigh.

Mao opened a file and looked at Gao for a few seconds before saying, "Comrade Gao Qing, at last I can thank you for the valuable information you have passed to us."

Gao and Mao talked for about thirty minutes. Mao told him the end of the war was in sight. The Allies had just invaded France and were making good progress inland. In the Pacific, the Japanese were steadily losing to MacArthur. Forget all that, said Mao. His priority was the Kuomintang. After the world war, Mao intended to re-ignite the flame of

China's civil war.

Gao listened intently as Mao outlined his future civil war strategy.

"The bulk of my troops will be fresh and all are volunteers. We are outnumbered by about eight to one, I have the backing of the Chinese peasants. Chiang Kai-shek has the support of the money-men, but they are soft. One peasant is worth ten of them. There is no doubt that we can defeat the Kuomintang, but we will never be in a position to beat the Kuomintang *and* the Americans unless Stalin helps us.

"That presents other problems. An ideological Capitalism versus Communism war would be a long and bitter conflict fought on Chinese soil. If Capitalism won, Communism would be finished. If Communism was triumphant, Stalin could, and probably would, annex China into Soviet control. Neither outcome would benefit China.

"What I would like," said Mao, "is for the world to go home after the war and leave us Chinese to sort out our own affairs.

"You can assist me greatly. I want as much information as possible on the Kuomintang forces, especially about their morale and fighting fitness. And I *absolutely must* know what the Americans will do when this war is over. Will they go home or stay in China and support the Kuomintang? If you help me take power in China, I will not forget your part in our victory."

That last sentence stayed with Gao. Mao had all but promised him an important position in his future Chinese Government.

*

Ten days after Gao's visit to Yan'an, Andriev telephoned, asking him to take the next ferry leaving for Chongqing. He must carry a black leather brief case. He did. Andriev, smartly dressed in western style clothes, was standing in the stern. On the deck at his feet was a black leather brief case. Gao joined him and set his own case down at his feet. As they shook hands Andriev slipped a small key into Gao's palm. When the ship could no longer be seen from the town, even through a telescope, Andriev touched his case with a foot, saying, "I have orders to deliver this to your hand." He stopped talking, stooped, picked up Gao's case and walked away. Gao stayed where he was.

The ferry edged slowly alongside Chongqing dock number one. From the stern, Gao watched Andriev approach the gangway and make a slight bow in his direction before disembarking but he didn't immediately leave the dock. He waited until the ferry began the upriver journey. When he was sure that Gao was safely on his way back to Dragon Gate Town, he summoned a rickshaw.

Back in the flat Gao climbed up to his hidey-hole in the roof and concealed himself by sliding the top of the wardrobe back into the closed position. He carefully unlocked the briefcase and found a large brown envelope. Opening that, he withdrew a thick sheaf of papers covered with encrypted text. He settled down for a long session of decoding.

The first page was a personal letter.

"Comrade Bashan, I place my trust in you. When you have read and understood, burn these papers. Only you, my secretary and I know about your primary objective. I have lost my contact in Britain able to supply accurate information on Axis military movements and war plans. This is urgent.

"You are the only available operative in the area who is fluent in Russian, Chinese, English and Japanese. I want you to capture a Japanese spy operating in China codenamed "Kogata" (Little Square). From him you must extract the exact location of a Japanese cipher machine. There must be one somewhere in China. Silence him only when you have the information. Your primary objective is to locate that machine. If you can "liberate" it, so much the better. Your secondary objective is to deliver Kogata's transmitter and codebooks to Andriev. Leave no trace of Soviet involvement.

"Everything we know about Kogata is enclosed. Ask Andriev for anything you need and on completion of your mission pass whatever you have liberated over to him. At present Andriev knows nothing except to fulfill all of your demands. Don't let me down. Stalin."

Gao continued to decode. "The Japanese have placed a spy, codename Kogata, somewhere in the mountains around Chongqing. He uses the callsign BBYQ. We want him stopped. If the Nips overrun China, the Japanese High Command might decide to invade the Soviet Union, therefore we must hinder their progress as much as possible."

Gao read on. "Kogata is careful and clever. He always transmits in code. No long messages. He uses several pre-arranged frequencies, changing several times during every message and he regularly changes his location. It has not been possible to pinpoint his base or his most-used frequency with any accuracy. However, we are sure of his most favoured transmitting areas.

1. The hills overlooking the northern Kuomintang army base.
2. Somewhere near to the American airfield west of the city.
3. The heart of the city

We think he has contacts in Chongqing and guards protecting him. Here follows a list of frequencies used and a map showing areas around Chongqing he has been known to set up his transmitter. This transmitter must be light and portable with a strong signal. Very advanced. We would like to get our hands on it. End of message'

It took two days of hard thinking for Gao to realize that he was going to need help with this mission, and there was only one man he could turn to.

3.

Two days later, in the dusk of evening, the familiar car with black windows was waiting to meet Gao off the ferry. He joined Madam Zeng on the back seat and thirty minutes later he was shaking hands with Comrade Zhou En-lai.

"It is a pleasure to see you again Comrade Gao," said Zhou. "What can I do for you?"

"I need help with an assignment that will, I think, help both our interests." Gao replied.

He went on to explain that he needed to capture a Japanese spy, codenamed Kogata, and outlined his plan. Zhou responded with ideas of his own. At dawn Gao was back on the ferry. Four days later, after explaining that he would be "in hospital" for anything up to a month, Gao left Dragon Gate Town and returned to Chongqing.

Dressed in his usual Chinese clothes, he carried a suitcase containing three American style shirts, a selection of neckties, socks, handkerchiefs, underwear, shaving tackle, the new navy-blue pinstriped western-style suit and brown leather shoes given to him by the Yun family, a black trilby hat and his pistol. The same car, with Madam Zeng beside him, took him to the Communist Liaison Office.

Gao's old card-playing army pal, Kong Yuan, and Zhou En-lai were waiting. He was ushered into a private apartment where, on the bed, a complete uniform of a Kuomintang Army Officer was laid out. Beside it was a set of identity papers, tags, money, visiting cards, swagger stick and pistol. A second set of papers and visiting cards sat beside the pistol.

If anyone had followed Captain Wen-biao (Gao Qing) when he was driven out in a different car, they would have tailed him for several kilometres across the city before seeing the car stop and wait for a sentry to open a pair of huge iron gates. Seeing the car enter the grounds of the residence occupied by the Kuomintang Lieutenant-General Liu Min shu, Chief of the General Staff in Chongqing, would have ended any thoughts of further surveillance.

The driver jumped out of the front passenger seat to open the rear door for Gao to alight. He then ran to press a bell. The heavy wooden door opened to reveal a young white-jacketed army orderly carrying a holstered pistol at his waist. In accordance with ancient custom as still used by the most important families, Gao made a tiny bow whilst offering a visiting card held in both hands, thumbs uppermost.

"Please inform Madam Wen-gian that her cousin has arrived." Gao said.

The orderly led him into the hall and took his cap, stick and gloves. Placing his visiting card on a small silver plate he replied politely, "Please wait here sir," bowed and hurried away. In the meantime, the driver had taken the car to the rear of the house.

Gao heard a slight rustling sound.

"Cousin Wen-biao, I have been impatiently awaiting your arrival," said a sweet, clear voice. A graceful lady, aged, Gao guessed, about thirty, was floating down a flight of stairs towards him. His eyes were first drawn to her amazingly beautiful face framed by long black hair. His gaze travelled downwards, taking in her slim and shapely figure wrapped in a black qipao decorated with silver phoenix birds. She looked magnificent.

Her hands reached out to wrap his right hand in both of hers, a normal thing to do when close family members meet. When she released her hold, he took a step back and made a small bow whilst making the familiar identity sign, his left hand over his abdomen, index finger curled under. She took his arm and led him upstairs into the drawing room where a maid was already serving tea. They sat opposite each other in deep leather armchairs and waited. As soon as they were alone, it was all business.

"I have a message for you," she said. "Your leader (Zhou En-lai) has obtained agreement from his superior (Chairman Mao) for the work to go ahead."

Gao nodded. "Anything else?"

"Yes. I must obey your orders. What is expected of me?"

"Care for my driver. He is part of this."

"He is already unpacking your luggage and I have arranged for him to have the room next to yours."

"Thank you. Have you anything else to tell me?"

"Yes. Comrade Zhou En-lai has arranged an appointment at nine tomorrow morning for Mister Chew to meet Major St. John-Smythe at the British Embassy."

Madam Wen-gian was the General's second concubine. Zhou En-lai had advised him that although she was not a member of the Communist Party and despite her position, she could be trusted. Her father, a peasant-landlord, had secretly joined the Communist Party in 1921. Madam, from a young age, had ingested her father's political opinions and taken them for her own. When, at the age of fifteen, the General chose her to be his second concubine, he was not to know that she had been on the verge of following her father into the Party. He still didn't know and Gao had been particularly asked by Zhou to keep it that way.

She had never betrayed the General by giving away secrets to the Communists, but she was always willing to assist in the war against Japan. She had been told that Gao was on the trail of a Japanese spy and needed help, nothing else.

"Tell me about your husband," said Gao. "After all, if I am to be posing as a member of his family, I should know a few facts."

"Oh, he is a good man. His wife with her two children and his first concubine and her two children live far from here in his native Guangdong Province. I live here alone with him, without children. He and Zhou En-lai first met and became friends when both men were involved in the Northern Expedition of 1926. That was the year the Communists and the Kuomintang first joined forces against a mutual enemy, the Warlords. In 1937 the Communists and Kuomintang combined again to fight against the Japanese, allowing the two men to renew their friendship. The General follows the teachings of Confucius, is good-tempered, honest and fair."

"I understand that he is on tour around the army bases and is expected to be away for several weeks," Gao said.

"That is correct. Please do not misunderstand. I have always been happy with him. I agreed for you to be here simply because Comrade Zhou En-lai explained that it would help the war effort against the Japanese...and that is all."

*

Exactly as the clocks struck nine, Major St. John-Smythe marched into his office and sat down. He looked at the visiting card Gao had handed to the receptionist, then at Gao. He didn't shake hands or give the usual British greeting of "Good Morning" or offer tea. Instead he barked in English, "What can I do for you, Chew?"

Gao was now dressed in Western clothes. His identity papers and visiting card gave his name as Colin Chew, a freelance Chinese-British war correspondent. To match the Major's bad manners, he deliberately made his voice unfriendly.

"Can you confirm the rumour that there is a Japanese spy operating in the city?"

"What?"

"The story is that there's a clever Japanese spy operating around the American airfield and sending all kinds of information back to Tokyo."

Gao could almost see the words Major St. John-Smythe was thinking, "What the hell is this crazy Chink going on about?" What he said was, "Why are you bothering me? Go to the Yanks." On a second thought he asked, "Why did you take this to the Communists?"

"I was born in China and speak Mandarin so it was easy for me to cultivate some good contacts there. Because I work for the British Press, they sent me to you. Incidentally, the Chinese Communists had already heard the rumour. They got it from the Russians."

"I haven't..." the Major stopped talking, coughed a pretend cough to hide his vexation, then growled, "Wait here."

He stood up and left the room. Gao smiled to himself. The Major's feathers had been ruffled on learning that the Soviets and the Chinese Communists had beaten the British to the rumour, therefore he didn't believe it to be true. Gao knew he was going to telephone, but wasn't worried. He had already briefed Andriev and Kong Yuan to arrange for their respective establishments, if asked by the British or Americans, to confirm that a better-than-average spy rumour had been reported.

Twenty minutes later the Major returned and sat down behind his desk. He reached for a notepad bearing the Royal Crest and began to write with a pencil. When he had finished, he lay the pencil to one side, tore off the top sheet and sealed it in an envelope, also bearing the Royal

Crest. On the envelope he pencilled "For Major Franks" before pushing it towards Gao, saying, "Take this to the American Embassy." He turned and picked up a file, Gao's cue to leave.

*

Back at the General's house Gao asked his hostess to steam open the envelope. The Major had written, "Dear Arthur, the bearer of this note has a spy story. Not much in it, but I think you should listen to what he has to say."

It was signed, "Jonathan St. John- Smythe, Major."

He hadn't even bothered to mention Chew's name.

Gao asked Madam Wen-gian to telephone the American Major Arthur Franks, saying she was calling from the residence of General Liu Min-shu to request an appointment for a Kuomintang Captain Wen-biao and a civilian journalist named Colin Chew. The subject matter was urgent and the British Major St. John-Smythe had referred them.

Five minutes later the telephone rang to check that Captain Wen-biao was known.

"Of course he is," replied Madam Wen-gian. "He is a close relative. Do you want to speak to him?"

The caller said he didn't. "Please advise Captain Wen-biao and Mister Chew that Major Franks will see them at two this afternoon."

Major Franks was an altogether different man from his British counterpart. Mild-mannered, scholarly, respectful, and nobody's fool. With his driver now dressed as Colin Chew - his usual work for the Communists was as a Chinese/English interpreter, and Gao posing as Kuomintang Captain Wen-biao, Franks met them at reception, smiled and shook hands.

"Colin Chew" handed over the letter from Major St. John-Smythe and both of them gave Franks their visiting cards. Franks led them to his office and vaguely waved to chairs, which they took to be an invitation to sit down. Franks sat behind his cluttered desk and read the letter. Laying it aside, he squinted through his glasses at his visitors and said in passable

Mandarin, "You know that we hear lots of spy stories and rumours."

"This one seems to have more substance," replied Chew.

"Why?"

"You cannot afford to ignore it. It's travelling fast and is very strong. The Russians, the Chinese Communists and the Nationalists have heard something and so have the British. I'm surprised that you haven't because the American airfield seems to be the primary target."

Speaking English, Captain Wen-biao interrupted. "Major Franks, when Mister Chew brought this to me, my first impulse was to dismiss it. Luckily I decided to check it out and found out that this is not just another rumour. There is a spy and he is particularly clever. All sorts of information is being passed to Tokyo."

"What have you got?" asked Franks.

"His code name is Kogata and he is using modern equipment that allows him to move about. He seems to have guards protecting him and a support contact in the city. He is dangerous and must be stopped."

Franks nodded, excused himself and left the room.

An hour later, Franks apologized to Colin Chew for having to tell him that, as a civilian, he was banned from all future meetings on the subject. "This is strictly a military matter now, but I expect Captain Wen-biao will give you an exclusive when it is all over."

4.

Early the next morning Gao was back at the American Embassy. Franks introduced him to the Officer Commanding the airfield, a Colonel. He in turn took Gao into a side room to meet with Major-General Claire Chennault and other American officers. The Colonel introduced Gao as "Captain Wen-biao, a relative of Lieutenant-General Liu Min-shu, the Chief of the Kuomintang General Staff in Chongqing. The Captain has brought us some important information." As it was an American Colonel doing the introductions, no one questioned Gao's credentials.

Gao spoke in English. "Gentlemen, we have discovered that a Japanese spy, code-named Kogata, is operating in this area and seems to be particularly interested in the Northern Kuomintang Army Base and the American airfield. I need your permission to take troops onto your airfield to flush him out."

It was all a bluff. He had no troops. This had been Zhou En-lai's idea - he knew his man. At the mention of his precious airfield, Chennault visibly stiffened, and at the end of Gao's talk, quickly came back to him.

"Captain Wen-biao, can you give us more information?"

Without mentioning the decoder Stalin wanted, Gao detailed everything exactly as Moscow had given it to him. After all, it *was* good intelligence.

A long discussion followed. At last the men around the table came to a decision. No "outside" troops. Far better to use Americans, they were better equipped. It was also agreed that as Captain Wen-biao could speak Chinese, English and Japanese, he should be involved as an interpreter. However, agreement must be sought from Chiang Kai-shek. "After all," said Chennault; "it's his country."

Chennault made a telephone call. Not long afterwards a line of vehicles left the American Embassy bound for "Cloud Chambers", Chiang's private residence. Chennault, Franks and Gao travelled together in a large car with five vehicles in front and five more behind. Chennault admitted to Franks that during his call to Chiang, he had used the bait of Chiang getting his hands on some advanced radio equipment, so permission was very likely.

During the journey, Chennault, who was known to love China and the Chinese, asked after General Liu.

"He is very well," answered Gao. "At present he is touring Kuomintang Army Bases and hoping to get to Guangdong Province to spend time with his families."

An hour later, Gao, posing as Wen-biao, was sitting around the same table as Generalissimo Chiang Kai-shek, Major-General Chennault and sundry other important brass. Half an hour after that, permission to dig out the Japanese spy was granted. And because the airfield was strategically more important, the Americans were given priority over the Kuomintang. If they failed at the airfield, then Wen-biao had permission to take all necessary steps, including the unlimited use of Kuomintang men and equipment, to neutralize Kogata and capture his transceiver.

Chiang had one last proviso - the operation had to be classified TOP SECRET. Chennault agreed.

Chiang signed orders stamped TOP SECRET and passed them over. This was a huge piece of luck. Gao had his authority signed by Chiang Kai-shek himself. Even better, they were TOP SECRET orders, which meant that Gao could go to any Kuomintang Army Unit and demand all the men and equipment he needed without having to explain his reasons. There was not a Kuomintang Officer anywhere who would dare to question orders personally signed by the Generalissimo.

Major Franks suggested that for security and operational reasons, during the American hunt for Kogata, it would be better if Wen-biao and his batman were allocated temporary quarters in the Officer Wing at the base. If the Americans captured Kogata, Wen-biao would then be able to interrogate him and take possession of his radio. Chiang and Chennault agreed.

*

Back at General Liu's house Gao bade Madam Wen-gian goodbye and moved out. A new English-speaking driver/batman from Zhou En-lai's personal staff drove him to the American airfield. Knowing that Major Franks would recognize his old driver as Colin Chew, Gao could no longer use him. Gao thanked him for his invaluable help before sending him back to his normal duties.

So far so good. Everything, and more, had happened exactly the way that Zhou En-lai had said it would. He had successfully planned Gao's infiltration into the confidence of the Americans. That was the end Zhou's involvement. Gao was on his own.

5.

Gao spent two weeks with the Americans. During that time they didn't get the slightest sniff of a Japanese spy, and he knew why. The Americans scared him away.

As soon as the meeting with Chiang Kai-shek broke up, the Base Commander hurried back to his office to issue orders that a second ring of barbed wire be laid 200 yards outside the existing perimeter fence. He also gave orders that patrols around the inside perimeter fence be trebled.

A new detachment of six hundred men was created under the command of a Major Tate, backed up by a Captain and six Lieutenants. Around the camp, on a twenty-four hour rota, fifty search parties, each comprising a Sergeant and three men, some with dogs, patrolled the area between the fence and the barbed wire.

Two helicopters flew overhead during daylight hours. All those involved, officers and men, were ordered to paint their helmets bright red so that the helicopters could easily identify the wearer as friendly. Those red helmets could be seen for miles. If Kogata had turned up to do a bit of spying, he would have quickly realized what the American were up to and skedaddled!

Franks was waiting to sign Wen-biao (Gao) onto the base and accompany him to his quarters. The room was small but functional. It had a single bed, footlocker, bedside cabinet, wardrobe, small table and a chair. On a horsehair mattress, bedding stood in a neat pile with a pillow on top. Further down the bed, a full set of American combat gear was laid out, including a newly painted bright red helmet. Four sizes of boots sat on the floor. Franks chuckled when he saw the boots and told Wen-biao to see if a pair fit. One pair did and very comfortable they were too. He kept them on.

This was officer accommodation. His batman immediately made himself busy putting things away and making the bed. He had a cot in the next hut with other batmen. His orders were to report anything of interest gleaned from the conversation of others in his hut and base area.

Gao was very impressed. In just one day, the Americans had assigned seven officers, six hundred men and all the machinery and materials needed to do the job. They had also painted six hundred helmets bright red.

On the way to attend their first briefing and meet the officers assigned to the detachment, Franks showed Gao around. Franks warned, "Keep to the perimeter paths, they will lead you to the places you need to go. Whatever else you do, don't go onto the airstrip unless accompanied. We Americans are outsiders, ignorant of oriental affairs. Some of our guys have only been in China a short time. They could easily think that your Kuomintang uniform is Japanese. If that happens, you'll be shot."

Headquarters proved to be efficient. Gao was issued with a pass for the base and another for the Officers" Club situated just outside the camp gates. He respectfully declined the offer of a jeep by explaining that he had his own car and driver. He gratefully accepted gasoline vouchers issued to all officers having their own transport.

He was introduced to Major Tate, a battle-hardened, cigar-chewing, tough-looking Marine with a cluster of campaign ribbons dating back to World War One. Tate automatically commanded respect despite his lack of height. During the briefing Gao heard almost word for word everything he had said to the meeting chaired by General Chennault earlier that day and concluded that Chinese TOP SECRET didn't mean much to the Americans. When Tate finished speaking he asked for questions.

As Captain Wen-biao, Gao stood up and asked in English, "Why the high profile security measures? I thought we were out to catch Kogata, not scare him away."

To which the Major replied, "*Your* job is to catch him. *Mine* is to stop him spying on us *and* catch him if he is stupid enough to try."

So that was that. The Americans wouldn't be capturing Kogata.

Gao could use most of the next fourteen days gathering information for Mao Zedong.

*

That meant spending a lot of time in the Officers" Club. Gao and his driver had to show their passes whenever they wanted to go through the main gate to get there and back. That meant remembering some new English words.

A fresh pair of passwords was issued daily at 0800 hours. Words like "Milkshake/Strawberry, "Earp/Holliday', "Marzipan/Vanilla', "Lollipop / Toffee-apple".

When challenging, the sentry would shout the first part of the password and they had to shout the second before showing their passes. Their oriental faces and Kuomintang uniforms, familiar to them, strange to Americans, attracted plenty of challenges from Japanese-spy-nervous trigger-happy guards.

Gao found the Officers" Club to be a gold mine of useful information. Almost all of the Americans had ideas about China's future. The majority thought that when the world war was over, Washington would keep a strong force of American troops in China ready to help Chiang Kai-shek should the civil war start up again. Some thought, and hoped, that they would all go home and leave the Chinese to sort out their own problems. A few had no opinion.

One day General Chennault spent a few hours with them. To Gao's surprise, the General deliberately sought him out. He loved China and its people and had a Chinese wife. Gao was a Chinese who could speak English and Chennault wanted to talk. So did Gao.

The name Claire Lee Chennault is now part of Chinese folklore. He was commissioned into the American infantry in 1917, then transferred to the Signal Corps and became a pilot. When, in 1937, he was forced out of the army because of a hearing problem, he volunteered his services to the Kuomintang. Almost single-handedly he formed the American Volunteer Squadron and recruited some fifty US civilian pilots to fly against the Japanese.

After Pearl Harbor, he was invited to rejoin the US Army Air Corps and absorb his volunteer squadron into his new command, the 14th Air Force, China. The skill and bravery of the American pilots quickly earned them the nickname "The Flying Tigers".

Chennault knew more about American politics and had a wider understanding of China than just about any other person on earth at that time. He was quite certain that after the war the Yanks would leave China to the Chinese.

In double quick time the USA had gone from an interested bystander to full participant in World War Two. After Pearl Harbor, Hitler, expecting Japan to launch an offensive against the USSR, had also declared war on the USA. As soon as Japan and Germany were defeated, the American people would quickly lose the taste for war and want the men back home.

Sitting comfortably in the best chair, he surmised, "It would be political suicide for the Democrats if Roosevelt kept us here to help Chiang fight the "Commies" and corpses continued to flow Stateside. The Soviets will be our next problem, not China. If Congress agrees to fund an American occupation of Japan and a European-based peacetime army facing East, they won't want to spend much on China.'

He went on to say that after the war, America would continue to support the Kuomintang. "After all," he concluded, "Chiang Kai-shek is the head of the recognized lawful government of China. Should the Chinese civil war start up again, I think Washington will supply the Kuomintang with everything needed to wage war against Mao, except human beings."

It was good stuff spoken by an expert and exactly what Chairman Mao needed to know. Gao's next task for Mao entailed him getting inside a Kuomintang Army base to check out the morale of the troops.

For Stalin, he had to capture Kogata and his equipment.

6.

The morning Gao returned to the General's house, Madam Wen-gian greeted him with the news that General Liu was due back home by nightfall. This required a quick change of plan.

His first decision was to stay and face it out with the General. To leave without meeting him would have raised eyebrows and created unnecessary questions, so he spent the morning with Madam, talking through their strategy. He told her everything. Kogata, the meetings with Chennault, and Chiang, his TOP SECRET orders, and not having a chance to capture the Japanese spy during his time with the Americans. In return, Madam worked out a way to explain his presence in the house.

After lunch and still in Kuomintang uniform, he climbed into the car and instructed his driver to take him a few hundred yards down the road and park where he could keep the entrance to the house under observation through his rear-view mirror. They waited.

True to his word, as dusk was falling, a four-car convoy of identical black limousines swept past Gao's parked car. Through the rear-view mirror Gao watched them turn in through the gates. Two minutes later three of the cars exited, leaving one inside the grounds. The General was safely back home.

They waited an hour then they too drove up to the house. Gao got out of the car and the driver drove around the back as usual. Gao rang the bell. The front door opened to reveal the same white-coated male army orderly, same revolver strapped to his waist. He smiled and let Gao in, but this time, instead of Madam Wen-gian descending the stairs to greet him, it was the General.

The General smiled, stuck out his hand and firmly grasped Gao's. "You must be Captain Wen-biao. Madam has been explaining your presence here. Come in my boy."

He was dressed in a loose white silk jacket and trouser set, white ankle socks and cloth homemade sandals. He was at ease and was easy to like. What Madam Wen-gian had said about him was true. He was unassuming, friendly and courteous. Gao now understood why Zhou En-lai and the General could be such good friends, despite their political differences.

Gao's cover story was simple. Although he was a member of Madam's family, until recently he had spent several years abroad. Returning to China, he had joined the Kuomintang Army and was now on a secret mission for the Generalissimo. After reading Gao's orders, the General not only accepted his story, he wanted to help.

"Tell me what you want my boy, and I will make sure that you get it," he said.

The next mid-day, guests arrived to celebrate the General's safe return. A grand feast, carefully overseen by Madam Wen-gian, was laid out in the huge dining hall. As each important person and consort arrived, Gao was introduced as the guest of honour, giving him instant credibility.

One of the guests was a Colonel Zhu Chi-chang. During the introductions, the General said to Gao, "Colonel Zhu is my most trusted officer and right-hand man. He will help you in your search."

To the Colonel, the General ordered, "Captain Wen-biao has top-secret orders signed by the Generalissimo. Make sure that he gets everything he needs. If any officer gives you trouble, refer him, or her, to me!"

And that was that. Gao was well and truly inside the Kuomintang. The only pity was that after completing his mission, he had to somehow extricate himself without leaving any evidence of his true identity.

7.

Gao stood behind the four army radio operators using the most modern radio equipment available to the Kuomintang. Eight more operators were resting in the hut next door. He had arranged three shifts of eight hours each, to conduct a round-the-clock search for Kogata. He spent as much time as he could in the army hut he had christened "Seeker", situated on the fringes of an army camp east of the city.

Because of the TOP SECRET status, his request to be isolated from the rest of the camp had been approved. It gave Gao protection from prying eyes and nosey officers asking awkward questions. Armed guards patrolled day and night, and their meals were brought to them in a jeep driven by armed cookhouse personnel. Gao had a small sleeping room at the end of the operational hut. The operators slept in an adjacent hut known to them as "Hide-away".

Ten days of searching the airwaves had resulted in him having to relearn how to snatch sleep in small doses. Hundreds of sounds were discovered, reported to him, and dismissed - he had only one target, the callsign BBYQ. Suddenly, at 0255 hours, it was there, loud and strong, exactly as described to him by Moscow.

Gao took over from the grinning operator responsible for finding Kogata. All four operators stood around Gao, watching him write down groups of Japanese characters. It was code, so none of them could understand their meaning.

It was gone.

The operators hurried to their sets and began to search. There was Kogata again. This time Gao listened on the monitor set and kept all four operators at their posts. In less than five minutes it had again stopped. They found him again on another frequency. At 0320 hours, nothing further was heard.

It had been a good night. They had a list of the frequencies Kogata had used and his particular operating sound - fast, fluent, no frills Morse-code perfection. Gao, strictly against army discipline but what did he care, opened a bottle of rice wine and shared it out.

"Well done men," he toasted. "Gambei!"

He reported to the Colonel. During that day eight more radios were installed with six tuned to the frequencies used by Kogata the previous night. He used his experienced men the second night, whilst eight more newly sent operators slept next door. They would be the day-shift. And sure enough, at 0255 hours, Kogata began to transmit, using yet another frequency. Six more frequencies were listed that night. More radios and operators arrived the following day and all around the city trucks carrying radio direction-finding equipment were carefully but unobtrusively placed. On the third night, fifty pairs of ears were now waiting, hoping to hear Kogata sing his song.

Nothing.

And nothing for the next forty-eight hours. Had Kogata realised that the Chinese were on to him? Gao already had the utmost respect for his Japanese opposite number, now he was beginning to wonder if he was in his league.

He needn't have worried. On the fourth night, Kogata began to transmit, using one of his known frequencies. Ten days later, after all the direction finders had reported their latest trace-lines, Gao had his most-used position, the city centre, number eleven Emei Road. Favoured time to begin transmitting, 0255 hours.

The CIS ordered extra plain-clothes agents into the Emei Road area and the army sent in one extra mobile patrol per hour. Everything was kept low key. None of them wanted to startle Kogata into flight. The Military Headquarters of the Kuomintang City Garrison had orders to wait until dusk, then quietly surround the Emei Road area with troops and armoured gun carriers and await further instructions. The whole operation was placed under the command of a Colonel with Gao leading a company of tough and ruthless killers. They had been American-trained within an urban environment and were perfect for this job.

From careful reading of maps supplied by the local Municipal Planning Department, the Colonel ordered Gao's company, without being seen from the windows of number 11, to stealthily move into pre-arranged positions until not one metre of road, alley, storm-drain, sewer or other escape route was left unobserved. The fronts, backs and sides of the six houses nearest to number 11 were also covered. At 0300 hours the direction finders confirmed that Emei Road was the transmitting point. On a whistle, all the houses previously covered had their front and rear doors battered open. The noise was like thunder in the quiet of the night, but the result was satisfactory.

Within a minute of entering number 11 they found their quarry trying to finish one last message. When the soldiers burst in, he pulled out a knife. Only a quick-witted young lieutenant, well-versed in Japanese psyche, stopped Kogata from sticking the long sharp blade into his own belly. Hara-kiri was the traditional Japanese act when faced with dishonour, and being captured alive was dishonour indeed for a Japanese warrior.

Within five minutes all resistance had been overcome with three men captured and two killed. At last Gao was face to face with a very much alive Kogata. His men had also captured Kogata's equipment, code books, *and a cipher machine!*

Gao ordered Kogata be handcuffed and taken from the house with his stuff. As he was inspecting the rest of the house, a jeep with US markings drew up outside. Andriev, dressed as an American Lieutenant-Colonel and two white-helmeted American Military Policemen quickly alighted. In American-accented Mandarin, Andriev called to the young officer who had stopped Kogata from killing himself, "Lieutenant. You are to hand Kogata and his equipment into my custody…'

*

The next afternoon Gao was in General Liu's living room reading the paper when Madam Wen-gian came to tell him her news. "I've just heard that Chiang Kai-shek went completely berserk during a meeting with the Americans. Apparently, after he asked when he could expect delivery of the radio equipment, the Americans denied any knowledge of the capture.

"Then," she chuckled delightedly, "the meeting was interrupted by a telephone call from the Soviets. They wanted to thank the Generalissimo for his generous gift of the Japanese radio and code books now on their way to Moscow. The caller went on to say that through their common efforts, the allies had moved a step closer to absolute victory."

Chiang Kai-shek had let loose a stream of abuse against the

surprised Americans. Chiang's information, backed up by several reports of the capture, had an American Colonel demand custody of Kogata and his precious equipment, so how had the Soviets got hold of it? Who had given the Americans the authority to demand custody of the Jap Spy? What was the name of the officer? Where was Kogata? Nobody had answers. Gao smiled and went back to his reading.

8.

Two days later Gao bade the General and Madam Wen-gian goodbye, saying that he had more secret orders to carry out. His driver returned him to the CLO where he reported to Zhou En-lai.

"Our planning went perfectly and I had some luck. During my time with the Americans and the Kuomintang I picked up a lot of information that will be useful to Comrade Mao Zedong. Please arrange for me to be on tomorrow's flight to Yan'an, then I must return to Dragon Gate Town. I've already been away a worryingly long time."

Captain Wen-biao and Colin Chew disappeared, never to be seen again. The limousine with black windows took Gao to the Kai-xuan Hotel in Yellow Corner Village. He alighted and watched the car speed away.

He entered the hotel anticipating a splendid afternoon with Zhao Ying before his evening meeting with Andriev. She was there and they did indeed make love but their time together was tinged with sadness. Andriev had thought it best if it was she, not him, who broke the news that his good friend Sparks had been killed in Burma.

Gao remembered something Sparks had said during their time in spy school.

"No man can escape death. When my time comes I want to be remembered as a loyal comrade with a brave heart who never shirked his duty".

His wish had come true.

"Does Chopper know?" he asked. Zhao Ying shook her head.

"Andriev thought it best to await your return so that you can tell him," she whispered.

Gao comforted himself in her warm body. Over and over. Needing to feel alive.

*

That evening he had an interesting meeting with Andriev. His arrival words to Gao were, "Congratulations Comrade Gao Qing. It is my pleasure to advise that Comrade Stalin has promoted you to the honorary rank of Colonel in the NKVD." He saluted. Gao was pleased. However, Andriev's second piece of news was far more important to him.

"I have a warning for you from Serpent. Chiang Kai-shek is absolutely furious about what happened in the Kogata case. He summoned all the senior officers from the CIS and the MISB and is reported to have roared, "What use are you? No bloody use at all! You are all fucking useless! How could you let the Americans and the Russians make such fools of us? I always knew you were an ineffectual bunch of bastards, now you have allowed me to lose face to the whole world! How did the Russians get to know our plans? Somewhere there is a spy in your headquarters, perhaps many spies. Maybe YOU, or YOU." He apparently nodded his head at random to whoever was standing nearest to him as he paced up and down the room and accused them of being a Russian spy. No one dared say anything.

"He is rumoured to have bellowed, "I want my army and my city cleared of spies. Dig them out! I want results, NOW! Do you understand? NOW! Otherwise, every one of *you* will punished!"

Serpent reported that Captain Wen-biao was not under suspicion. It was he who had brought the news of Kogata to the attention of the Allies and it was he who had pinpointed Kogata's exact position in Emei Road. He had followed his orders to the letter and was not present when the Americans took Kogata into their custody. Plus, and it was a big plus, he was a relative of General Liu *and* he had been trusted with TOP SECRET orders personally signed by the Generalissimo. Nobody dared bring the

Captain's name into any discussions.

Andriev told Gao that Serpent was keeping his head down and seemed to be safe. Gao must do the same.

"Do not use your radio. Zhao Ying and I must be your only contacts. The CIS and the MISB have joined together to find every secret radio in the area, no matter if it is British, American, Russian, Japanese or whatever. The Generalissimo wants heads to roll and they will. Just make sure yours is not one of them."

At last he came to the bit Gao wanted to hear.

"Stalin sends his congratulations on a job well done. Not only did you manage to deliver the equipment and books, you sent a very much alive Kogata. He couldn't be more pleased."

9.

The air journey to Yan'an was uneventful except for some mind-shattering information told to Gao by the flight attendant. He was the only passenger and due to minor engine trouble they were late taking off. This meant that for the last hour of their journey they were flying in daylight. As they neared Yan'an, the flight attendant pointed downwards. Through the porthole Gao saw vast fields of white. The Flight attendant shouted above the engine noise: "Opium."

Gao couldn't contain his surprise. He shouted back, "Did you say opium?"

The flight attendant nodded. "Grown by the Communists."

He told Gao that for many years Mao and his Communist Party had relied on opium for their main source of income. There was a huge army tucked away in Yan'an needing something to do. Mao had ordered the growing of opium on a vast scale.

The terrain in a place near to Yan'an called, Nan-Ni-Wan (South Mud Bay), was perfectly suited for growing the poppies, and every year huge amounts of raw opium was harvested. Mao is reported to have explained his reasons.

"If we break our backs growing vegetables, fruit, grain and cotton perhaps we can send a hundred carts to market and get ourselves a few small bags of coin. If we grow opium, one cart taken to market will return a hundred carts full of banknotes."

Gao learned that Mao supplied Communist supporters with opium. They sold it for a huge profit. After taking their cut, the rest of the money was channelled back to Yan'an. Although Mao didn't care who bought or used the drug, he wanted most of it to end up in the Kuomintang controlled areas. Opium helped to destabilize the economy and weaken morale. Chiang Kai-shek was completely unaware of the fact that a large number of his officers, men and families used opium, thus helping Mao buy the arms he was going to use against the Kuomintang when the civil war restarted.

Gao was shocked to the core of his being. He hated drugs and drug dealers, and yet, here he was, following a man who was responsible for the biggest drug industry in China, perhaps the world. Then he had another thought. Perhaps the two drug dealers Brown and Blue that he and Chopper had handed over to Colonel Chen were Communist supporters. What a dog-shit bloody awful mess! He felt the beginnings of an intense dislike for Mao Zedong. The aircraft landed. Could his training help him keep his temper under control and his mouth shut? He hoped so.

CHAPTER 7.

Nanking, 1944–1945

1.

The ferry was late, delaying Gao's return to Dragon Gate Town. He had stood for over an hour on the dock, waiting among an ever-increasing crowd of would-be passengers. He decided to rent a rickshaw. Not to go anywhere, just to sit in until it was time to board the ferry.

His randomly chosen rickshaw puller was an honest-looking fellow, and anyway, Gao was sitting in his conveyance. He handed money to the man and asked him to run off and get a newspaper. The man loped off and quickly returned with a paper and the change. Gao dropped a tip into his hand, nothing much, but a little more generous than usual. The man made a deep bow and respectfully asked if he could give any further service. Gao shook his head then had a second thought. He looked closely at this man who normally would never be noticed.

Aged about thirty, he looked like any other rickshaw puller, with one exception, his natural air of independence and self-respect. Gao was prompted to ask, "Have you eaten?"

For someone to ask such a thing was something that never happened to people like the rickshaw puller. He looked suspicious but also grateful for the question. With a small shrug of his shoulders he replied, "Yesterday I ate noodles. Tonight I will eat rice."

Gao made to give him more money but with a dignity usually unknown to the Chinese poor, he held up a right hand in refusal. "No Master, no. I do not take money for doing nothing. I must earn it. But I will forever remember your kindness."

Gao replied, "While we are waiting for the ferry, we could be eating. Go to the nearest street food vendor and get some rice and vegetables for both of us."

Gao ate slowly, watching the man wolf his down. The poor chap was starving but between mouthfuls he didn't miss the chance to talk business.

"If I could be your private rickshaw puller. Ahhh! That would be very good."

Gao looked at him for a few minutes in silence. He had an idea.

"I am thinking about your offer," said Gao. "Please tell me your name."

"My given name is Liming (Dawn) and my family name is "Tian" (Sky)."

"A good name," Gao said. "Does this rickshaw belong to you, or do you rent it?"

"I saved for years to get it, and now it is mine."

"So business is good for you." A statement needing a reply.

"I must work hard to support my old mother and invalid sister. Mother is sick and confined to bed. We cannot get a doctor to visit because we are already in debt to him and the herbal shop…'

At that point Gao pulled some notes from his pocket. Dawn quickly waved them away.

"No Master, I cannot accept your kind gift. I must earn it. This is the teaching given to me by my parents."

"You must know Chongqing very well."

"Yes, Master. There is nowhere in Chongqing that is hidden from me."

"What about Dragon Gate Town?"

"The same. I once lived there."

"Can you read and write?"

"No Master. My family needed me to work. No time for school."

Actually, Gao really did need an assistant and this fellow called Dawn might be a good choice. He could be his helper, private rickshaw puller and messenger to keep him in touch with Chongqing. It was a bonus that he was illiterate. Gao asked one more question. "If I employ you for good wages, could you keep my secrets? Can I be sure that my business will stay my business and nobody else's, not even your closest family would hear anything from your mouth?"

"Master," eagerly answered Dawn. "I promise to never utter one word. I would rather have my bowels cut out than betray your trust."

Gao decided to take a later ferry. He wanted to see if Dawn's mother really was ill and the man wasn't just another clever liar. Dawn easily pulled him up the hill into the poorest part of the city to his home, but they were too late. Mother lay dead. His weeping sister lay prostrate over the body and it was easy to see that her left leg and arm were under-developed, almost useless.

Dawn cried for just a few seconds then dried his eyes.

"Master," he said. "The poor have no time to grieve. There is so much death around here, our funerals are quick, cheap and simple. Like most of her generation, mother arranged and paid for her funeral years ago. I have family debts to settle and a sister to support so I really want to work for you, but not today. If it pleases you, I will return you to the ferry then bring myself and my rickshaw to your home tomorrow evening."

Gao put out his hand, but not to shake Dawn's. They hooked little fingers and shook twice. Dawn now believed that if he broke his promise, he must commit suicide and go to the eighteenth layer underground, the Chinese version of Hell.

Gao pulled some notes from his pocket.

"This is an advance on your wages. Settle your affairs. I will expect you in Dragon Gate Town by noon the day after tomorrow. Agreed?"

Dawn nodded. This time his tears flowed unchecked.

*

As good as his word, Dawn and his rickshaw arrived during the morning of the third day. He stopped outside the Dragon Gate Garments Factory, climbed into his rickshaw and snoozed whilst waiting for Gao to appear. Gao did, at lunchtime. Dawn grinned delightedly. His happy face and readiness to do Gao's bidding without seeming to be subservient confirmed Gao's first impression of him. Dawn was a man of honour and integrity. They hooked little fingers again but this time it was not because of an oath but a spontaneous confirmation of their mutual trust.

Gao took Dawn to meet Fa-fu. On the evening that Gao had met Dawn, the big man had boomed, "Thank goodness you are back. I need your education more than ever. Now that there is money to be made from rebuilding, every greedy rat and cockroach in town has crawled out of the slime looking for easy pickings."

Gao had told Fa-fu about Dawn. He, as usual, showed his generous side by offering a share of a room above the restaurant. "My waiters live there. He will have company and food in exchange for free rickshaw rides for me when you do not need him."

When the proposition was put to Dawn, he looked dubiously at the big man, wondering whether he could pull such a weight up the hills - decided that he could and smilingly agreed. So that was settled.

That afternoon Dawn set up his business outside the factory and was soon taking fares. Gao didn't mind him earning extra money when he didn't need him, and anyway, Dawn handed his takings over to Gao. Dawn wanted to repay the advance on his wages as quickly as possible so that he could concentrate all his energies on creating a good home for his sister.

Dawn's determination to retain his independence quickly earned Gao's respect. In addition to his rickshaw earnings, Dawn and Gao agreed the terms of Dawn's employment, including allowing Dawn to take a detour to check on his sister every time Gao sent him on a message to Chongqing.

Gao made trips to Chongqing too, but only to pay overnight visits to the Yun house. It was something he particularly looked forward to after the night he felt someone slip into the bed and snuggle up beside him. It was the silently giggling Little Dove. In bed, the normally chattering young lady became quiet, sedate and shyly explorative, making their nights together so wonderful, he couldn't stop her from slowly melting into his heart.

2.

The intelligence services had swamped Chongqing with agents dedicated to the task of uncovering illicit radio transmitters and arresting spies. They even appeared in Dragon Gate Town. There was never news of a genuine capture. Of course there were arrests of known political troublemakers and petty criminals to show the Generalissimo that they were successfully carrying out his orders. Kangaroo courts were quickly arranged to give the expected guilty verdicts before the victims were shot.

A joke circulated saying that the CIS and the MISB had dug out four transmitters. One especially set up by the CIS so that their agents could "uncover" it, one created by the MISB for the same reason, and two commercial stations run by a local entrepreneur. Another joke said the idiots running the intelligence services couldn't detect dog-shit on their shoes. Nevertheless, it was a nasty few weeks.

Chiang Kai-shek soon forgot about radios. He had many other problems to occupy his mind, and one of his biggest was Lieutenant-General Joseph Stilwell.

Joseph Warren Stilwell was born in 1883 in Palatka, Florida. Although he trained at West Point, he was more scholar than soldier. A fluent Mandarin speaker, he was an acknowledged authority on China.

From 1932 to 1939 he was Military Attaché to the United States Embassy in Beijing. In 1942, he was appointed Commander of the US ground forces in China, Burma and India, as well as the 5th and 6th Chinese Armies. A Democrat, he was also given the political appointment of Chief of Staff to Chiang Kai-shek.

"Vinegar Joe" Stilwell lived up to his nickname. He was a brilliant strategist with a sour personality. Almost from his first day in the job, acute problems arose between him and the Generalissimo, and also between him and Brigadier-General Claire Chennault.

With the loss of Burma, supplies had to be airlifted over the hump of the eastern Himalayas and, of course, there was never enough of them to go round. The Japanese were in full flow in 1942. Of the supplies that did arrive, each US commander wanted the lion's share for his own forces. Stilwell was more concerned about keeping the Japanese from making any more land gains. Chennault thought that air supremacy was the way to victory and expected priority for his needs. Neither man was ever satisfied with his allocation even though everything was divided more or less fifty-fifty.

By the beginning of 1943, the lack of supplies and troop replacements had made China's position desperate. On all fronts, Chinese military and civilian morale was dangerously low. If the Japanese had launched just one major offensive at that time, the combined US/Chinese forces would have found it almost impossible to mount any kind of resistance. Luckily, the Japanese were unaware of the true state of affairs. At just the right time for the Allies, the Japanese facilitated a lull in the fighting to consolidate their hold on previously hard-won territorial gains.

Roosevelt had meanwhile decided to support Chennault by promoting him to Major-General. That gave Chennault the authority to demand more of the available supplies, enabling him to launch many successful air strikes against the Japanese.

For all concerned, 1943 was, generally, a year of recovery and reparation.

At some time during the early weeks of 1944, an unofficial truce occurred between the Chinese Communists based in Yan'an, and the Japanese. Historical documents do not show exactly how. Was it by negotiation or simply allowed to happen? No one knows.

Documents do show that the Japanese had realized that Mao

Zedong was not a danger to them. He had no intention of losing his growing army by fighting against the better-equipped Japanese. Only the relatively small Communist 8th Route Army and the much smaller New 4th Army were fighting alongside the Kuomintang against the Japanese.

The truce hugely aided the Japanese. Most of their forces doing nothing except keeping watch on Mao's Yan'an army were shifted south for an offensive against Chennault's airfields.

Built by hundred of thousands of Chinese coolies, these airfields were numerous and well placed to make strategically significant raids on Japanese positions as far afield as Formosa (now Taiwan) and Manchuria.

Taking the airfields was just one part of an overall Japanese attack plan. Whilst they slowly gobbled up the airfields, they also cleared the railway tracks needed for swift transportation of everything required by an army on the move. This gave them the opportunity to amass a vast store of armaments and supplies.

Meanwhile, not foreseeing what was to come, Chiang Kai-shek finally gave in to General Stilwell's demand that he be allowed to use the best of the Chinese battalions for an offensive in Burma. Stilwell continued with his plans and went into Burma four days *after* the Japanese launched their East China offensive on May the 11th 1944.

The Japanese advanced steadily against patchy opposition, gaining ground and taking most of the remaining airfields. By the end of November the Chinese position was more desperate than ever. The Burma offensive was called off and two of the best divisions flown back to China. Chiang Kai-shek had Stilwell replaced by Major-General Albert Wedemeyer. It was a gamble that paid off. Wedemeyer quickly reorganized the Chinese forces and in a series of counter-attacks, stopped the Japanese advance.

3.

Whilst all this was going on, the Soviets were looking with some alarm at the Japanese successes. Was Russia next? Whilst still having to contain the Germans in the north, they were forced to deploy troops all along their southern borders.

Stalin wanted to know what the Japanese were planning. The tank battle at Kursk had shown Stalin the value of advance information. If the Japanese were to attack, he wanted his armies to be in the right place, ready and waiting.

In September 1944, Dawn brought Gao an innocent-looking package from Zhao Ying. Inside Gao found coded details of his next assignment. Stalin wanted him to get himself into the city of Nanking, infiltrate the Japanese Headquarters and learn all he could about their future plans.

Gao decoded further and found that he had help. Sadly not Chopper. His old partner was now a lieutenant in the Kuomintang army. His American employer had been promoted and recalled to the USA, leaving Chopper without a job. Before departing for America, his boss introduced Chopper to a Kuomintang Commander and, with Moscow's blessing, Chopper was given a plum officer post in Chiang's personal guard.

Gao had managed to spend an hour with him to find that he was happy with his position. Army life was a soft touch compared to the hard life of a coolie. And his wife and ten-year-old son had been allowed to travel to Chongqing for a joyful reunion. Gao's news about Sparks saddened Chopper but Gao had brought good news too. Chopper was no longer active. He was now a "sleeper" to await further orders.

Gao's help on this mission was a man named Takeo Tsuse. Code-named "Kawa" meaning "River" in Japanese, he was an unusual political mixture. Rich industrialist Japanese family background, pre-war Moscow University graduate, spy-school graduate, devout Buddhist and a committed Communist. After spy-school he had returned to his home city of Kyoto and campaigned for peace but Pearl Harbor had happened anyway. To his disgust he had been conscripted into the Japanese Navy and given an officer rank of full lieutenant. After being wounded during the Battle of Midway he was promoted to Lieutenant-Commander and put behind a desk in the Japanese Military Headquarters, Nanking.

Kawa had memorized plenty of secret stuff and had collected lots of classified bits of paper, all locked away in his desk. Security was so tight he dared not risk trying to take anything out of the building.

Gao's job was to get into Nanking, contact Kawa and pick his brains. But that was not all. Gao also had to get a floor plan of the building, break into Kawa's office, shared with three other officers, take possession of the bits of paper stored in his desk and get out again. All without being noticed. Gao didn't like the sound of this mission but knowing it was important to Stalin, he had to do his best.

4.

Gao dressed Dawn in a pair of black trousers and a white shirt for their trip. Dawn immediately cut down the trouser legs to make shorts and got rid of the arms of the shirt. "Too hot," he explained. His body-skin was like leather and he always went barefoot. He didn't notice seasonal temperatures or weather changes and the soles of his feet were harder than US combat boots.

Gao wore his normal Chinese dress of black gown, black skullcap, socks and leather shoes. With him in the rickshaw he had his briefcase and brown suitcase containing a change of clothes for them both and a raincoat for himself. He carried no pistol or other give-away clues to his true profession. He was a simple Chinese public servant delivering a file containing important legal papers to his opposite number in Nanking.

The papers weren't applicable to a real transaction but they were authentic. Gao had drawn them up himself! He had also drawn up the passes to get them through the checkpoints, but here he was taking a small risk. He knew that they wouldn't stand up to *very* close scrutiny.

Gao and Dawn were on a ship authorized to take passengers and cargo all the way to Shanghai, stopping several times on the way. In 1937, the Japanese had declared their desire to create a "Great East Asia Co-Prosperity Sphere" within the Japanese Empire. This ship was running under that declaration. Chinese merchants and government officials were allowed to cross into and out of the Japanese controlled areas provided they had proper authorization. At the border the ship picked up Japanese guards who stayed with the ship until dropping them off on the return journey.

Gao and Dawn arrived in Nanking without too many problems. The Japanese guards had been through the ship checking papers and had taken one unlucky man into custody. Gao's papers passed their first check and were stamped. Good. Many stamps meant less scrutiny.

They disembarked. Dawn went off to see to his precious rickshaw whilst Gao followed other passengers towards customs. His luggage was carefully checked and passed. Heart bumping, he continued on his way to immigration. From his side of a barrier he could see people milling around or greeting new arrivals. Nowhere could he see a military uniform. He was now at the front of the queue, causing his attention to switch to the black uniformed Chinese official. He handed over two sets of papers, one set for him and another set for Dawn.

"Where is your companion?" the official asked in Mandarin.

From the side of his eye Gao saw a movement, took a quick look then pointed at a grinning Dawn standing on the other side of the barrier.

"There," Gao replied. "He has been taking care of the rickshaw."

Unexpectedly, a man of about Gao's age appeared and stood beside Dawn. He was dressed in a black old-fashioned Western-style suit with tails, white wing-collar shirt, black cravat, black top hat and very shiny black shoes under white spats. He lifted one black-gloved hand and waved his black umbrella and called in Japanese,

"Mister Gao, it is good to see you again."

Gao nodded and smiled a greeting, saying in Japanese, "It's been a long time."

That was sufficient for the official. Any Chinese able to speak Japanese, had his own rickshaw and was welcomed by a man dressed in clothes favoured by the Japanese Emperor *must* be legitimate. He hurriedly stamped Gao's papers and let him through.

The Mandarin Hotel was still standing and giving good customer service. Most of those staying there were high ranking Japanese officers. Very few civilians and almost no Chinese, so eyebrows fluttered in surprise when Gao checked in and they lifted almost to the hairline when he asked for a single room for Dawn.

It was politely pointed out to Gao that in Nanking, rickshaw-pullers *never* stayed in hotels.

"This one does," said Gao firmly.

More forms. Everywhere in Nanking forms had to be completed. Eventually a porter picked up their luggage and led the way to their adjoining rooms. Kawa was not with them. He explained that duty called. He would be along later. That suited Gao. He needed time to settle his nerves and collect his thoughts.

5.

Kawa arrived at eight p.m. dressed like a traditional Buddhist. In his robes, with a shaved head and the usual large cloth bag favoured by all Buddhist monks slung across his shoulder, he could easily blend into any oriental country.

He smiled at Gao's too obvious up-and-down look and said in Japanese, "Being a practising Buddhist, I am perfectly entitled to dress like this. I always do when off duty. It is an excellent way to travel around without being noticed or recognized. All Buddhist monks look the same."

He sat, opened the cloth bag and pulled out some photographs and two rolls of paper. He tapped one roll with his forefinger. "Map of the city," he explained. He then tapped the other. "An enlarged section, showing the Military Headquarters."

He unrolled the first to show Gao the general layout of Nanking and point out the important places. Then he unrolled the second.

"This is the Military Headquarters, and here is the building I work in," he indicated with his finger. "And if you look at these photographs, you will see that there is a high wall topped with barbed wire running all around the complex, impossible to get over.

"This is the front entrance, well guarded, so no way in. However, I've given much thought to the problem and I've found a weakness."

He went on to explain that the mix of buildings had once been a Kuomintang Military Base when China was at peace with the world and Chiang Kai-shek only had the Chinese War Lords to worry about.

They kicked around their ideas and discussed all possibilities. Gao had to admit that Kawa had probably found the weakness, but he needed to check it out for himself. He was free the next day. Kawa was not. From 0800 hours he was rostered to begin his twenty-four hour stint as Senior Duty Security Officer. At first Gao thought they might have to waste a day, but Kawa assured him that provided he didn't do anything stupid, it would be safe for him and Dawn to go out.

A thought suddenly struck Gao, prompting him to ask, "How long is it between your Security Officer duties?"

"Every twenty-one days."

"Does it ever vary? I mean, do officers swap shifts?"

"Yes, quite often. Sometimes I will swap or do an extra shift for someone as a favour."

"How often do you get asked?"

"It varies. Once or twice, sometimes three times in a month."

"So it wouldn't be unusual for you to ask for a swap if we needed it?" Gao asked.

"No. I am sure I could change without any problems or attracting attention."

*

The next morning Gao treated Dawn to a rickshaw ride. He sat beside Gao, taking in the sights of Nanking. The once-beautiful city had been badly scarred. Many of the splendid plane trees lining the main thoroughfares had been blasted to stumps and every building had damage. In the riverside area there was hardly a decent structure left standing and the old shantytown had quadrupled in size to house the homeless and the thousands of coolies used to load and unload ships.

All along the riverbank hundreds of flat-bottomed sampans either moored to posts or tied to each other housed thousands more people. The owners of these little houseboats plied their trade along the river by day and after tying up for the night, took a modest rent from those wanting somewhere to sleep. Throughout the orient, for centuries, this has been an accepted way of earning money. Anyone willing to pay extra could stay for breakfast. Paying double bought a sleeping-place next to a female family member and breakfast. By the end of summer, the river stank of sewage and rot. It would continue to stink, getting daily worse, until the monsoons washed it clean.

Gao paid the rickshaw fare and they walked. Dawn was interested in everything but Gao wasn't sightseeing. He wanted a good look at the section of the city surrounding the Japanese Military Headquarters. It didn't take him long to realize that unless Kawa was right about the weakness, this was going to be a tough nut to crack.

After lunch, Gao gave Dawn a ferry ride across the river. In his bag he carried binoculars supplied by Kawa, and he needed them. As it flows past Nanking, the Yangtze River is about one-and-half kilometres wide. Gao walked along the river bank until he was opposite the Military Headquarters. Whilst Dawn kept watch, he hid in some bushes and took a look through the binoculars. He didn't take too long. To be caught would have meant being shot where he stood. Nevertheless, he had to chance several looks from different angles as he sketched his impressions. It took most of the afternoon until it was time to catch a ferry. They couldn't afford to be caught out and about after curfew.

The next day he and Dawn returned to the Military Headquarters, this time approaching from the other side. They walked around the perimeter one way, and back the other. It was a big place, about one kilometre square. At the only entry, a horizontal barrier could be lifted to allow vehicles through. Guards were everywhere. Passes were meticulously checked. Floodlights.

Kawa was right, no way in for him. He was right about the wall too. It was three metres high with broken glass and barbed wire on top. All along the base, a concrete path had been laid. Gao couldn't possibly climb over it or dig under it, so forget that idea.

According to the map the wall also ran along the rear of the complex but Kawa told Gao that the Japanese had made some changes. The two side walls had been extended out into the river. Work had taken place just before the start of the monsoon season when the water level is always at its lowest.

On each side, a two metre high extension ran down the slope of the riverbank and into the river for about thirty metres. The two sides were then squared off with another wall to make a filth-free safety area for officers to bathe. For added security, the Japanese had laid barbed wire on the tops of all three new walls.

The resulting enclosure ran along the entire kilometre length of the complex. Sand had been brought in to make an artificial beach. To keep the water in that area clean, no sampans or other boats were allowed to moor within two hundred metres of the place.

Kawa was right again. There *was* a weakness - maybe. It was through an ordinary waist-high gate let into the inner rear wall to allow the officers access to the protected patch of sand. Of course it was guarded, usually by two men, one on duty and one resting.

Kawa had pointed out that inside the complex, single storey buildings had been built directly against the original rear wall. They would hide most of Gao's activities as he approached the complex from the river.

Gao arranged that he and Dawn should eat all their meals in his room. After dinner, Dawn sat quietly whilst Gao prepared for the arrival of Kawa. It was time for Gao to pick Kawa's brain clean of any secrets. He placed a pile of plain paper and a dozen pencils on the table. From room service he ordered a big vacuum flask of boiled water, three mugs and plenty of loose green tea.

Kawa arrived, carrying his cloth bag stuffed with reference books. He began to tell Gao everything he knew whilst Gao wrote it all down. Kawa had not realized just how much information he had stored in his brain. He told Gao that memory retention had been his best subject in spy school. After four hours of him remembering and Gao writing, it was time to adjourn for that night. Kawa left his books with Gao and returned the next evening to finish emptying his head.

On the third night they began to plan. Gao suggested that they went through the whole thing by him asking questions and, as Kawa provided the answers, Gao wrote everything down.

First question, "Does the tide affect the water level of the river?"

Kawa pulled out a book and checked.

"Yes, quite a lot. More than seven metres in the centre of the river."

"What is the date and time when the darkness spring tide is at its height?"

Another check.

"Ten days from now at 0130 hours," said Kawa.

"At this time of year, how much of the wall and barbed wire is covered at high tide?"

"The lowest neap tide water levels cover the side walls to about one-quarter. At high spring tide it comes up at least three metres more. That means it just about covers the barbed wire on top of the wall."

"How thick is the wall with the wire on top?"

"One metre."

"About how much of the beach is left uncovered at the highest tide?"

"Ten metres."

"How fast is the water running just before and after high spring tide?"

"At this time of year it is quite fast, but not dangerously so."

Good. That was the end of the tide and beach questions. Next came security.

"How tight is security around the perimeter?"

And so on through the list. They made good progress.

Kawa went on to explain that the Chinese had been demoralized to such an extent that they were generally well behaved and obedient. The Japanese did not expect trouble.

Security was high at the main gate, mainly for show, using highly trained Japanese Military Police. Inside the complex and around the domestic areas, security was lax. Although the guards patrolled in pairs, there had not been a known case of a break-in, so they did not expect to encounter trouble. Once inside the complex, an intruder who looked as though he should be there could wander around unchallenged.

Security, with regular body searches, was much tighter when going in or out of the administration and operational buildings. That was why Kawa didn't dare try to bring anything out.

Passes were almost never checked at the little gate. Junior Officers up to the rank of Lieutenant Commander had morning use of the beach to bathe, shave and swim for an hour from 0700 hours, and again in the evenings for one hour before sunset. Senior officers and Japanese female personnel used it from 0900 hours to 1700 hours.

In the mornings and evenings there was always a crush of junior officers anxious to make full use of their hour on the beach, and another rush to leave before the deadline. Officers were never stopped provided they were properly dressed for the beach in black shorts, white singlet with a rising sun badge sewn on the left breast, white knee length socks and black gymshoes.

At the end of the session, they had worked out a plan. After Gao translated it to Dawn, the uneducated rickshaw puller asked a missed question.

"How can you move around dressed in shorts and singlet carrying break-in tools going in, and a load of papers going out?"

A good question and another problem to solve.

Dawn asked three more questions.

"In what drawer of your desk are the papers stored?"

Kawa explained his office layout.

"How do you bow and who to?" and, "How do you salute and when?"

Lessons in Japanese etiquette and military customs followed.

*

The break-in was to take place the night before the highest tide of the lunar month, and with luck, Gao would exit the complex two nights later. Whilst Kawa and Dawn had important parts to play, if it all went wrong, Gao was the one who would be shot. And because the plan was a bit scrappy, he could very easily be discovered. Nevertheless, he decided to chance it. Stalin was waiting

For the seven days prior to the break-in, Dawn pulled his rickshaw all over Nanking and particularly the route between the hotel and the Military Headquarters. He quickly got to know his way around. At night he parked his rickshaw in a side street alongside the complex wall and went to sleep. Gao wanted him to be seen by the sentries as not being a danger, just a tired rickshaw puller. He was never challenged.

Kawa changed one of his Senior Duty Security Officer days so that he would be on duty on the night Gao planned to break into his office.

There were things to do. Not wanting to be too close to the Military Headquarters when making his preparations, every morning Gao and Dawn crossed the river by ferry to find the things he needed. First he found a cheap flat-bottomed punt-shaped boat for sale. With it came a single rear oar. The boat was in poor condition but perfectly shaped for the plan. He needed the platform at the bow end.

From a local ship's chandler he purchased two twenty-five-metre lengths of heaving line. He also toured the street markets until he found two well-made cloth shoulder-bags, one big and brown and a smaller black one. From other stalls he bought a sand-coloured light cotton jacket and matching trousers, cloth shoes and some black cloth to make a hood with eyeholes to cover his head completely.

From another trader he paid for a white pouch with string ties. It had to be big enough to hold three or four handfuls of carefully selected gravel, and it had to be white because he needed it to be seen by Dawn.

His last purchase was a Japanese-made waterproof wristwatch with a black leather strap. Kawa advised that this was a standard item worn by all Japanese officers. He had also suggested that Gao have his head shaved.

Purchases over, and hairless, Gao went to the riverbank to find four round medium-sized pebbles of the estimated weight he needed. He popped two pebbles into each shoulder-bag. And finally, he returned to collect his boat. He dropped everything into it and rowed up river until he found a good mooring spot for the boat and an almost deserted clearing where he could do a little bag throwing.

Because it was an important part of the plan, he spent an hour a day in the clearing perfecting his bag-throwing technique, and it was a good thing he did. His first attempts at throwing the bags, weighted to their estimated loads, were pitiful. If he hadn't practised, the plan would have failed for sure.

The last time he had done any single-oar rowing was as a boy. It was time to relearn that particular skill. His first attempt was rubbish and his muscles really hurt. So, after a daily hour of bag throwing, he rowed the boat up and down the river. At the end of each day, he used a large rock as an anchor. The boat wasn't worth stealing, so it was safe where he left it.

It was going to be quite dark for his row across the river. He needed something to aim for. As it happened, it was easy. The floodlights at the main gate lit up the dark sky. They were only switched off during air raids.

He expected no problems with cold air or water. In late September the days are hot and the nights are warm. By the time the Yangtze reaches Nanking, the water has meandered through six thousand kilometres of China being warmed by the sun.

6.

The evening came when Gao had to go, ready or not. With no chance of a trial run, he was going with a plan that was, at best, underdeveloped. For the umpteenth time he looked at his new Japanese wristwatch, 2330 hours. Dressed in the sand-coloured jacket and trousers, black cloth shoes and black hood, he began his journey across the river. The currents were quite strong, but he had every confidence that he would reach the other side.

In the bottom of the boat lay one length of heaving line and the two shoulder-bags. The big brown bag held the white gravel-filled pouch, two of the pebbles, a few hand tools, a bottle of freshly boiled water and a tin containing cold fried rice wrapped in lotus leaves. The smaller black bag was empty except for the other two pebbles.

Before setting off, he had extended the length of the painter by knotting it to one end of the other heaving line. The other end of the extended line was securely tied to the large rock he had used as an anchor. On the bow platform, the rock and long line was coiled, ready for use.

His hours on the river had enabled him to regain his boyhood rear single oar rowing skills and he made good progress. Then, sudden panic. A ship was bearing down on him, making for the sea. He paddled like crazy and just managed to get clear before the ship's bow wave hit his flat-bottomed boat. Luckily he knew what to do. He quickly shipped the oar and jumped overboard to steady the boat until the river returned to normal. He hauled himself over the stern and back into the boat. That was his only scare. He arrived at the barbed wire with plenty of time to spare.

He manoeuvred the boat to the end of the enclosure farthest away from the guarded gate. With its flat bottom, the boat slid a fair way over the barbed wire before stopping. As he had planned, the flat platform at the bow jutted out, giving him an easy jump into clear water on the other side. But first he had to pick up the anchor-rock and throw it as far forward as possible. It splashed and sank, holding the boat where he had put it. So far, so good.

Leaving his stuff in the boat, he took a big leap off the bow. To his immense relief he splashed into clear water. Rising to the surface, he brushed the water off his face and listened. There was no reaction from anywhere. He searched for the anchor line, found it and raised the rock into his hands. Resting it on his chest, he swam on his back towards the beach until he could wade ashore.

Absolute high tide was due in thirty minutes. He rose to his feet, picked up the line and began to pull. The little boat, no longer bearing his weight, easily floated over the barbed wire and forward to the beach. When it was high and dry, he untied the rock-anchor and carefully placed it into the boat and began to unload everything he needed until all that was left on board was the rock and the oar.

He tied one end of the second heaving line to the end of the first. The boat was now attached to the painter and fifty metres of heaving line. To the free end he tied the black shoulder-bag. Holding the bag in his right hand, he looped as much of the line around the bag as he could. This was the time to find out if the pebbles were heavy enough and all that throwing practise had been worth while. Standing just above the waterline about five metres from the side wall topped with barbed wire, Gao threw the black bag. It immediately disappeared. All he could see was a few metres of line snaking away into the darkness. Holding his end of the rope, he waited. A tug on the line, then another. His breath came out in a huge gasp of relief. Dawn was holding the other end. He let go of his end and went to the boat.

Slowly the line was pulled tight. With him pushing, and Dawn pulling, they manoeuvred the boat out to the farthest end of the wall and simply floated it over the wire. Dawn had been instructed to retie the rock-anchor to the long heaving line and drop it into the river about a metre from the bank. The boat would float inconspicuously away on the end of the fifty-plus metre length of line and stay there. It was 0140 hours.

7.

In the corner of the beach, where the inner and the extended walls met, Gao dug in the sand where Kawa had buried certain items. During the time he had been preparing his end, little by little, Kawa had carried out things that Gao would need and buried them. He found the mandatory officer-issue olive coloured Japanese Army wash-bag. It was about forty centimetres square and fifteen centimetres wide with a flapped lid secured by two straps and buckles. It also had a long shoulder-strap. In the bag Kawa had packed shaving gear, a hand mirror and a small towel, otherwise it was empty. He needed it to be empty because he planned to cram the brown cloth shoulder-bag into it. Also buried, wrapped in separate bits of brown paper, were the pair of shorts, singlet, socks and gymshoes needed to get him through the gate.

Despite being surprised to learn from Kawa that the beach was not checked at least once during the night, Gao nevertheless took the precaution of burying himself in the sand with only his head showing, resting on his gear. Kawa had assured him that because nothing had ever happened to raise security awareness, complacency had set in. Year on year, increasing troop requirements at the many Japanese battle fronts all over the Pacific had resulted in bare minimum numbers at Headquarters. This had reduced guard and patrol levels to an absolute minimum.

At 0530 hours he sat up to eat his rice and drink from the bottle before burying the tin and the bottle deep in the sand. It was almost daybreak. He took off his clothes and buried them where he could easily find them again in the dark. Naked, he slid down the beach on his backside and into the river. When the first officers appeared on the beach, he didn't want to be seen. So, as dawn broke, he sat with the water lapping at his nostrils with only the top part of his shaved head showing.

At 0700 hours the gate opened and men began to fan out over the beach. Most stayed near to the gate. Gao watched one officer wander along the water's edge doing exercises. It was Kawa.

He too stripped and walked into the river. Ten minutes later they left the water, collected their shaving gear and sat in the water, shaving. They rinsed and dried themselves before dressing in the Japanese shorts, singlet, socks and gymshoes. They looked at each other and laughed. Who could tell them apart? Gao had just one more thing to do. He stuffed the brown shoulder-bag into the wash-bag supplied by Kawa.

They began the long walk to the gate. Other officers were doing the same. They ambled, wanting to be among the last to file in. They chatted, or rather, Kawa talked and Gao nodded. The gate loomed. Gao followed the fellow in front of him while Kawa kept the conversation going from behind...

"...I doubt that the sea temperature in Shanghai is much different. The warm waters of the Yangtze and Wampoo Rivers join together at Shanghai to heat up the East China Sea. That is why Shanghai suffers from so much moisture and humidity...'

The guard was in front of Gao, to the side, gone from sight. He was through. So was Kawa. Gao was inside the Japanese Military Headquarters at Nanking. The two men stiffened their backs and marched at speed, like good Japanese officers should. Kawa took the lead to his living quarters.

"I have a Japanese army batman and a Chinese servant," he warned. "Be careful what you say. As far as they are concerned you are helping me with a naval problem. Let me do the talking."

They went upstairs, along a corridor to the end and into a fair-sized room. Kawa, as the Senior Officer in charge of the block, had the room to himself. Gao's face was unknown to everybody living or working in the block but that was not an unusual occurrence. Many of the officers were newly commissioned arrivals from Japan awaiting transport to other Japanese occupied locations. Kawa threw Gao a freshly laundered white shirt. He took off the singlet and put the shirt on.

At 0800 hours, Kawa took over as the Senior Duty Security Officer, leaving Gao to spend the day in his room poring over charts and reference books, trying to look busy. In fact all he could think about was how he was going to get into Kawa's office. Kawa had left orders for the Chinese servant to collect Gao's lunch from the Officers" Mess. He did and it was delicious. The servant took away the dirty dishes. They didn't converse.

All day the batman came and went. Gao didn't speak to him either. Neither man seemed to mind. In the Japanese Military, there was a huge gulf between Officers and men, and an even wider gap between officers and servants.

Darkness arrived, so did Kawa. His batman helped him change from day to night uniform. Kawa was still on duty so he didn't have much time. "I'll be back," he promised before hurrying out. The Chinese servant bowed himself off duty. Later, the batman also left. At last Gao was able stop looking at meaningless charts and confusing reference books and concentrate on the matter at hand.

Once again he mentally ran the plan through his head looking for flaws and making allowances for the "what ifs". What if this happens? What if that goes wrong? He snoozed. The next thing he knew was Kawa shaking him awake.

"Time to go," said Kawa. "Put these on."

Gao yawned and looked at his watch, 2230 hours. He took off the shorts, shirt, socks and gymshoes and pulled on the brown overalls and cloth shoes recently taken off by the servant. From the Japanese wash-bag he pulled out the brown cloth shoulder-bag. It still contained the two pebbles, the hand tools and the white gravel pouch. The servant was a plump man so there was room for him to hide the brown bag inside the overalls, against his skin. From somewhere Kawa had found a grubby conical-shaped straw coolie hat. Gao put it on his head. "Ready," he said, trying to look confident. Inside him, enormous butterflies nested in his belly. As an afterthought he said, "Don't lock your room. I might need to disappear in a hurry."

Kawa led the way down the stairs, out of the block and across the compound to the administration area. Gao shuffled along behind him, bent over to hide the bulge of the brown bag and trying to look like a servile, subhuman Chinese moron. From somewhere, Kawa picked up a broom and handed it to Gao.

At the block containing his office, Kawa pointed Gao in the direction he needed to go and in poor Mandarin, shouted, "Get that mess cleared up. When I return I want to see it scrubbed clean!"

Gao shuffled down the side of the building towards the correct window. Where was the patrol? He slid into shadow. It wasn't long before two men nonchalantly walked by. Back under the light, Gao looked at his watch. 2335 hours. He had until five minutes after midnight before they were due round again. He hid the broom and coolie hat in the shadows then stepped out to begin his first attempt at burglary.

He ran his eyes around the window. It was a tight shut western style sash with the catch in the secure position. Five iron bars, about fifteen centimetres apart, ran vertically down the outside of the window. They had probably been fitted during construction. In those days there had not been much need for security. Each iron bar was held to the wood by a single screw at the top and bottom. Since then, many layers of paint had been applied, but not recently. The paint was chipped and cracked. He doubted that anything he did to them would be noticed, provided he could get inside the building and out again without being caught.

Screwdriver in hand, he estimated that two bars must be pushed sideways to allow him to squeeze through. Immediately he encountered a difficulty. The screw-heads were filled with old, hard paint. He couldn't turn the screw. It meant using up precious time removing the old paint. Never mind. He had all night. He checked his watch, only fifteen minutes before the patrol was due.

Luckily he had a small pocket knife. He used it to break down the paint. Another time-check. Ten minutes left. He attacked the other screw. Five minutes left. He stopped and stepped back into the shadows. On time, the patrol went by.

Using the driver, the first screw slowly began to turn. As soon as it was loose, it came out quickly and easily. He carefully put it into a pocket and started on the second screw. It began to move then suddenly made an awful screeching noise. Heart pounding, Gao stopped working and stepped back into the shadows, expecting the patrol to return and investigate the strange noise. They didn't.

He used the time trying to figure out a way to silence the screw. All he had was spit. He checked his watch. Ten minutes left. From his dry mouth, he mustered up as good a globule of spit as he could and spat it over the noisy screw. He returned to the shadows. At 0035 hours the patrol went past.

To his joy the screw moved easily and quietly this time. He got it out and carefully put it into his pocket. Now it was time to pull the bars to one side. He wanted them to move easily and noiselessly. They didn’t. The first began to screech as soon as he tried to shift it. The second bar simply refused to budge. No option but to loosen the top screws. By this time he was sweating profusely and getting more and more agitated.

The patrol passed. The time was now 0105 hours. He pulled himself up onto the window ledge and held on. Another problem. The brown bag hidden inside the overalls was in his way. He could hold on with both hands but was in danger of falling off the narrow window ledge if he let one hand go. He hooked his left arm around a bar and tried to use the screwdriver. It fell out of his hand and disappeared into the dark.

He dropped down to look for it, getting ever more frustrated. Under the overalls he felt sweat running down his back and from his armpits. Panic was setting in. He stepped back into the shadows to regain his composure. At the same time, his eyes searched the ground for the errant tool. There it was. Snatching it up, his anger wanted him to chuck it away into the darkness but he couldn’t do that, he could only stand and fume.

Time passed. Regaining his composure, he persevered until he got the bars to move. The catch was easily shifted with the help of the pocket knife. The window slid upwards sufficiently for him to squeeze through the bars and into the room. Wanting the bars to appear untouched unless *really* looked at, he jiggled them back to their original positions before he closed and secured the window.

He was now in a room used by the cleaners. He distinctly smelt old cigarette smoke. He slowly opened the door and peered out into a long corridor. All was still and quiet. As he left the room, he mentally noted what the door said in Chinese. "Gong-ju-jian" meaning "Tools Room".

Carrying a broom to look like a cleaner, and following Kawa's directions, he silently went up the stairs, along the right-hand corridor to room number ten. Exactly as Kawa had said it would be, the door was unlocked. He crept to Kawa's desk and opened the bottom left-hand drawer. Undoing the buttons on the overalls, he stuffed papers into the cloth bag until the drawer was empty. He closed the drawer, buttoned the overalls, picked up the broom and let himself out of the office.

Back to the Tools Room he stopped to catch his breath and settle his bumping heart. He needed a good swallow of rice alcohol. All he got was a whiff of disinfectant and cigarettes. He checked his watch. The Patrol was due. He waited, watching through the window. They came, and went. He was reaching up to slide the window catch to the open position when someone banged the door open and switched on the light. He nearly died of fright.

It was a wizened old woman dressed in almost identical clothes to him. She didn't seem the slightest bit surprised to see him there. She smiled, and said, "Having a quick smoke?" Obviously the room was a recognized Chinese hidey-hole. She picked up a canister of scouring powder and left.

He switched off the light and exited out of the window and squeezed himself between the bars. He then replaced and tightened up the screws. Before disappearing into the shadows, he checked the time. Almost 0300 hours. Dawn would be feeling anxious. He put on his coolie hat, picked up the broom, and made his way to the side wall and followed it to the junction with the inner rear wall. Dawn should be somewhere close on the other side.

Whilst waiting for the patrol to pass, he undid the overalls and freed the brown bag. It was now stuffed full with papers, pebbles, tools and the white gravel pouch. He needed the pouch and pulled it out.

When it was safe, he lobbed the gravel pouch high in the air, urging it to fly over the barbed-wire-topped-wall. A minute later a brief gravel shower hit the ground not more than a metre from where he was standing. Dawn was there.

He took a firm grip on the brown bag and threw it with all his strength. It sailed smoothly and silently out of sight. Moments later a second handful of gravel showered down. All was well.

He could visualize Dawn picking up the bag and quietly taking out the tools and pebbles. Placing the bag in the rickshaw, he would settle down and sleep. When sufficient people and vehicles were out and about, he would throw the pebbles and the tools into the river before taking the rickshaw, the bag and himself to the hotel.

Still carrying the broom, Gao shuffled himself around the complex until he was back at the block containing Kawa's living quarters. After quietly shuffling up the stairs and into Kawa's room, he collapsed onto a chair, exhausted.

Kawa shook Gao awake at 0600 hours and whispered, "Everything all right?"

Gao mumbled, "All gone."

Kawa passed Gao a pair of naval officer-issue trousers, white cap, white shirt, black tie, black socks and shoes. At the same time, he whispered, "My batman and servant will be here at 0630 hours. Put these on and come to breakfast."

Gao looked at him, wondering if he had heard right. Kawa whispered, "Don't worry, I will look after you."

They marched to the office of the Senior Duty Security Officer where a full breakfast was laid out. Kawa quietly explained, "I said that we have work to do and had breakfast for two set up here. It is a common occurrence."

In fact they didn't have anything to do except wait until 1900 hours when they would again go through the gate, this time *to* the beach. Kawa would return to the complex alone. At high tide, with Dawn's help, Gao planned to use the boat to get himself safely over the barbed wire and back across the river. Hopefully they would soon be on their way back to Chongqing. They were.

Gao's only concern was how to get Kawa's papers past the various checkpoints. Dawn dealt with that. He simply sat on the bag. During the journey he stayed with the innocent-looking rickshaw and reported that it, and he, never got a second glance.

Back in Chongqing, Gao handed over a scruffy brown bag stuffed with creased bits of paper to Andriev. With a grin Gao joked, "Believe it or not, these papers are important. Stalin wants them as soon as possible."

He never did find out if the contents of the brown bag helped Stalin make up his mind about Japan. On the 6th of August 1945, the Americans dropped the first atomic bomb on Hiroshima. Realizing that the Japanese were on the verge of surrender, Stalin took full advantage of the situation. He declared war on Japan and ordered his forces to attack.

By the end of hostilities, for minimal Russian casualties, Stalin had annexed a huge slice of eastern Asia, including a chunk of northern China.

The Nanking mission had been perfectly executed. Not as dangerous as Gao had first thought, but very scary. Without Kawa and Dawn, he could not have succeeded.

CHAPTER 8.

Magicman, 1945

1.

On the 30th of April 1945, Hitler committed suicide. A week later, the war in Europe was over. Everywhere there was happiness and celebration. Jin and Gao took Dawn and every employee of the garment factory, and their families, to Fa-fu's. Fa-fu and Jin supplied the food free and Gao treated everyone to as much wine, beer and other drinks as they wanted. It was truly joyous evening, something they had not had for many a year.

May is the wettest month of the year in Chongqing. The monsoon humidity dampens everything and there is a smell of dankness and mould. Although the air temperature is high, the people cook hot chili meals to combat conditions such as rheumatism and arthritis.

May mornings usually begin with a thick fog, making road travel dangerous but Gao felt safe sitting in the rickshaw being pulled by Dawn. He was a marvel at avoiding collisions, making Gao almost believe that Dawn could see through the murk. He safely delivered Gao to the Kai-xuan Hotel.

He was responding to an urgent summons by Zhao Ying. Leaving Dawn sat in his rickshaw keeping a watchful eye on every person and vehicle appearing from out of the fog or disappearing into it, Gao walked into the hotel.

Zhao Ying was waiting. With a "shush" sign she jerked her head upwards and pointed with her nose. Behind the closed door of her apartment she whispered, "There is someone waiting in the back room. He's a Feilibov recruit. Short, fat, balding and dressed in a navy blue Western style suit." She turned and fished out two pages of writing paper from under the mattress and passed them to Gao. "This is his written report."

He glanced down, then looked closely before asking, "Is this his handwriting?"

Zhao Ying nodded.

The report was written in the most beautiful Chinese language handwriting that Gao had ever seen. With no alterations, every character was perfectly formed using a dip-pen and black ink. Such writing takes many hours of concentration to produce.

The report was clear and concise and began by explaining that the writer was the Chief Engineer in Chiang Kai-shek's most important munitions factory. Because of his position, the writer knew what was being manufactured in the factory, in what quantities and where the finished products were bound.

It went on to explain that wherever munitions were sent, units of the army were there to receive them, therefore the size and number of shipments gave a good indication of how large the army was in that area. During recent weeks, huge amounts of munitions had been sent to the 18th Army Unit based in the Yan'an area. The shipments were a strong indication that the Kuomintang was building up the army around Yan'an in preparation for an attack against Mao's Communists. End of report.

Gao stopped reading and looked at Zhao Ying. She urgently whispered, "I'm worried. Recently this man has repeatedly requested a meeting with Bashan. His name is Zhang Chao with a codename Magicman. His information has always gone to Stalin, never Mao, so why this report? And why does he want to meet Bashan? On what authority? Bashan's identity is a closely guarded secret. Even I do not know who he is."

"That is for your own safety," Gao replied. "The less you know about Bashan, the safer you are. Can you confirm that this is Magicman's handwriting?"

"Yes. It is very distinctive and I've seen it before."

"Have you ever seen him?"

"No. This is the first time for him to come here," replied Zhao Ying. "His description fits, but him being here doesn't. Why would he court trouble by personally bringing this report to me? It would usually go through the pipeline to Andriev."

With a deep-thinking frown, Gao said, almost to himself, "Perhaps it is bait to get to Bashan… or the Chinese Communists. If what he says here is true, it is of great interest to Mao. Maybe he wants to make money by working for both sides. On the other hand the report could be false. If he is the real Magicman, and a traitor, can we easily get to him?"

"Yes."

"Is he married with children?"

"Yes."

"Then he must have a good reason to openly ask for a meeting with Bashan. This report is purely a Chinese Communist affair, nothing to do with Moscow. He should be trying to talk to someone in the Chinese Communist Party, not Bashan. And that brings up another question. From where did he hear the name, Bashan? How close is this Magicman to the Russians? Have you told Andriev that he is here asking about Bashan?"

"No, not yet. After reading his report I realized that it is a Chinese affair. That is why I asked for this urgent meeting with you. *We* are helping both Communist Parties, perhaps he wants to do the same thing. Or he already is, and he knows that we are also involved with the Chinese Communists."

Gao ticked items off on his fingers. "One, if Magicman is genuine, I need to know what he knows about Bashan and why he needs to speak to him. Two, if he isn't Magicman, everyone must be told that we have an impostor among us. Three, if he is Magicman, he might risk his own life but would he risk the lives of his family? Four, I agree that this sounds wrong. Should I follow it through to the end or send him away?... No, I can't do that, too dangerous. Five, under no circumstances can Bashan's identity be revealed. Six, is Magicman working for both Communist Parties or is this a trap set up by Moscow to catch *us* out?"

A decision had to be made, and Gao made it.

"Tell Magicman to go to the Green Bamboo Teahouse in Jie-kou Square tomorrow afternoon at two o'clock. Book a private room. Then get this report to Zhou En-lai and tell him where it came from. If the Chinese Communists know this Magicman, then this is their affair and nothing to do with us. If they don't, they must treat this report with suspicion and keep away from him."

"Shall I call Andriev and get him here?"

"Not yet," he replied. "Magicman might be doing what we're doing, working for both sides. If he is, we don't want to put him in danger. Let me speak to Magicman tomorrow, then we'll know more."

Zhao Ying went downstairs to pass on Gao's message to Magicman. Whilst they were talking, Gao quietly went down the stairs and out of the main entrance to Dawn. He was guzzling food and drink sent from the hotel kitchen.

Gao described Magicman to Dawn and told him to get Magicman as a passenger or follow him to his destination, then return to the hotel. If Magicman made several calls before going to his home or workplace, Dawn should remember the addresses of those stops.

Gao went to the hotel reception and picked up a telephone positioned where he could see the switchboard operator. He asked for an outside line. Making sure that the operator was not listening in, he telephoned Chopper and arranged to meet him for lunch.

Meanwhile, Zhao Ying had sent Magicman on his way. She had also sent a message down the pipeline to the Communists.

2.

Gao had randomly picked the restaurant and the two friends sat at a corner table where they could talk without being overheard. Chopper looked really smart. He explained that all officers attached to Chiang's personal guard had recently been issued with a complete set of new kit, including uniforms.

They chit-chatted for a while, simply enjoying their time together. They didn't drink any alcohol with their meal, just green tea, and it wasn't until they were on the last cup that Gao began to explain the reason for their meeting.

Chopper listened as Gao told him everything that had happened earlier in the day, before asking, "Do you want back-up?"

Good old Chopper.

"Perhaps yes. Perhaps no," Gao replied. "I don't know what I am walking into."

He told Chopper that he had already telephoned Serpent and had him standing by. He gave the number to Chopper and advised, "Serpent is expecting you to call and give him instructions, and I need you to be near your normal contact telephone from two o'clock tomorrow afternoon. Wait for a call from either Dawn or myself. If it is my voice advising that the goose is safely in the cage, all is well. But if a man calling himself "Red Sky" telephones, I need urgent help - and I mean *urgent.*

"If, by 1700 hours, you don't hear from Red Sky or myself, it means that neither of us can make a call. If that happens, contact Andriev and tell him everything about Magicman."

After lunch, Gao returned to the Kai-xuan Hotel where Dawn told him that Magicman had gone directly to a private house and stayed there. He gave Gao the address. In return Gao spent a couple of hours teaching Dawn how to use a telephone. To Gao's surprise, Dawn carried a superstitious belief that telephones could read thoughts. However, the instant that he recognized Gao's voice coming out of the earpiece, he was converted.

After teaching Dawn how to use a private telephone, Gao took him to a public telephone and showed him how that worked. When he fully understood, Gao gave him sufficient small change to make several calls from a call box and had him memorize Chopper's contact number.

They stayed the night in the hotel and left at first light. Dawn pulled Gao along the almost empty fog-shrouded roads to Jie-kou Square. Before the streets filled with people Gao had positioned Dawn near to a public telephone call box where he had a good view of the front entrance to the Green Bamboo Teahouse. When he was settled and Gao was sure that he understood his instructions, Gao returned to the hotel to collect Zhao Ying. By this time the fog had thinned to mist and it was raining hard. A normal monsoon day.

At one o'clock Zhao Ying and Gao began the return journey to Jie-kou Square, arriving twenty minutes later. Zhao Ying was on his arm as they casually walked around the square sheltering under a huge umbrella. At one-fifty, a man fitting Magicman's description arrived in a rickshaw and alighted outside the teahouse. Zhao Ying nodded her confirmation that it was the same man she had met at her hotel the previous morning. That was her job done. Gao summoned a rickshaw and sent her back to the hotel.

At two o'clock precisely, Gao walked into the teahouse. As usual it was filled with people enjoying their ritual afternoon of gossip, business meeting or reading. For over a thousand years the Chinese middle classes have frequented teahouses. They are the Chinese equivalent to a continental bar or a British pub, with one exception, no alcohol, just best quality green tea.

Gao was led upstairs to a private room. Sitting uneasily, was Magicman. He stood up. They shook hands and sat down. Gao ignored the tea and the dishes of nibbles laid out on the table and got straight to the point.

"My name is Chen-ye," he used the false name he had used when posing as a silk merchant with the false papers in his pocket. "I know your name is Zhang Chao and I also know your codename. Please tell me, how did Feilibov find you and bring you in?"

Gao could safely talk about Feilibov, who was now back in Moscow.

"I cannot tell you that," answered Magicman.

"I agree, so can you describe Feilibov to me?"

"I can."

And he did. Gao asked questions, Magicman gave the right answers exactly, leaving no doubt in Gao's mind that this man had known Feilibov.

Gao asked the most important question. "From whom did you hear the name, Bashan?"

"I cannot tell you that, either."

Gao was not satisfied with that answer, but had to accept it. It was true that Magicman should *not* be talking about Bashan. He should not even know the name!

They talked around in circles for about thirty minutes, each of them weighing up the other. There was no doubting Magicman's claim that he had been close to Feilibov. What Gao didn't know was that whilst they talked, men were on their way to the Kai-xuan Hotel to arrest Zhao Ying.

Magicman suddenly asked, "Are you Bashan?"

"No," Gao replied, looking directly at him. "I am not Bashan. I am only a messenger."

Disappointment showed in the man's eyes.

Gao continued, "I have been sent to ask why you want to meet him. Where is your authority? Why should you meet Bashan when others cannot?"

"Is Comrade Bashan refusing to meet me?"

"No. He is not refusing. He sends his regards to you with the message that he must be careful. You can tell me what you want to say to him. I have orders to pass on your words exactly as you give them to me."

Whilst Magicman and Gao were talking, down in the Square, Dawn was witnessing lots of men, easily identified by their almost identical western-style dress code, quietly surrounding the teahouse. Four to the back, four to each side, six outside the main entrance waiting to move in and the rest covering the three roads leading into the Square. He hurried to the call box.

To Gao, Magicman was explaining himself. "Since being recruited by Feilibov, I have always worked within the single-cell system with just one contact to pass on my information. However, I sometimes get important and urgent tip-offs. Usually, when that happens, by the time I manage to pass it on, it is too late to be of use. Do you understand so far?"

Gao nodded his agreement and sympathized, "It must be frustrating."

"That is why I want to speak to Bashan, to explain why it would be to his advantage to widen my scope to pass on the urgent stuff."

Gao nodded again.

Magicman continued, "The munitions business is very much like an international club. We all know each other, perhaps not face to face but through trade. War is our business but not all of us are in the war. Nor are we all on the same side. In the munitions club, business news travels quickly from country to country via allies to neutrals to enemies.

"With a wider report line, I could have passed on the information that Italy was about to surrender unconditionally many hours before the news broke internationally. Please tell Bashan that I am an old Communist Party member. I hate Feudalism, Fascism and Capitalism. For over twenty-five years I have worked for the Communist cause. Surely he can spare an hour to speak to me personally."

Gao nodded again. "I will pass on everything verbatim. It is too dangerous for meetings like this to last too long. If you don't mind, you leave now. I will settle the bill and follow in a few minutes."

They stood to shake hands. Magicman left whilst Gao remained standing. He was almost persuaded that Magicman was genuine, but not completely. The man hadn't explained why he had given Zhao Ying information for the Chinese Communists when he knew that she belonged to Moscow. Nor had he explained why he hadn't asked Andriev for a wider report line, or from where he had got the name, Bashan.

Gao went to the window to check on Dawn in time to see him running back to his position. He waved and pointed. Gao saw Magicman hurry out of the teahouse and approach two men. One of them said something, Magicman replied, then summoned a rickshaw. The two men ran towards the teahouse, waving at others to follow. Gao stood for just a few seconds more to see Dawn take off with his rickshaw, following Magicman. "Well done Dawn," he thought. "Whatever happens, you're safely out of it."

He ran from the room and down a back passage towards a window. He quickly checked that the window overlooked a rear passage and opened it to see men with pistols down below. He ducked back and, with nowhere else to go, ran into the toilet and locked himself in a cubicle. He needed time. How to get it?

Men noisily searching. They reached the toilet. It sounded as if a thousand men had entered, crushing themselves into the small space. Gao heard shouted instructions, men leaving, making room.

A thud on the cubicle door. "Come out. You cannot escape!"

"Can't a man shit in peace?" Gao shouted back.

"Cut it short and come out. NOW!"

"All right, I'm coming."

Gao counted to thirty, rustled paper, rubbed his hands up and down the silk of his gown to make it sound as if he was putting his clothes back to normal and pulled the flush. He counted again, this time to ten, slipped the bolt and opened the door.

Immediately pistols were shoved into his face and hands spun him around a hundred-and-eighty degrees. His arms were put behind his back and he was handcuffed.

"Why are you doing this?" Gao shouted. "Is shitting now against the law?"

He was turned to face a man holding up an identity card.

"CIS. You are under arrest."

"What charge?"

"Pretending not to know eh?"

"What charge?" he repeated, and got a punch in the face. Blood ran from his nose into his mouth. He sprayed a mouthful over as wide an arc as possible. Accompanied by curses, a rain of punches began to land everywhere on his upper body and head. At last they stopped. Gao raised his head and sprayed again. An arm swung, smashing a revolver-butt down onto his head. Close to unconsciousness, he fell to the floor. Had he made enough time? He needed time.

He was half carried, half dragged. He didn't resist, he simply made himself as heavy as he could, making it difficult for his captors to get him down the narrow stairs and out into the street. An American-made jeep with Kuomintang Army markings was waiting. He saw two Kuomintang officers. One was Chopper. He was standing beside the Jeep accompanied by Serpent. Both men wore white gloves and each was holding a revolver. A third military man, unknown to Gao, was standing in the jeep where the back seat used to be. He had the butt of a mounted machine gun tucked into his shoulder.

The men holding Gao stopped in their tracks, puzzlement showing on their faces. Chopper waved them away. "Leave this man here with me," he ordered.

A CIS man stepped forward. "And you are…?"

"I repeat," said Chopper with military menace. "Leave this man here."

"We are from the CIS and he is our prisoner. We have orders to arrest him."

"And I have orders that take precedence over yours. This case is outside your jurisdiction and I have been sent from Garrison Headquarters. Hand him over."

Serpent moved forward and took Gao's arm.

Chopper continued, "Ask your Commander when you get back to base."

To Gao, he stiffened to attention, transferred the revolver to his left hand and threw a very fine Kuomintang salute, and with the deepest of respect obvious in his voice, said, "Your Highness Commissioner, I was ordered to see you safely home."

If Gao's head hadn't been hurting, and his split lip and nose were not bleeding so much, he might have burst out laughing. It was almost the same trick that they had played on the officer when they had saved Little Dove. It had helped them get the girl out of trouble, would it work this time?

Gao had to admit that using the term "Highness Commissioner" was a good touch, very good indeed. Like many of the old Chinese Emperors, Chiang Kai-shek was known to send out trusted High Commissioners on covert investigations. They were usually members of high-ranking elite families, and their civil authority was absolute except in the presence of the Generalissimo.

The CIS immediately stopped holding Gao and stood back, fear and shock clearly showing on their faces. For a few seconds no one moved. Breath was locked in lungs and voice-boxes were immobilized. Gao broke the spell by giving a snort of contempt.

"Bungling idiots!" he snarled. "Get me out of these handcuffs!"

Someone quickly obeyed. Gao moved forward with Chopper on one side of him and Serpent on the other. They climbed into the jeep. Chopper fired the engine and they sped away.

Actually nobody had checked Gao's papers nor made a positive identification. He was dressed in his best silk finery last used when he had posed as a silk merchant, so he could have been anyone, even an important someone. Chopper's use of the title Highness Commissioner was quite believable. Only an important personage would have a jeep with a machine gunner and two officers waving revolvers come to his rescue.

Chopper drove across town, into the ferry dock and stopped. He introduced the gunner. He was a soldier, but not in the Kuomintang army.

He belonged to the Communists. After their meeting, Chopper had risked exposure to get him sent by Zhou En-lai.

"I needed a gunner. Where else could I get one?" said Chopper.

Gao thanked the men for saving him from probably a very nasty death. They simply shrugged their shoulders and said, "Not worth mentioning." Gao got the same response from the grinning gunner. He was busy in the bottom of the jeep changing into civilian clothes. He jumped out of the jeep, made a small "be seeing you" gesture and went off.

Gao, Chopper and Serpent couldn't be so casual. Gao said to the other two, "We have to think about our next move. All three of us have been compromised."

"I had no choice," said Chopper. "You were in trouble. Your man Red Sky was good. He stressed urgency and I only had the jeep. Serpent and the gunner were standing by outside the camp and we had to move fast. I broke every traffic law to get to you. Only police and army vehicles can be driven like that."

Serpent asked, "What do we do now?"

"Well," said Gao, peering into the rear view mirror. Whilst most of the blood on his face had dried, his split lip and badly cut nose were still bleeding and his clothes were a mess. He gingerly felt the wound on his head where he had been clubbed. His fingers came away bloodstained. "I cannot move around the city looking like this. I need to go into hiding. Luckily I can return to Dragon Gate Town."

After further discussion they came to the conclusion that there was nothing for it but for Chopper and Serpent to return to their jobs. "No names were given and nothing was said that gave a clue to our military placements," said Serpent. "Perhaps we can get away with it if we keep our heads down." That brought them to their last item of business.

Chopper asked, "What about the traitor?"

Gao made a small shoulder shrug, anything more was too painful. His whole body ached and breathing was difficult.

"Leave him to me," he said. "I don't want to put you in any more danger. As soon as I can, I will contact Andriev and tell him that he has a traitor in his organization. If the Soviets or the Chinese Communists don't deal with him, I will."

So that was it, meeting over. They shook hands and split up. Serpent hailed a rickshaw to return to his unit. Chopper and Gao waited until he was safely away, then Chopper drove off in the jeep. Gao spotted a tap protruding from a toilet wall. It was used by the cleaners. The water came straight out of the river so it was dangerous to drink. He just splashed most of the blood off. Nonetheless, he still looked as if he had been run over by a horse and cart.

It was getting dark, made darker by the monsoon clouds. It began to rain again. Gao took the ferry, keeping to the shadows. There were few passengers. He did not attract any particular attention.

Jin was still in the garment factory. He took one look at Gao and moved forward to catch him in his arms. He was surprisingly strong for his size. He slowly got Gao up the stairs and onto the bed. Gao was grateful to him for not asking questions. Jin's only comment before he turned out the light was, "Getting falling-down-drunk is one thing. This is ridiculous!"

3.

Back in Chongqing big events happened whilst Gao was out of circulation. Serpent returned to his job and was never at any time suspected of wrongdoing. Chopper was not so lucky. An alert CIS man involved in the incident outside the Green Bamboo Teahouse noted the military number of the jeep. All Kuomintang military vehicles had an identification number stencilled onto the side of the engine cowling. When it became obvious that Gao's so-called title of High Commissioner was a trick to help him escape, the CIS asked Military Ordnance to trace where the jeep was based.

When they had it pinpointed, the CIS dispatched a company of soldiers to the Headquarters of Chiang's personal guard to check it out. With the soldiers were two of the CIS men who had stood close to Chopper. He was easily identified, but being quicker witted than they, he ran to the same jeep and took off. On a mountain road Chopper was forced to stop. To avoid being caught and tortured into betraying Serpent and Gao, he put a bullet into his own brain.

Gao later learned the fate of Zhao Ying. Magicman, after leaving the Square, went straight to where Zhao Ying was being held. He wanted to conduct her interrogation personally. She had been chained naked to a wall in an "X" position and expert torturers were standing by.

For many hours she withstood the most horrendous suffering. Her only words were a constant stream of abuse at Magicman for his traitorous activities. Finally, no longer able to stand her insults and his loss of face, Magicman shoved the barrel of his revolver into her mouth and shot her dead. Her final words had been to curse Magicman straight to hell. She was a true Comrade and a wonderful person.

*

Dawn had an altogether different adventure. For many days he followed Magicman. Where Magicman went, Dawn and his rickshaw also went. Dawn heard of Gao's arrest and thought that he had been killed. He then heard the details of Zhao Ying's death. Such events cannot be kept secret for long. As far as Dawn was concerned, Magicman had been responsible for the deaths of the two people he most liked in the whole world. Only his sister was more important to him. He wanted revenge.

Nobody ever notices a rickshaw puller. They are just a means of getting from one place to another quickly and cheaply. Whenever Magicman hailed Dawn, as he did many times, he never realized that this particular rickshaw was always nearby, waiting to be called.

Dawn, on the other hand, knew the identity of his passenger and was constantly on the lookout for an opportunity to do Magicman a damage. He had the vague outline of a plan, and because it meant sacrificing his precious rickshaw, he took off the small license plate issued by the local taxation department. It showed a number that could be traced back to him.

His chance came one wet and windy day. Chongqing is a mountain city with steep hills and slippery road surfaces. Magicman climbed into Dawn's rickshaw and ordered him to an address uphill. On the way up a particularly steep slope, Dawn saw a big truck coming down at speed. Instead of pulling over to the side to avoid the truck, Dawn swung his rickshaw sideways into the path of the lorry and watched it disappear under the wheels.

Magicman's big belly was squashed flat. Dawn, jumping up and down with delight, watched the legs thrash and the mouth screech in pain for many minutes before death arrived. Laughing like an idiot, he ran across the city to his home.

*

For two weeks Gao barely moved. Three broken ribs were no joke. To everyone, including the doctor sent by Fa-fu, he had been beaten up and robbed. As soon as he could, he ventured out to telephone Andriev. Speaking Russian, he told him his version of events. Andriev said that Magicman had disappeared. Then he told Gao about the deaths of Zhao Ying and Chopper. Gao was devastated. He had loved his dear friend Chopper in a way that only men who have experienced such a fine friendship can understand. And although he had never been *in* love with Zhao Ying, he had grown to love her very much.

He asked Andriev to send at least three thousand yuan to Chopper's family. Chopper had received very little personal pay from the Soviets. The least they could do was make sure that his wife and son had money.

Two days later Gao telephoned Andriev again to check if he had sent the money. He hadn't. Moscow had refused permission. Without their agreement he dared not send government money. He planned to send five hundred yuan out of his own pocket. Gao was upset with those cold so-and-sos in Moscow, but knew that it wasn't Andriev's fault. He asked Andriev to add five hundred more from him. He would repay Andriev when next they met. Andriev agreed.

Gao returned to his bed, wishing the world would go away and leave him alone. Of the four who had left spy school with high hopes and honest intentions, only he was left. Hunter had died in Xing Jiang during the autumn of 1944, then Sparks and now Chopper.

Depression set in and it was just after this time that his hair began to turn white. For several weeks he moped, until, quite suddenly, his life changed completely.

Gao awoke to a noise and there was Dawn standing beside his bed with a huge grin on his face. His joy was *huge*! Never ever would he be as pleased to see someone as he was on that morning. Dawn was the medicine he needed to begin living again.

Dawn told him everything he knew about the bravery of Zhao Ying and how she had died. He followed up that story with his part in the death of Magicman. After running home, he and his sister had a difficult time. Without his rickshaw he had no livelihood. He found work on a building site carrying bricks up and down ladders all day for small pay, all the while yearning for a chance to return to rickshaw pulling. When he wasn't working he naturally gravitated to the dock area where his old rickshaw pals gathered to smoke and chat whilst waiting for customers to come off the ferry.

One day, one of the pullers told a strange story. A jeep had pulled up with three soldiers and a civilian in it. One of the soldiers changed clothes then hailed the puller to take him to the Communist compound. When he returned from that job, only the civilian was left. It was getting dark when the puller saw the man slowly walk up the gangway onto the ferry but not go inside. He stayed out in the rain.

"Y'meet some funny people in this job," he said, finishing his story.

Dawn asked the storyteller what the man looked like.

"The description he gave sounded just like you," grinned Dawn, "so I thought I would come to Dragon Gate Town and check. And here we are."

A few days later Gao was in the office working alongside Fa-fu and a lawyer. They were breaking down the small print of a contract to find out how they might be cheated. The telephone rang. It was Andriev. Please meet him on the ferry later that evening. Gao did. Andriev broke the news that Gao's time in the Chongqing area was at an end. Bashan had successfully completed his tasks and come out alive. It was time to move on.

He had two weeks to wrap up his affairs in Dragon Gate Town. Shanghai, still under Japanese control, was to be his next home. His new job brought him a chance to use his languages and a change of career - Managing Director of the Dagong Bao (Big Public) newspaper. He had always thought it to be an independent organ well known for printing the truth. To his surprise he learned that it was Soviet controlled. Gao's job was to ensure that whenever possible the newspaper covertly presented communism in a good light.

The day after that he received a surprise visit from Little Dove and Clever. They arrived by a private sedan chair carried by eight strong men and were accompanied by six girl servants. They brought with them a letter from Little Dove's father. It was an invitation to his birthday celebration feast at the Yun house five days hence.

The two very different but equally attractive girls, dressed in expensive silks, were a surprise to Jin. He had no idea that Gao was so well connected, but it didn't stop him trying to sell a few choice items of his best stock. Female clothes were his speciality. He soon had the two giggling girls trying on various styles. After an enchanting visit, a happy Jin waved the young ladies away to the ferry. Little Dove and Clever had Gao's promise to attend the feast and stay for a few days.

Gao told Dawn about his imminent move to Shanghai and gave him a choice. He could accompany Gao and take his chances in a new city, or Gao would buy him a rickshaw and he could stay in Chongqing.

Gao knew it was a big decision for Dawn to make, so he left him to think about it. Two days later, Dawn surprised Gao by announcing that he wanted to travel to Yan'an and join the Communists.

The next day, Gao gave him as much money as he would accept and they said goodbye. Brave Dawn died during the battle for Nanking. At the end of the civil war, Dawn was honoured by Mao Zedong and given the highest Chinese Communist posthumous award of "Revolutionary Martyr". For a long time Gao sent money to Dawn's sister until, one day, she peacefully died in her sleep.

Jin Ze-ren just shrugged his shoulders. He knew Gao's situation, and in some ways he was glad to see Gao go. To him, Gao's presence in his factory had always meant danger.

"Come the revolution." he said in his clipped way of speaking. "We'll meet again." They didn't.

Fa-fu was tearful, making Gao weep. He hated leaving the big, generous, extraordinary man. They promised to keep in touch, and they did. When, in 1949, Chongqing was "liberated" by the Communists, Fa-fu was accused of being "A Residue of the Old Society" and executed.

*

Gao decided that he would spend his last days in Chongqing at the Yun house. Fa-fu held a farewell banquet in his honour to which many of the people he had met during his time in Dragon Gate Town attended. His last act was to tell Andriev where to find the transceiver and spy stuff. Andriev promised to have it moved. Then he was away, leaving part of his heart behind. Never had he been happier in any other place.

The Yun family welcomed him with open arms. His first unpleasant duty was to report the death of Chopper. He simply said that he had died bravely defending his beliefs, without explaining further. The news brought tears from Little Dove.

After dinner that evening, the day before the feast, they were sitting in the living room drinking tea when Little Dove's mother asked him his age.

"I am twenty-eight," Gao replied.

"That is perfect," she enthused, clapping her hands. "Little Dove is twenty-four. You two are a perfect match."

He looked at Little Dove. Wordless for once, she sat at his feet, a vision of loveliness, blushing profusely behind her hands. He was surprised at the suggestion. Though he loved Little Dove with all of his being, his work had stopped him from thinking of marriage.

She looked up. Their eyes met and he saw her happiness. Impulsively, in full view of the family, he reached out to hold her hand. No more was needed. He was now an official prospective bridegroom.

Master Yun nodded to his wife. She rose and left the room, to return a few minutes later with a small, beautifully carved wooden box. She knelt and opened it to reveal a pair of matching solid gold neck-chains and two wedding rings. With solemn ceremony she selected a neck-chain and placed it over the head of her daughter, saying, "These chains and rings were once used to marry my mother and my father. Theirs was an arranged marriage, but no two people were ever more in love."

She placed the other chain over Gao's head. Then came the rings. "This is your official engagement," she said. "May you be as happy and as fruitful as my parents."

Everything so far had come as a complete but wonderful surprise to Gao, but not to the family. Master Yun explained, "Little Dove decided a long time ago that she wanted to be your wife. She has often discussed it with us and we agreed that if you wanted her, there would not be any objections. We thought to wait until after the war, but now that you are off to Shanghai, this seems to be the appropriate moment. She wants to go with you and because we want her happiness above all else, we agree. Now it is done."

Gao stood up and gave deep bows of respect and gratitude to his prospective in-laws. Then he bowed to each member of the family in turn until he came to Little Dove. He dropped to his knees and kowtowed three times with his head touching the floor just in front of her tiny feet. He then kneeled upright and took her tiny hands in his.

"Dearest Little Dove," emotion made his voice waver, "how strange life is. Who could have guessed that when Chopper and I saved you from that officer, it would lead to this day? Now it is I who must show gratitude to you for making me the happiest of men and giving me a future. I promise you my heart, my fidelity and my life-long love."

*

Master Yun was unable to arrange a marriage for them before their departure. Chonqing's unwritten rules of good behaviour demanded a gap of three months between betrothal and wedding. Little Dove's mother did not want their happiness to be spoiled by spiteful gossip, so they agreed to marry in Shanghai. Mother Wu, Little Dove's faithful personal maid, insisted that she must go to Shanghai too. Mister Yun and Gao agreed.

Gao and Little Dove stood at the rail of the passenger ship. She linked arms and dropped her head onto his shoulder. He felt wonderful. The ship blew a long throaty whistle and slowly left the dock. With their free arms they waved farewell to the Yun family gathered on the dockside. Clever was not the only one crying. So too were Little Dove and her mother.

And Gao. Perhaps he could at last live a *normal* life.

CHAPTER 9.

The Military Map, September 1945

1.

About six weeks after the Japanese surrender, Gao was standing on the corner of a Shanghai intersection looking at the sad ruins of war. Every building had sustained damage and many had been completely demolished. Piles of debris lined every road and there wasn't a street lamp that worked. Wires and cables lay everywhere on the streets or hanging loose above people's heads. Except in the city centre and the sections of the city that had housed the Japanese Headquarters and barracks, there was no electricity, gas or running water. The people were forced to get water from the old wells or the river. Disease was rife.

Gao's two journalists, Ge Low, and Yi Fan, stood behind him. They sighed deeply. So did he. It was a sad sight. Beautiful Shanghai had been deeply hurt by the war.

As Managing Director of the Dagong Bao newspaper, Gao had wasted no time after the surrender in having the newspaper call on the Chinese people to provide evidence of Japanese atrocities. There were tales aplenty. For the last six weeks he had used the front page to graphically describe mass-murder in gory detail.

On the inside pages, he and his staff had exposed those Chinese who had collaborated with the Japanese or had behaved badly towards their own people. The readers were encouraged to tell the newspaper everything they knew about profiteers, bullies, gangsters and collaborators. These two major editorial campaigns made Dagong Bao a popular read.

He turned to look at an abandoned truck parked outside the old Japanese Imperial Army Headquarters. A red-sun flag, the hated symbol of Japanese occupation, still hung inside the cab and could clearly be seen through the dusty windscreen. He strode over, opened the offside door of the truck and angrily yanked the evil thing out. He handed it to Low. Low held it out whilst Fan lit a corner of the flag with his cigarette lighter. When the flag was almost burned, Low let it fall to the ground. Fan stamped on it. Japan was the most hated nation at that time, and although the Chinese were desperate for revenge, they doubted that they would ever get it. Their only satisfaction was the two atom bombs dropped by the Allies.

Gao spotted his Editor, Ah Fong, running towards him.

"Director Gao," he panted, "we have found the Japanese gold store!"

"Gold store?" Gao asked. This was of great interest. "Where?"

Ah Fong gabbled out his news. "Near to here, in the crypt of the old church attached to Saint John's University. There is no gold there now, only crate-loads of Nationalist bank notes, and guess what? I think I saw the green safe that disappeared from our old offices."

"Are you sure it's the same one?" Gao asked.

Fong nodded vigorously, "I haven't had a chance to check it properly but it looks very much like it."

Gao and his men hurried the two hundred metres or so to the once beautiful, but now so shabby gardens of the university. The seat of learning, founded by an early British Missionary, had survived the war in reasonably good condition.

Fong led them into the church. A generator had been set up to provide lights to guide them down into the crypt. Two Nationalist Army soldiers barred their way. Gao flashed his go-anywhere pass issued by the newly established Shanghai Interim Nationalist Government that gave him unhindered access to all parts of the city. One soldier saluted and stood to one side.

"How the hell did it get down here?" Gao asked nobody in particular as he reached out and ran his fingers down a line of rivets. All of them took a long look at it to make absolutely sure that it was indeed the right safe.

Fong ran his hand over the lid and said, "The same decoration. Randomly placed little iron stars painted silver surrounding one unpainted iron daisy flower. This safe belongs to our accountant, Su Ke, no question about it."

This young man was all right. He was helpful, honest and thorough. He continued to check the safe. "It looks more like a travelling trunk than a safe. That's strange, I can't find a keyhole or anything that resembles a lock. How do we get into it?"

"Let me help," Gao said with an amused smile. "I had Su Ke show me how to open it the first day he brought it into the office."

He moved forward and pointed, "Look at the decorations on the lid. There are one hundred stars hiding a secret. Can you see it?"

Blank stares all round. He pointed again. "One, two, three, four, five, six, seven special stars. *Now* what do you see?"

"Ahhh!" exclaimed Fong. "Now I see it. The Great Bear in the night sky."

Fan saw it too and cried out in astonishment, "I have looked at that lid many times without ever seeing it. Now I do, as plain as day, but how does it help us?"

Gao pressed the seven stars in the correct order from bottom to top then slid the metal daisy to the right. There was a click and the heavy metal lid jumped free of the locking mechanism. He opened the lid and looked inside.

Totally astonished, he exclaimed, "The trunk belongs to Su Ke but not the contents!" He lifted out a handful of tableware. "Gold knives, forks, spoons and," he pointed at other items, "silver salvers and sauce boats, gold candlesticks. This is no longer a safe, it's a treasure chest."

He replaced the tableware and lifted out a cloth bundle. Placing it on the floor, he carefully pulled back the folds to reveal at least fifty gold watches of all sizes and types and dozens of gold watch-chains.

Fan growled through clenched teeth, "Those Japanese bastards. This was their so-called surrender, taking stolen treasure back to their own scabby country. It looks like this lot was supposed to go too, but for some reason they left it here."

*

Watched by the guards, the four men slowly and carefully emptied the safe. As each item emerged, a description of it was written down on a notepad. Two hours later the floor area around the safe was covered with treasure.

Beside the safe they had a stack of paper-filled files that had been packed around the inside walls and along the bottom of it. Presumably to protect the contents.

The files proved to be a different kind of treasure. Gao picked one at random. The first page was stamped "TOP SECRET', written in Japanese, and issued by Japanese Army Intelligence from someone named Yamada, instructing someone else known as OWL, to ease himself back into Chinese society as a reserve force for future use. When circumstances allowed, Owl must contact Tokyo. It didn't say how contact was to be made, but Gao guessed that it must be by radio.

The last line read, "...all the important targets are marked on the attached military map of Shanghai. Also marked are the places where caches of weapons, ammunition and bomb-making equipment are hidden."

Luckily Gao was the only one among the group able to read Japanese. Tucking the file under his arm, he had the rest moved to a dark corner, out of the way. Nobody thought them important enough to be added to the list and Gao didn't suggest otherwise. He turned to the guards and instructed them to send a message to Army Headquarters requesting a senior officer be sent to take charge of the treasure.

He continued, "Both of you will sign to confirm that everything we pulled out of the safe has been recorded on this list. My two colleagues and I will also sign it. When we leave here, I will take the list and hand it over to the civil government. That way, everyone will be sure that nobody acted improperly."

The guards smiled and nodded. Gao could sense their relief. If anything went missing, no one could point the finger of blame at them. He shut the lid of the safe with a bang and told the guards to make sure that when the officer arrived, he left the safe where it was.

"It belongs to our accountant," Gao explained, walking towards the exit.

"Director Gao," Fong's voice stopped him. "The safe is a most unusual thing. I bet there isn't another like it in all of China. Did Su Ke tell you anything more about it?"

Gao smiled and replied, "Well, yes he did. Wait, I'll open it again."

Everyone watched as he pressed the stars and slid the daisy to the right. The lid sprang open. He fully raised it and pulled away part of the felt lining on the inside of the lid. Pointing, he said, "Look here. English letters that sound like Jay, Ess and Dee. The initials of the first owner."

He stood back to let everyone see. Even the guards took a look. When all of them were looking at him again, he told them that the travelling trunk, for that is what it was, had been especially made for a rich Scottish businessman named John Sinclair-Dunbar.

In the mid-nineteenth century, before his intended trip to China, Mister Dunbar commissioned an expert blacksmith and the best Edinburgh locksmith to make it for him. When he returned to Scotland he left the trunk behind. For almost a hundred years it had changed hands until Su Ke brought it to the newspaper offices.

As they walked away, Fong remarked, "It is a truly wonderful piece of engineering but I think an ordinary safe is more convenient." He was right. Gao had thought the same thing when he had first laid eyes on Su Ke and the trunk.

*

About two weeks before the official Japanese surrender, Su Ke had turned up at the newspaper offices. A high official in the newly established Interim City Government had sent him with a letter saying that Su Ke was a first class accountant, and so he proved to be. When he had brought in his "safe", requesting permission to keep it near to his desk, Gao had asked where he had got such a thing. "Spoils of war" was Su Ke's reply. By the time he had explained its history and how it opened, Gao had agreed.

At that time, the newspaper offices had been located in the northern suburbs. On the day the Japanese surrender was announced to the world, Gao left Su Ke in charge of the office. He, his Editor and two journalists had been invited to interview a Chinese Army General and some politicians about how the forthcoming takeover of the city would go.

It took them most of the day. When they returned to the northern suburbs, they found only a ruin where their offices used to be. People living nearby said that a company of Japanese army looters had descended on the district and not long after they had departed, a huge explosion had destroyed the offices. Strangely, in or out of the ruins, there was no sign of Su Ke or his green safe. Both had disappeared without trace.

As they walked out of the crypt, Fan was saying, "These are strange times. No sign of our accountant yet his safe turns up full of treasure. And even stranger, not the slightest bit damaged…'

The boys went on talking, creating possible scenarios. Gao had stopped listening. His mind was on the files.

2.

The next morning Gao received a telephone call from his old comrade Feilibov. To his surprise Feilibov was in Shanghai. "Come to lunch," he said to Gao. "I have things to discuss with you."

"And I have something to show you," responded Gao, pulling the

Japanese file from his desk drawer.

Feilibov continued, "I am at the Russian Embassy. Do you know the British-made iron bridge that crosses the mouth of Suzhou Creek as it meets the Wampoo River?"

"Yes, I've crossed it many times."

"The Soviet Embassy has just opened for business. We are in the building directly across the road from the main entrance of the old Astor Hotel. My office window overlooks the river. I don't mind the stink made by the people living on the thousands of sampans. I can look at the docks and ships coming and going. A wonderful sight. See you at noon."

At eleven-thirty Gao left his office and walked down the Bund, that very beautiful thoroughfare running from south to north beside the river on his right, with the sturdy British-built Victorian buildings across the road on his left. All the buildings were damaged but still standing. At noon exactly, he was shaking hands with Feilibov.

Gao noted Feilibov's silent surprise at the change in his appearance since their last meeting. His white hair and the lines on his scarred face belied his age of not yet twenty-nine. Only his youthful body stopped him from being mistaken for a man of sixty.

Feilibov opened up the conversation. "So how are things with you?"

"Very well," Gao replied. "I feel more at ease here. All over the world the dust of war is settling and everywhere there is peace. I will hate it when the civil war between Chiang Kai-shek and Mao Zedong starts again. Sadly, we Chinese have to face that one last conflict before absolute peace comes to China."

"How do you think the civil war will go?"

"Hard to say," replied Gao. "It depends upon the Soviets and the Americans. If the Soviets send an army to support the Communists, the Americans will fight alongside the Kuomintang, making it a very long war. Fortunately, neither the Soviets nor the Americans are looking for a fight. The Americans are already shipping troops and equipment back to the USA. My guess is that the world will leave the Chinese to sort out their own affairs and the Communists will win... maybe."

"And how is the newspaper?"

"Very good. Circulation continues to increase and advertising revenues are picking up."

Feilibov stayed silent for a while, before asking, "What about the Japanese?"

"Aaahh! That is an altogether different question. They are slowly trailing their way back to their own country. The Soviets and the Chinese hate the Japanese in equal measure. That is why the two governments have agreed to send important Japanese prisoners and their Chinese collaborators to the Siberian gulags. Why keep them in comfort when their lives can be made as unpleasant as possible? The Last Emperor Pu Yi is currently in Siberia.

"China and Russia are also interacting on Japanese espionage cases and I have been given permission by the Shanghai Interim Government to follow up any case that seems suspicious. As a newspaper Managing Director I can nose around with impunity, that is why I can openly visit you here. However, there is always the chance of a hidden enemy, and..." Gao pulled out the Japanese file from his briefcase and handed it to Feilibov, "here is one. Codenamed Owl."

"Strangely, Colonel Bashan," said Feilibov, "that is exactly the subject I wanted to talk to you about." He smiled his old mocking smile and said in his best sardonic manner, "Congratulations. For once in your life you are ahead of me."

When Feilibov had finished reading, Gao told him about the other files stacked in a corner of the crypt.

"This looks like a Chinese matter that need not concern Moscow." Gao said. "I have to report it because I shall be working with the Kuomintang Intelligence Services and perhaps the Chinese Communists too. If the Owl file is anything to go by, the Yamada files will be more useful to us here in Shanghai than our people in Moscow. I would like permission to keep them for as long as we need them."

Feilibov nodded his understanding and left the room to contact Moscow. The answer gave Feilibov and Gao clearance to take any action needed to gather vital information that would help the prosecution council at the planned war crimes hearings. If the Yamada files helped capture war criminals, they could keep them in Shanghai. Moscow would be satisfied with transcripts of items of interest.

After lunch, Feilibov told Gao that there was someone in the embassy he should meet. They entered a secure room where a man in his mid-forties sat at a table. He rose as they entered. Andriev was also there.

Feilibov explained, "I had Andriev bring this talented man here especially to meet you, Newspaper Director Gao. It gives me great pleasure to introduce you to Mister Yang, well-known Shanghai photographer. He has something to show you."

Yang opened his briefcase and pulled out a file containing a dozen enlarged black and white photographs. He spread them out over the table and invited Gao to look. Each photograph showed images of small groups of high-ranking Japanese Officers.

"The ex-masters of Shanghai," said Yang. "These are the men who ordered the deaths of over a million innocent Shanghai men, women and children. You can use them for your newspaper."

The photographs showed men at leisure with, apparently, not a care in the world. Some drinking, some playing games and others standing in small groups, chatting. All were in uniform. Gao picked up a photograph. "I don't know *this* face," he said, pointing to one man playing table tennis, "but *that* man," he pointed at his opponent, frozen in time, standing side-on to the camera, "seems familiar to me. Why would my memory tell me that he is Chinese not Japanese?" He looked up and raised his eyebrows questioningly.

Yang momentarily hesitated before pointing to the man Gao didn't know.

"This man is Yamada, the evil genius behind Japanese Military Intelligence. His ping-pong opponent is China's greatest traitor, Pu Li, cousin of the Last Emperor, Pu Yi. It seemed to me that Pu Li was much trusted by the Japanese."

"If that is Pu Li, why is he dressed in a Japanese army uniform?"

"My guess is that he wanted to please his masters," said Feilibov.

Yang answered honestly. "You're right. They often ordered me to attend their gatherings to take photographs. I hated doing it but was too frightened to refuse. During those times, I too was made to wear a Japanese officer uniform. It made them feel more at ease."

After more talk, Yang shook hands and left, leaving the photographs on the table.

Gao stood by a window looking out, but not seeing, still thinking of the table tennis players in the photograph. Yamada, as head of Japanese Intelligence in Shanghai had been the writer of the letter to Owl. Now he knew what *he* looked like. Who was the other man? Gao was sure that he knew him, but not with the name of Pu Li.

Click! A light switched on in his head and illuminated the face of Su Ke, the missing accountant! Could he also be the traitor Pu Li? He stared at the photograph. There was no doubting the possibility.

A guard let Fong into the room. He turned to Feilibov and asked permission to talk to Gao. Feilibov nodded.

Fong was overflowing with youthful excitement. "Director Gao, I bring you astounding news. Our accountant, Su Ke, has turned up in a military hospital badly wounded and suffering from memory loss. When found, Su Ke was filthy and wrapped in rags. *What* a coincidence. First the safe, and now the owner."

*

Feilibov, Fong and Gao discussed how best to deal with the situation.

"Best to see him in hospital where he is most vulnerable to pressure," said Feilibov.

Gao agreed, with a comment that they must go as soon as possible. That is why Gao and Fong were at the hospital that very evening. They learned that Su Ke had been in hospital for some time recovering from amnesia and badly infected gunshot wounds. They spotted him raised up on pillows at the far end of the ward. Su Ke heard their steps and turned his head.

He looked surprised, then pleased, croaking, "Director Gao, I am so happy to see you." His little eyes in his round face began to fill with tears. "I thought I was going to die without you knowing what had happened to me."

He *seemed* to be sincerely pleased to see his boss. So much so, soldiers in other beds sighed their sympathy with him, but Gao wasn't moved. His mind's eye was looking at the photographic image of a man playing table tennis.

Su Ke had changed dramatically since the day of his disappearance. He had lost a lot of weight and weeks of black beard covered the bottom half of his face. The skin of his upper face, which Gao remembered as tanned by the hot summer sun, was now almost ivory white. One thing hadn't changed, his distinctive speaking voice.

"...that day, after lunch, a group of Japanese looters burst into the office. I sat absolutely still, hoping they would take what they wanted and leave, but they didn't. One raised his rifle, butt-end towards me and..." he raised his hand to his head, "the next thing I remember was lying naked on cold concrete in a pitch-dark room. I later learned that it was a cellar below a building."

Fong held a tin cup and helped Su Ke to sip a little water. "During the next several days I was kicked and beaten with rifle-butts so many times I just wanted to die. Suddenly I was taken up some stairs to a room where I saw my safe."

More sips of water.

"An officer ordered me to open the safe, otherwise I would be tortured. Oh, Director Gao! I am not a brave man. I couldn't face torture just to protect the money and the other contents, so I showed them. After that, with other unfortunates, I spent long, long days chained to a wall in the cellar and kept alive by small amounts of rice and water."

More sips and a rest.

"One day the Japanese came and packed all of us prisoners into a truck. On the road to…I don't know where, I managed to drop off the back. The guards shot at me."

He pulled back the sheets to point at wounds in his groin and the fleshy part of his waist, then turned and pulled up his white hospital gown to show another wound.

"That one went through my shoulder blade and out…" he turned to face Gao and pointed to a wound above his right breast, "…here." He pulled the gown straight before continuing. "The truck didn't stop so I crawled as far away from the road as I could. Sometime later, a Chinese lorry stopped near to where I was hiding. The driver, needing a pee, found me, and here I am. I have been suffering from short-term amnesia. Yesterday I recovered my memory and gave my name. And here you are."

Gao turned towards some screens surrounding a near-by bed. "Have you heard enough?" he asked.

"Yes," came the voice of the photographer.

"What did you hear?"

"I heard the voice of Pu Li, Yamada's table tennis partner."

As quick as a young cat, the man Gao knew as Accountant Su Ke jumped from his bed and headed for the window. Gao was quicker. He got a handful of Su Ke's hair and pulled him back onto the bed where Fong helped to hold him down. It needed them both. Su Ke was fighting like a wounded tiger, scratching, biting, punching and kicking.

By now the four guards brought along from the Soviet Embassy especially for such a moment had arrived to take over. Su Ke was dragged to his feet and with his hands behind his back, handcuffed. Then he was shackled. Nobody was taking any chances with this suspected high-level traitor.

Yang stepped from behind the screen and stared hard at Su Ke.

"He looks whiter and thinner but absolutely yes!" he exclaimed. "This man is the traitor Pu Li. He was responsible for the deaths of many of his own people."

"Take him away," Gao said.

As they passed the men in their beds they shouted and booed. Some tried to get out of bed to beat the prisoner. Luckily there were sufficient nurses to keep order. Gao instructed Fong to deliver Pu Li to the Russian Embassy for questioning.

Gao asked himself, "Is Pu Li the Owl?"

He answered his own question. "No, I don't think so."

3.

The next morning Gao was late into the office. Now that the crypt was empty of treasure, it was no longer guarded. He and Feilibov had spent part of the night retrieving the Yamada files, and the remaining hours of darkness going through them.

Fan was waiting to report. "The orphanage director telephoned. There are hundreds of kids needing help. He asked us to launch an appeal in our newspaper for clothes and money to get them through the winter."

Gao nodded, "Give it to Low. He's good at the sort of thing. Anything else?"

"Yes. The Director of the City Museum telephoned to say that on the day the Emperor declared unconditional surrender, twelve irreplaceable ancient miniature paintings were taken away by the Japanese. From the information the Director has gathered together, the Japanese intended to take the pictures back to Japan but for some reason they didn't, they hid them somewhere. Would the newspaper help him get them back?"

"Yes, of course. You take care of it. Start with an editorial then follow up with an interview with the Museum Director. Keep me informed of progress."

That was Gao's day. He went home to bed.

*

The next morning Gao was busy checking copy when Low returned from the orphanage accompanied by Mister Chen, the orphanage Director. Chen was himself an orphan who had grown to manhood with an intense desire to help other unfortunate kids. With Chen came two of his charges, a short, square and strong looking boy about nine years of age and a tall, skinny lad. Both had shaved heads, wore simple clothes and home-made cloth shoes.

Gao stood up, pleased to see Mister Chen. They shook hands. Chen introduced the boys and Gao shook hands with them too. They beamed with pleasure at being treated like adults. They were a likable looking pair. Guo Li (Shorty) had an intelligent, cheeky face with a huge grin. Wei Jia (Lofty) was more serious.

"Would you like some tea?" Gao asked.

Mister Chen and the boys nodded. Low went to the kitchen to boil some water. When they all had mugs of steaming tea, Low explained the reason for the visit.

"Director Gao, the boys have found something. Director Chen thought it best to bring them here to personally hand it over to you."

Shorty got up from the floor where the boys had been sitting and solemnly handed over a bag which Gao recognized as Japanese military officer issue.

"Uncle Director," began Shorty before Gao could ask any questions, "we were out exploring and found this."

Shorty was the leader of this twosome. He told Gao that he and Lofty often went exploring. They liked to find new places to play and imagined themselves to be Marco Polo. Earlier that morning they had found a new path and had followed it to an old burned-out temple.

They were running around, playing at war, when Lofty tripped over a lump of wood, went flat on his face and saw a hole in the ground that looked interesting. The boys cleared away the rubbish blocking the hole to uncover some stone steps leading down into darkness. With Shorty leading the way, their curiosity forced them down the steps.

Shorty's foot knocked something. It was a flashlight. When he switched it on, it worked. This helped them to safely reach the bottom. They followed a passageway that went under the old temple into a large cellar. The boys began to get agitated at this point in their story.

The beam of light had picked out a man half-sitting, half-lying, in a corner, surrounded by empty food cans. At first the boys backed away, frightened. When the man didn't move to chase them, they gained enough courage to go nearer. It was a Japanese Army Officer, but not dangerous. He looked very ill.

"We must get help," said Shorty.

One of the boys spotted the bag that Gao was now holding. Shorty said that they should take it with them to make the adults believe their story. They were children. They did not have the thought or inclination to disarm the man. As they neared the top of the stairs, they heard a gunshot. Quickly returning to the cellar, they found a bloody still-twitching corpse, pistol near to hand.

The officer had followed the Japanese code by preferring death to surrender. As more and more Japanese soldiers were found, the Chinese discovered that such suicides were normal.

Low took up the tale. "I was at the orphanage when the boys returned. They quickly told their story but pleaded with us not to tell the authorities. They feared some sort of punishment for being somewhere they shouldn't be, and for stealing the bag. So Director Chen and I thought it best to bring the boys to you."

Gao nodded his approval and smiled at the boys. "Don't worry, we three adults will keep your secret. Does anyone else know?"

The boys exchanged worried looks before Shorty admitted, "Yes. When we came up the steps and into the open we met Mister Yang the photographer. We know him because he came to the orphanage to take pictures. He asked why we looked so upset and where we had found the bag, so we told him. Did we do wrong?"

Gao patted both shaven heads. "Don't worry lads, you did everything right. We adults will take over now."

He looked in the bag, not expecting much, to find several pencils and a notebook. Only he could understand the significance of the spidery writing. It was sufficiently interesting to make him want to deliver it to Feilibov. That very afternoon he left Low in charge and delivered the bag to Feilibov whilst on his way to see the orphanage for himself.

The ramshackle two-storied wooden building stood within a dusty courtyard. In the yard, about a hundred shaven-headed children of varying ages from toddler to adolescent were cutting winter logs with old saws and an axe with a makeshift handle. The moment they realized that a visitor had arrived, they stopped working to crowd around, curious to know all about Gao. Director Chen hurried to his side.

"Children," he shouted, "this is Director Gao. He is going to write about us in his newspaper, so..." he scowled in mock menace, "...you behave yourselves and be nice to Uncle Gao."

The children were poorly clothed and undernourished but obviously happy. They loved Director Chen and he loved them. Inside the building more children were cooking whilst others cleaned and the eldest girls cared for the babies. Gao calculated that there must have been close to two hundred kids crammed into that one building, with more arriving every day.

Shorty and Lofty ran off to tell their companions about their adventure and soon had an admiring crowd listening intently. Gao and Director Chen reached the office. Kids whose turn it was to be orderlies brought in mugs of tea.

Mugs empty, Director Chen showed Gao around. There wasn't much in the orphanage but what they had was spotlessly clean and tidy. Gao had expected desperation but no such thing existed in this place. Thanks to Director Chen and his small band of helpers, these kids weren't beaten down, yet anyway. Hopefully they never would be.

The orphanage was an eye opener and somehow spiritually uplifting. Gao decided to devote a series of fund-raising editorials until Director Chen had all the money he needed to get those kids through the winter.

The following day, the newspaper told the people of Shanghai that the City Museum and the Orphanage needed their help. The front page was filled with the museum theft, telling the reader all about the missing pictures and that a reward was on offer for information that led to their recovery.

The whole of page three screamed out how the people could help the poor unfortunate kids facing a long, bleak winter with little or no food, clothes and bedding. Low and Fan had worked until late in the evening getting everything written exactly as they wanted it. Gao had added a note saying that the absence of an adequate police force should not stop people from reporting everything they knew to the Interim Government. Or they could contact the Military, the Soviet Embassy – the only embassy open in Shanghai at that time, any newspaper office or other important organizations. All had agreed to work together until Shanghai was functioning normally.

4.

Feilibov was treating Gao to lunch in the Astor Hotel restaurant. He asked Gao, "How is Little Dove? Will you be married soon?"

"Not for a while. There is so much for the new administration to sort out. Civil weddings are a long way down the list. In the meantime we live together. Little Dove is currently fulfilling one of her little girl dreams. The University reopened two weeks ago and she enrolled to read Classic Chinese Literature. As for me, Little Dove makes me the happiest of men and I enjoy my work. What more could I want?"

After lunch they returned to Feilibov's office to find Andriev waiting. He laid two files on the desk. "The translation of the book found in the Japanese officer's bag," said he. "A copy each."

Feilibov passed one file to Gao. They read for about ten minutes. Gao had a hope that the Jap officer had written something about Owl, or the Military Map, or the missing paintings. None of these things were mentioned. Most of it described the officer's feelings of dishonour after the surrender. Then, right at the end, he mentioned a spy, codenamed 87. Just 87. He, or she, had been left in the city.

When they finished reading, their eyes locked and simultaneously they exclaimed, "*Eighty-seven?*" followed by Feilibov's groaning, "Another one. The city must be riddled with them."

Andriev returned, this time shepherding a very nervous girl of about fifteen. He coaxed the girl to sit down. She did, on the edge of the chair, bolt upright, as though waiting for an executioner's bullet. She barely opened her mouth to produce a frightened squeaky voice.

"Master, my grandfather sent me to tell you that he thinks he knows something about the stolen pictures."

"Who is your grandfather?" Feilibov asked softly.

"He is the gate-keeper at the old graveyard."

*

They wasted no time. Taking the girl with them in a Russian Jeep, they drove at breakneck speed, arriving twenty minutes later outside the graveyard. This particular cemetery had many important people buried in it, so it had a keeper. With the girl nodding her agreement, Feilibov, with his European face and his identity card, easily convinced the old man that he was indeed from the Soviet Embassy. The old man made a hand gesture for them to follow him. They passed many graves until he stopped and pointed at a new tomb, saying, "Perhaps the pictures are buried there."

He explained why. "Two nights ago a big truck drove up to the gates. Before I could dress and go to check their papers, two Chinese men brandishing revolvers burst into my house and told me to stay where I was. "Don't poke your nose into our affairs," threatened one, "or you and the girl will be shot." Taking my keys, they left, locking the house door behind them."

Not daring to go outside, the old man climbed the stairs to the attic and looked out of the window. Flashlights gave enough light to see five people. It was almost dawn when he heard gunshots followed by the truck being driven away.

When full daylight arrived, he returned to ground level and climbed out of a window. His keys were still in the padlock. Before he went to investigate where the men had been working, he opened his house door to tell his granddaughter to stay hidden.

He continued to tell his tale. "Three bodies were lying near to this spot, see the blood? I've moved them into the storage room. It's cooler there. I think they were workers forced to help. Please, you dig. Whatever you find I don't want any reward. It is my job. Soon gossip will reach those men and they will return to kill my granddaughter and me. We must leave here. I go to pack. Here are the keys."

The Interim Government sent a squad of soldiers with tools. It didn't take them long to unearth a number of large black leather bags, no paintings. The bags held files containing documents belonging to the despised puppet police force.

They had questions. Why didn't the men burn the papers? Or bury them outside the city? And why this graveyard? The gatekeeper had been sure that the two men with guns were Chinese, probably members of the dispersed puppet police force that had used brutal methods to keep order for the Japanese.

They came to the conclusion that the only possible reason why the papers were buried in this particular graveyard was their hope that one day the Japanese would be back and they would easily remember where they had buried them. What arrogance! They threatened a man and a girl with pistols, defiled a grave to bury the papers and killed three men, still thinking that they were invulnerable, able to do whatever they liked. Well, their time was over. The two who had buried the bags, *and* all their pals, would be hunted down, tried for treason, and if found guilty, executed.

5.

The absence of a police force meant that the newspaper was, for most people, their only reporting centre where they could get a fair hearing. For the same reason, as a trusted newspaper Director, the city government gave Gao information that needed his so-called expertise. In return he was allowed to follow up on cases, for example, to attend the behind-closed-doors discussions on the graveyard documents.

The meeting was a long one. During one of the hourly breaks, news came that Pu Li, alias Su Ke, had been shot dead whilst trying to escape. That was upsetting. Gao had hoped to get information from Pu Li that would crack the three outstanding cases - the missing museum pictures, Owl and the Military Map, and 87. Now Pu Li couldn't help. He had tried to escape one time too many.

About three weeks later, Feilibov phoned Gao and asked him to get to the Embassy as soon as possible. He did. Feilibov came straight to the point. "Some time ago the MISB arrested a female on suspicion of spying for the Japanese. She has been a tough nut to crack. After questioning, the MISB handed her over to the city government. When they couldn't break her, they sent her here. She is with Andriev in a secure interrogation room under the building."

Five minutes later, through a two-way mirror, they watched three people. One was an exhausted young-ish woman, wearing just an olive coloured overall, sitting on one side of a table. Her bruised face was testimony to hard questioning by her previous interrogators. Now it was Andriev's turn. He sat opposite the woman. The third person was a female stenographer sitting in a corner, taking notes.

"How long has the woman been here?" Gao asked.

"Two hours," replied Feilibov. "Andriev has been working on her since then. We waited for you to arrive before springing our surprises."

The voices came to them through a speaker.

"Are you sure you have never heard of Yamada?" asked Andriev.

In a weary but defiant voice, the prisoner replied, "I have never heard that name."

"You do know that, under Chinese law, to be caught lying results in double the punishment?"

"Yes."

Feilibov nudged Gao as Andriev slid a photograph out of a file.

"Tell me about this," he said.

In the photograph Gao could clearly see Yamada sitting beside a woman looking very much like the prisoner.

Andriev pointed. "This man is Yamada and you are the woman. You were known as Yan Ku in those days. Do you still deny knowing Yamada?"

The woman was shocked. She stuttered, "I…I don't understand…"

Andriev held the photograph up to eye level in front of her face and said quietly, "Look carefully. There is Yamada and there is you."

The bravado had quickly disappeared. All that was left was a frightened woman saying nothing. Suddenly she asked, "Where did that photograph come from? It must be a fake."

"Oh no madam, this photograph is genuine. It is of you sitting beside Yamada. Would you like to see more?"

A second photograph was produced, then a third. From Gao's vantage point, he could see that the second and third images were definitely of this woman in bed with Yamada.

There was a long silence before Andriev asked her, "Nothing to say?"

The woman murmured more to herself than out loud, "I was told that all photographs of Yamada and that woman had been destroyed."

"Well," answered Andriev in a mocking tone, "someone has lied to you. These photographs came out of Yamada's own files, and I can tell you that we have many more hot and sexy pictures of you with Yamada. Would you like to see those?"

Yan Ku was astonished. For about ten seconds her mouth dropped open and her huge eyes stared at Andriev, then she recovered sufficiently to say, "*You* have Yamada's secret documents? Why you? This is the Soviet Embassy not City Hall. How did you get your hands on them?"

"We recovered Yamada's files from the crypt of Saint John's University Church. We also have the puppet police force files from where they had been hidden. We expect to find your name in those files too."

Hearing this, Yan Ku's defences completely crumpled. She wasn't to know that the Soviets did *not* have the graveyard files.

Her words started slowly then gathered speed as she said them. "Yes…I… am Yan Ku. Yamada was…my lover. … I just wanted to stay alive…and I still do. If you spare me, I can help you."

"Are you the person known as Owl?" asked Andriev.

"No."

"Are you the person known as 87?"

"No."

"What do you know about the missing paintings?"

"Nothing…except…" she stopped in mid-sentence. Gao got the impression that she was frightened to say too much in case she condemned herself to death.

Andriev leaned back in his chair and said quietly, "Unless you convince me that you can be of use, I will send you back to City Hall for trial and execution. Tell me everything about your life with Yamada and I will recommend leniency."

With great slowness and hesitation, Yan Ku began to talk.

"The paintings…you ask me about paintings. Everything was rush, rush, rush. All of us were scared. Even the all-powerful Yamada was in a panic to get out of Shanghai alive. The paintings and a big travelling trunk full of Yamada's personal stuff had been loaded onto the last lorry left in Shanghai.

"I was supposed to travel with Yamada in his staff car and he gave permission for the top Chinese puppet police officers to ride on the lorry with their black leather bags. Pu Li wanted to go too, but Yamada wouldn't let him. In the end, Yamada had to shoot at Pu Li to chase him away. Pu Li fell to the ground, wounded. Then there was something wrong with the engine of the lorry. It wouldn't start.

"Yamada was furious. Before he drove off in his staff car, he ordered a Japanese officer and some soldiers to unload the lorry and hide everything. The officer and soldiers took off with the paintings and the trunk. The Chinese puppet police officers, carrying their leather bags, hurried away in the opposite direction. By that time Pu Li had crawled off somewhere…to die I suppose, leaving only me standing next to the useless lorry. That's all I know about paintings."

Gao remembered the abandoned truck still standing outside the old Japanese Imperial Army Headquarters. So that was why the trunk containing the treasure and Yamada's most important files was still in Shanghai. Engine trouble. It also explained how Pu Li had got his bullet wounds and proved his story to be a complete lie.

"How was Pu Li dressed?" asked Andriev.

"Like a Japanese officer."

Andriev opened a map of Shanghai and laid it on the table. Handing Yan Ku a pencil, he instructed, "Mark the places where the caches of mines and explosives are hidden." His voice turned hard and menacing. "Don't lie or cheat. If any more untruths come out of your mouth, I will send you back for trial followed by a bullet in the brain."

Using the pencil, Yan Ku quickly marked places on the map, skillfully, with a professional touch. She was unconsciously revealing her knowledge of maps, which suggested that she was more than a simple courtesan. A spy perhaps?

When she had finished, she whined, "I could only mark the places as I remembered them. Some may be wrong. A few days before Yamada left Shanghai he was busy clearing out his office. I saw him give Pu Li the real map to pass on to…I don't know who. Yamada had no time to do it himself. That is why I don't think Pu Li is the Owl. And he definitely isn't 87."

Andriev abruptly changed the subject.

"Who is 87?"

"I don't know. Honestly I don't. Yamada told me I was being watched around the clock by someone called 87. He said that if I did anything suspicious, 87 would kill me. I think 87 is a man. I believe him to be an assassin and still in Shanghai."

Later that day, when Andriev had drained the last bit of information out of Yan Ku, she was handed back to the city government with a recommendation that she be sent to Siberia to join the other collaborators. He also suggested that she take a message to the last Emperor, Pu Yi, informing him that his cousin, Pu Li, was dead.

"Give him something to think about," said Feilibov.

They all agreed. None of them had any sympathy for the Chinese who had collaborated with the Japanese invaders. Feilibov also said that he and Gao should immediately go and re-check the big trunk.

Gao protested, "I personally checked it thoroughly. There was the treasure and the Yamada files. Definitely no map." Then a thought, "Do you mean a hidden compartment like a double bottom?"

Feilibov flashed a sardonic smile, "Come, come, Colonel Bashan. You must keep up."

Fong arrived at the Soviet Embassy a minute before they were ready to leave.

"Director Chen from the orphanage telephoned to report that some of his children have found names carved on the walls of an abandoned house near to the old temple. It seems that the Japanese had used the house as a secret prison. Lofty found the name of his missing father. He cried so hard and appealed for revenge so vehemently that the Director went to have a look for himself and found these words, "*Soon to be shot. Avenge us. The traitor is...*" Director Chen was not able to read the name. It had been obliterated by something sharp, like a knife." Anxious to hear of any further developments, Fong hurried away.

"Little by little the rats are being uncovered," said Feilibov. He told

Andriev to take some men to search the abandoned house for more clues whilst he and Gao took another look at the trunk.

*

If there was a secret compartment, they couldn't find it.

"There is only one thing left to do," said Feilibov. "Get someone to blow the bloody thing apart!"

In a short time, an explosive expert from the Soviet Embassy was with them. Continuously talking to himself, he said it helped his concentration, he checked the trunk, made some calculations in a notebook, and finally announced, "I can explode a small charge that should blow out the bottom without damaging any contents."

It was agreed that the trunk should be blown apart.

The expert began to wire up a small bit of explosive that looked like putty. All the while he kept up a monologue. "Excellent design. Never seen the stars in the night sky used as a lock. Very clever. Great Bear or Little Bear, Orion or Orion's Belt, Southern Cross or Northern Lights. All heavenly bodi …'

"WAIT!" Gao shouted. "You have given me an idea."

He knelt down beside the open trunk. "Let's try the Little Bear," he said. "What's the pattern of stars for the Little Bear?"

Between them they sorted out the correct positions of the stars that made up the Little Bear. Gao pressed them from bottom to top. The daisy wouldn't budge.

"Try top to bottom," said Feilibov.

He did. The daisy slid to the left. There was a muffled click and the bottom of the trunk sprung open. The space was empty. They left the trunk intact and returned to the embassy.

Waiting for them was Fong. "Bigger news has come," he said excitedly. "The lost paintings have been found. Twelve altogether. They are now in our office guarded by Low and Fan."

"Who found them?" Feilibov asked.

"Mister Yang the photographer."

Feilibov turned to Andriev. "Did you find anything in the abandoned house?"

"One or two bits and pieces."

When Feilibov had seen what Andriev had brought back with him from the abandoned house, he said, "Well done. Now go and get Mister Yang. Tell him his reward is waiting for him in my office."

6.

Feilibov warmly welcomed Mister Yang and ushered him to a comfortable chair.

"It is so nice to meet you again," he gushed. By now Gao knew Feilibov well enough to know that his pleasantries meant big trouble for the photographer, and he didn't waste any time. He nodded to Andriev, "Search him thoroughly."

A shocked Mister Yang protested, to no avail, as his belongings began to pile up on the desk. Feilibov picked up each item and carefully inspected it. A handkerchief, a ring of keys, a broken penknife, some small denomination coins, a ten yuan banknote, a passport, an identification card, a camera and a tripod. Nothing seemed special.

Yang continued to complain. "This is an outrage! For what reason did you order the search? Haven't I always been happy to help? How can the simple and innocent contents of my pockets be of interest to you?"

Feilibov didn't answer immediately. Instead he nodded to Andriev, who left the room.

All eyes returned to Yang as Feilibov began his interrogation.

"Mister Yang, please tell us where you were before the war."

"In the northwest city of Lanzhou growing fruit trees. Why do you ask?"

"Was life good to you in those days?"

"It was a peaceful life and business was good."

Feilibov thought for a few seconds. "Sounds like an idyllic life," he said, seeming to be thinking aloud. "Now tell us, Mister Yang, where and how you found the missing museum paintings."

"The reward has got everybody looking for those pictures, including me. I found them in the house where the names are carved on the walls. They were under an old bed, wrapped in sacking. The kids didn't notice the bundle. I did. When I opened it, I found the paintings."

That sounded reasonable.

"I think you have just told me a lie. You did not find the paintings in the house but in the cellar of the old temple where the Japanese officer committed suicide. The boys didn't think to search the place, they just wanted to get out and report finding the bag. When you went in, you searched and found the paintings. Isn't that the truth?"

Yang shrugged his shoulders and snorted, "What rubbish! By chance I met those boys and they told me about the dead man. That was nothing unusual, left-behind Japanese are being found all over the city. I suggested that they hurry off and report to Director Chen. I didn't go down those steps. I am squeamish around dead bodies so why would I want to look at a dead Japanese?"

"You would do well to tell the truth Mister Yang," warned Feilibov. "Tell me why you scraped your name off the wall after the word "*traitor is*"?

A seemingly puzzled Yang replied, "What name? What you are talking about?"

Gao knew that Feilibov was keeping something up his sleeve, and he had to admire Yang. He was a very convincing innocent.

Feilibov slowly opened a drawer of his desk, reached in and picked up something. Holding it in his clenched hand, he closed the drawer, held his fist thirty centimetres above the desk-top and opened his fingers. Something fell from his hand onto the flat wooden top with a tiny metallic ring. He picked up the piece of metal, reached out for Yang's penknife, opened it and matched the piece of metal to the broken blade. At the same time he asked, "Can you tell me where you broke your knife?"

"I can't remember." For the first time, Yang looked uncomfortable.

Feilibov looked straight into Yang's eyes, daring him to lie.

"Can you explain why the broken piece of the blade was found in the room where the traitor's name was obliterated?"

The silky tone belied a dangerous Feilibov.

"I...I cannot explain..." Yang began to cough, "...please can I have my handkerchief?"

Feilibov pulled a handkerchief from his own pocket and passed it over.

"Please use mine, it is freshly laundered."

Yang stopped coughing.

"Director Gao," Feilibov called, "come and look at this." He pulled open the desk drawer again, picked out a small pair of scissors and Yang's handkerchief. He closed the drawer. Taking a corner of the handkerchief, he began to cut at the material with the scissors where two sides of the hem met and were sewn together. A tiny black pip dropped onto the table. Feilibov stopped Gao from picking it up.

"It is an extremely fast-acting poisonous pill. One need not cut it out like I have just done. Anyone can die instantly simply by chewing the corner of the handkerchief."

With icy eyes, Feilibov said to Yang, "*Now* will you tell me the truth?"

*

Yang began. "As I told you, I was forced to work for the Japanese and even to wear their uniform. I hated it, but what could I do? I took photographs when told, including pictures of their prisoners, so it wasn't long before some Shanghai people thought me a traitor. I wasn't, but how could I prove my innocence? I *had* to obliterate my name. When I explained my situation to Yamada, he gave me the suicide pill. He said that if I were ever in deep trouble, the pill would instantly send me to eternal peace."

With slow deliberation, Feilibov opened the drawer again. He slid everything off the desk back into the drawer and slammed it shut. The sudden noise made Yang jump.

Feilibov leaned forward and said with a menace that would frighten a snake.

"Mister Yang, you are stupidly trying to lie your way out of trouble. Be assured that you never will, because I know who you really are. Director Gao, let me introduce you. Yang is not his real name and he was not a fruit tree grower. His only truthful statement is that he was born in Lanzhou, the product of a liaison between a Chinese woman and a Japanese professor teaching in Lanzhou University. However, for now we'll play his game. We will continue to call him Yang and we can also use his two codenames. You see, Director Gao, the wartime Japanese gave Yang the codename of 87. Before he left, Yamada changed 87 to Owl."

Yang silently stared at Feilibov. Gao listened intently. The guard looked ahead, apparently impervious to the drama taking place in front of him.

Feilibov began again. "This is what happened, stop me if I'm wrong. At some time after the lorry wouldn't start, you saw the Japanese officer with the paintings and decided to follow him. When he disappeared into that hole in the ground and didn't return to ground level, you followed him down. He would have known you as a trusted friend to the Japanese, so it would have been easy to get him to tell you that he had orders to guard the paintings with his life. Exactly why Yamada gave the order I don't know, nor do I care, but it meant that you didn't dare touch the paintings. The officer would have killed you. In any case, at that time you probably didn't have much interest in them.

"By the time the boys went down those stairs, the officer was close to death from lack of food and water. He probably no longer cared about the paintings; he wanted his agony to end. The boys arriving in the cellar was his opportunity. To him, surrender equalled dishonour. Suicide was his only alternative.

"Meanwhile, *you* had read the newspaper and realized that the paintings were of use. To your surprise, you found that the boys had got to the cellar first and the officer had killed himself. When you were alone, you went down to the cellar, recovered the paintings and re-hid them somewhere else. That was how it happened, wasn't it Yang?"

Silence.

Feilibov walked out from behind his desk to the side of Mister Yang, alias 87 and Owl. Leaning down until his mouth was close to Yang's right ear, he shouted, "WHERE IS THE MILITARY MAP?"

Yang winced at the sudden shout into his ear a second before his eyes showed surprise. He blurted out, "How do you…" before managing to get hold of himself to say, "…I destroyed it."

"LIAR! WHERE IS THE MILITARY MAP?"

"I destroyed it."

Feilibov stood and pulled Gao to one side and whispered in his ear. "The map is too valuable to be out of his possession. It is with him in this room, but where?"

Gao's eyes scanned the room and alighted on the photographic equipment. He took up the camera and opened the back. There was no film, nor anything else. Putting it to one side, he picked up the tripod. It took him about five minutes to find, in a hollow leg, a roll of developed film wrapped in tissue paper. He checked it against the electric light bulb.

"Yes!" he exclaimed. "It's the Military Map. Got you, you bastard. You're bound for Siberia."

*

There were things Gao didn't understand. "Why did Yang bring those photographs to you?" he asked.

"Simple," said Feilibov. "He really is a good photographer. He wanted to ingratiate himself into the new elite circle of Shanghai, but knew, with his reputation, he would never be accepted. So, using the photographs as bait, he decided to try us Russian newcomers and get himself into diplomatic circles. And it was going well for him. I introduced him to you and from the photographs, you recognized Pu Li.

By betraying his friend at the hospital, Yang hoped to disprove any rumours still circulating about him being a traitor.

"Your newspaper would have printed the story of his part in the unmasking of Pu Li and of him finding the missing museum paintings. That would have made him a double hero instead of the merciless assassin that he really is.

"Unfortunately for him, everything went wrong. You had already found the Yamada files. Then we got our hands on the graveyard files. I had a good read of both. There was sufficient information in them to point me in Yang's direction. But I have to admit that Andriev finding that little bit of broken penknife was a huge stroke of luck. All we need now is one last piece of evidence."

Everything was quiet. For over an hour they waited until Andriev returned to the room. He beckoned in two Soviet guards carrying a mud-covered package. The guards placed it on Feilibov's desk and stood back.

"We dug this up in Mister Yang's back yard," said Andriev. Fishing a penknife out of his pocket, he cut several strands of twine stitches until he could pull back the folds of thick canvas. Revealed was a Japanese transceiver.

"I will make sure that the boys get the reward," Gao said.

* * *

Yu Tianming.

West Hill Dictatorship Team...autumn 1967.

These are Yu Tianming's words now.

We heard the guards approaching. Old Gao whispered, "I will tell you more tomorrow. I have a story about the government official who sent Pu Li to me with that letter of introduction."

But as we all know, "tomorrow" can mean "never"...

Old Gao shook me awake. It was dark, very dark, so I had no idea of the time.

"Shhh," hushed Old Gao. "Listen."

I heard the sound of heavy engines labouring up the steep climb to our prison. Soon afterwards the first of a long line of trucks appeared and every light in the place was switched on. The trucks seemed to encircle the prison then stop.

Peering through holes in the wall of our cell, Old Gao and I witnessed troops criss-crossing our courtyard carrying rifles with fixed bayonets. Two machine guns, each manned by two soldiers, were set up.

Men in prisoner uniforms hobbled into the yard. Their legs were already shackled, yet in their arms and over their shoulders they carried shackles. Behind them more shackled prisoners appeared, carrying handcuffs. Perhaps two hundred leg shackles and two hundred pairs of handcuffs were dropped to one side of the yard, making two piles of metal.

Old Gao whispered, "They're going to cuff and shackle the whole bloody lot of us. What the hell is going on?"

From noises elsewhere, it seemed as if the same thing was happening in other courtyards. We looked at each other, unable to make sense of it. Suddenly officers began to shout, "Number two, number three, number four…come out."

"Number five, number six, number seven…come out."

Men and women walked into our vision. Many were barefoot. Clothes were filthy, worn and holed. Men had long beards. Both sexes had long matted hair. Some showed signs of beatings and others were crippled. All were pitifully emaciated.

Pairs separated whilst in prison, recognizing a loved one, reached out, desperate for the tiniest of contact, to grasp a finger or touch a cheek. Soldiers kept them apart. One by one they were handcuffed and shackled before being led away, out of our sight.

"Number fifty, number fifty-one, number fifty-two…come out."

So it went on, through the remains of the night and into the dawn.

I heard Old Gao murmur, "Is this what we fought so hard for? Why Chopper, Sparks, Hunter, Dawn and Zhao Ying gave their lives? … No! Definitely not. Mao Zedong has betrayed every one of his brave freedom fighters."

I said to no one in particular, "Once accused, there is no escape."

Old Gao was saying, "At some future time there must be a reckoning."

"Number one-hundred-and-ninety-nine, number two-hundred…come out."

That was the end, except for us. Two officers, accompanied by soldiers, moved towards our cell. Old Gao and I stepped back. The door opened, soldiers entered, followed by the officers. One of the officers looked at Old Gao's hands, then mine.

"No number!" shouted the officer checking my hands. He looked at me and asked, "What is your number?"

"Seventy-four."

"What is your name?"

"Yu Tianming."

"You are not on this list. Why are you locked in here?"

"I suppose I must be a bad element."

I was frightened but Old Gao had taught me to never show fear. What will be, will be. Fear makes no difference.

"Stand back against the wall," commanded the officer. "We have orders to take the prisoners on this list. You are not on it, so you stay here."

From outside came the shout, "Number one, come out!"

Very calmly, Old Gao gave me his last long look, encapsulating everything we had become to one another and walked out. His demeanor was of someone filled with confidence. Of being the victor, and in a way he was. He had never succumbed to their bullying and beatings. Nor had he revealed his secrets to anyone but me.

"He is being taken away to be shot," I thought to myself and took a desperate few steps forward. A soldier roughly pushed me back.

An officer shouted, "You are not wanted. Go away. Ask your leader for guidance."

The cell was empty.

To my surprise the cell door was left ajar. For a while I sat on my straw bed wondering what to do. I feared walking out in case it was all an elaborate hoax to tempt me into trouble. Loneliness enveloped me like a thick black mantle, forcing me into action. I pushed open the door, looked around and walked out into silence and solitude. The prison already had the neglected feel of abandonment.

I walked through the various courtyards, offices, interrogation and torture rooms. No prisoners, no soldiers, nobody. From somewhere, I sniffed the succulent, mouthwatering smell of cooking and realizing that I was hungry, I followed my nose to a kitchen. Four peasant workers sat around a wooden table eating a rice and vegetable mixture. I coughed and walked in. They were surprised to see me. "What are you still doing here?" asked one.

"Left behind," replied I. "My name and number weren't on the list. What's happened? Where has everybody gone?"

At last one of the men gave the traditional Chinese words of greeting that were music to my ears. "Have you eaten?"

Very quickly a big bowl of leftover food together with a tin can filled with green tea was placed on the table and I was invited to eat. For over a year I hadn't seen food like that. I emptied my bowl in no time. Sadly there was no more food. Happily my tin can was refilled.

The men were a friendly bunch. They told me that the prison had closed. The prisoners had been taken to a mass rally to be sentenced. Some to ordinary prisons, others to labour camps. Many would be shot. I had been set free without being given a sentence. What to do now?

"Nothing for it but to make your way back to the city and report to your work unit," said one man. "Go down hill to the road and turn right."

Another added, "We are leaving too. Our employment here has finished. Who cares? This is a bad place. I'll be happy to be gone."

The men nodded their agreement and rose from the table. One by one they shook my hand and wished me good luck. Each picked up as many kitchen utensils as he could carry and walked off. I filled my tin can one more time, relishing the remembered tea-taste. No rush, I wasn't expected.

*

When I had drunk the last drops of tea, I followed the advice I had been given and went the shortest way down the hill. From somewhere I heard just the faintest of sounds. I couldn't make it out exactly. Voices shouting at a sports meet perhaps?

I kept going downwards, heading towards the noise. After maybe ten minutes, I saw, in a clearing near to a village, a semi-circular crowd of people being held back by soldiers. My heart sank. I had seen similar scenes before. It was an execution.

Whenever there is an execution anywhere in China, police and militia round up locals to witness the killing. Of course, some people cannot be kept away from such events - the rest are forced to watch. It is a sure way to instill fear and obedience into the masses.

I arrived quietly from behind and stood on a grassy knoll where I could see everything. I was looking for just one man, and there he was, his white hair and beard giving him away. I watched, mesmerized. Many of the prisoners had already been dispatched. A pile of handcuffs and a second pile of shackles testified to that. Bodies almost filled a horse-drawn cattle cart. This was real Communism I was witnessing. Not the brave New World promised by Mao Zedong but a land consumed by hatred and murder.

Old Gao stood alone, separated from the other condemned prisoners. My heart was bumping in my throat, but I couldn't help a huge surge of inspirational admiration for him. He was not the least cowed. Although he knew it was close to his time, his head was high, his back was straight and he seemed to be at peace within himself.

He saw me standing on the little hill and a soft smile came my way. He nodded his message. I received it. "Good friend, live on. One day you will be able to tell my story."

I tapped my temple with my right index finger to say, "It is all in here."

It was cruel. Those to be murdered witnessed the deaths of others going before them. They went two at a time, dragged forward by soldiers. They stood still to have their cuffs removed and their hands bound with thin twine. Then the shackles were taken off and they were forced to kneel in the blood of the already dead.

An officer read out a list of their supposed crimes that I couldn't hear much of, followed by the death sentence. Immediately other officers stepped forward, one behind each man or woman. They raised their pistols and shot their victim in the head. The body usually fell forward, writhed for a while then stilled. Men dressed in prison garb moved forward to carry the body and throw it, like garbage, onto the cattle cart.

When only Old Gao was left, the same officer who had conducted his interrogations moved forward and waved the other officers away. He personally wanted to conduct this murder. He was holding a pistol in his right hand and a thin bamboo stick in his left.

I couldn't hear the reading of Gao Qing's crimes or death sentence. The sentencing officer stepped back. Old Gao was still standing, his face showing no fear. The handcuffs were removed and Gao's hands were bound. The shackles were taken off. The crowd was silent.

I think I spotted anger on the face of the killer. I now knew him well enough to know that he wanted to see fear and hear pleas for mercy. Old Gao did not give him that pleasure. Killer stepped forward and viciously kicked Old Gao in the groin. Not once, but twice. Gao's body doubled over. Through sheer strength of will, Gao straightened up. Raising his head, he spat into Killer's laughing mouth. A roar of approval from the crowd.

Killer had just lost much face. He smashed his pistol into the face of Gao, bringing forth a murmur of disapproval. With no other way to fight back, Gao sucked in the blood from his shattered nose and sprayed it out over Killer. I remembered him telling me that he had done the same thing to the CIS officers. A huge roar of approval, even I was delighted, despite knowing that the end was near.

Without being told, Gao walked to the right place and knelt in the blood, waiting.

EPILOGUE

I did live on, carrying Old Gao's friendship in my heart, his story in my head and his death in my dreams.

I reported to my work unit and it was as if I had never been away. Nothing was said about my imprisonment or absence. My desk was still as I had left it, except that Gao Qing's file had disappeared to be replaced by another. As far as the authorities were concerned, that was the end of it. Only I knew that it wasn't.

I settled down to pick up the pieces of my life. My only loss was my girlfriend. After a few weeks of good fattening food, sun and fresh air, I found another one. I started smoking again, and I kept my promise to myself. Every week up to her death, I wrote a long letter to my mother.

In my spare time I began the difficult job of tracing how Gao Qing had got on after the Owl episode. I went to Shanghai and learned that he and Little Dove were eventually married but not before the birth of their first son.

In January 1950, upon the orders of Zhou En-lai, now the Premier of the People's Republic of China, Gao took his wife and son to Taiwan where he continued to work for the Dagong Bao newspaper. His second son was born there.

In 1952, the family moved to Hong Kong for a few weeks before returning to China. Premier Zhou En-lai had given Gao a good job in the Foreign Affairs Bureau in Beijing.

During one of Mao's many political purges of the fifties, it was noticed that Gao Qing's personal file had a gap, with nothing reported from 1939 to 1952. That was sufficient for him to be arrested.

Without trial, he was imprisoned in the West Hill Dictatorship Team prison. The so-called "non-communist" thirteen years was used as evidence that he was working for a foreign power and not for the Chinese Communist Party. Gao Qing said nothing. His accusers took his silence to be positive proof that he *must* be guilty.

At that time, Premier Zhou En-lai was, without doubt, the most loved and respected man in China, something Mao could not accept. Mao Zedong *and only* Mao Zedong must have the love of the people, therefore Zhou En-lai's public image must be destroyed.

To do that, Mao needed hard evidence. Gao Qing was a Zhou En-lai placement, therefore he must know something about the Premier. That was the thinking. However, no evidence was ever uncovered against Zhou En-lai.

Gao Qing was kept in prison. In due time, the *assumption* that he had been in the pay of a foreign power became a *proven crime* that could not be forgiven.

Little Dove and her sons were taken away, never to be heard of again, yet Gao steadfastly refused to talk. By the start of the Cultural Revolution, Mao had such a strong power base, even Zhou En-lai was powerless to help Gao. Nevertheless, despite his own Party leaders betraying him, Gao Qing remained silent.

Zhou En-lai continued to hold the office of Premier until his death in January 1976 and Mao continued as Chairman till he died eight months later.

*

Whenever my financial position allowed, I travelled thousands of kilometres looking for Chopper's relatives. In 1982, I eventually found his wife and son living in the poorest conditions in a remote mountain village in Sichuan Province. Chopper was last seen in a Kuomintang uniform, that made him a Counter-Revolutionary Turncoat Traitor. His wife and son, as reactionary family members, were exiled and forced to do hard labour without payment.

I wrote a long letter to the newly created Rehabilitation Office of the Central Party Committee. I told them that Comrade Huang Chi (Chopper) was really a revolutionary hero. Fortunately, Deng Xiao-ping, then the unopposed leader of China, had a recollection of the exploits of Gao Qing. He ordered a full inquiry. In 1992, Chopper was cleared of all wrongdoing.

After more than forty years of Communist persecution, Chopper's wife, now in her middle eighties, was invited to meet with the local Communist official. He read out the rehabilitation document. It said that Comrade Huang Chi was recognized retrospectively as a Revolutionary Martyr. On hearing this, Chopper's wife passed out. She and her son had suffered for nothing.

Chopper's son, in his middle fifties and semi-illiterate, was given a job at the village shop for the smallest of wages - forty yuan a month (about £3.00). To him, never having had a wage, it was a fortune!

The Japanese officer named Takeo Tsuse, codenamed Kawa, survived the war and returned to Kyoto where he rose to high political prominence. He continued to supply Moscow with top-grade information until his retirement in 1978. His present whereabouts is unknown.

I don't know what happened to Serpent.

Every member of the Yun family and all of their servants were arrested and sent to the countryside for "re-education". In Communist jargon that meant slave labour. Their crime? They were rich, or worked for a rich family.

For many years a Communist Provincial Governor lived in their house. Today, where the beautiful house once stood, there is a concrete office block.

*

So now you know the story of Gao Qing. After almost forty years of waiting, I have at last honoured my promise to the best friend a man could wish for. I hope I have done him justice.

"At some future time, there has to be a reckoning!"

www.ingramcontent.com/pod-product-compliance
Lightning Source LLC
LaVergne TN
LVHW010609100826
845148LV00014B/2896

* 9 7 8 1 6 8 5 6 0 0 6 2 4 *